LDAP System Administration

LDAP System Administration

Gerald Carter

Beijing · Cambridge · Farnham · Köln · Sebastopol · Tokyo

LDAP System Administration
by Gerald Carter

Published by O'Reilly Media, Inc., 1005 Gravenstein Highway North, Sebastopol, CA 95472.

O'Reilly Media, Inc. books may be purchased for educational, business, or sales promotional use. On-line editions are also available for most titles (*safari.oreilly.com*). For more information, contact our corporate/institutional sales department: (800) 998-9938 or *corporate@oreilly.com*.

Editor:	Mike Loukides
Production Editor:	Matt Hutchinson
Cover Designer:	Emma Colby
Interior Designer:	Bret Kerr

Printing History:

March 2003:	First Edition.

ISBN: 978-1-565-92491-8
[LSI]

Table of Contents

Part II. Application Integration

Part III.   Appendixes

Preface

In 1999 I began experimenting with the *Lightweight Directory Access Protocol* (LDAP) and immediately became frustrated by lack of documentation. I set out to write the book that I needed, and I believe that I accomplished that goal. After teaching instructional courses on LDAP for the past few years, I have come to the belief that many people share the same frustration I felt at the beginning of my LDAP career. Managers and administrators alike can sometimes be dazzled (or disgusted) by the plethora of acronyms in the IT industry. The goal of this book is to cut through the glossy vendor brochures and give you the knowledge and tools necessary to deploy a working directory on your network complete with integrated client applications.

Directory services have been a part of networks in one way or another for a long time. LDAP directories have been growing roots in networks for as long as people have been proclaiming the current year to be the "year of LDAP." With increasing support from vendors in the form of clients and servers, LDAP has already become a staple for many networks. Because of this gradual but steady growth, people waiting for the LDAP big bang may be disappointed. You may wake up one morning and find that one of your colleagues has already deployed an LDAP-based directory service. If so, this book will help you understand how you can use the services that LDAP provides. If you are at the beginning of a project, this book will help you focus on the important points that are necessary to succeed.

How This Book Is Organized

This book is divided into two sections of five chapters each and a section of appendixes. You will most likely get the most out of this book if you implement the example directories as they are covered. With only a few exceptions, all client and server applications presented here are freely available or in common use.

Part I : LDAP Basics

Part I focuses on getting acquainted with LDAP and with the OpenLDAP server. In this part, I answer questions such as: "What is lightweight about LDAP?," "What security mechanisms does LDAP support for preventing unauthorized access to data?," and "How can I build a fault-tolerant directory service?" In addition, the first part of the book helps you gain practical experience with your own directory using the community-developed and freely available OpenLDAP server.

Chapter 1, *"Now where did I put that...?", or "What is a directory?"*, is a high-level overview of directory services and LDAP in particular.

Chapter 2, *LDAPv3 Overview*, digs into the details of the Lightweight Directory Access Protocol.

Chapter 3, *OpenLDAP*, uses the free server distribution from OpenLDAP.org as an example to present practical experience with an LDAP directory.

Chapter 4, *OpenLDAP: Building a Company White Pages*, provides some hands-on experience adding, modifying, and deleting information from a working directory service.

Chapter 5, *Replication, Referrals, Searching, and SASL Explained*, wraps up the loose ends of some of the more advanced LDAPv3 and OpenLDAP features.

Part II : Application Integration

Part II is all about implementation. Rather than present an LDAP cookbook, I bring different applications together in such a way that information common to one or more clients can be shared via the directory. You will see how to use LDAP as a practical data store for items such as user and group accounts, host information, general contact information, and application configurations. I also discuss integration with other directory services such as Microsoft's Active Directory, and how to develop your own Perl scripts to manage your directory service.

Chapter 6, *Replacing NIS*, explains how an LDAP directory can be used to replace Sun's Network Information Service (NIS) as the means to distribute user and group accounts, host information, automount maps, and other system files.

Chapter 7, *Email and LDAP*, presents information related to both mail clients (Eudora, Mozilla, Outlook, and Pine) and servers (Sendmail, Postfix, and Exim).

Chapter 8, *Standard Unix Services and LDAP*, explains how to use an LDAP directory to share information among essential network services such as FTP, HTTP, LPD, RADIUS, DNS, and Samba.

Chapter 9, *LDAP Interoperability*, examines what to do when your LDAP directory must coexist with other directory technologies.

Chapter 10, *Net::LDAP and Perl*, provides the information necessary to roll your own LDAP management tools using Perl and the Net::LDAP module.

Part III: Appendixes

The appendixes provide a quick reference for LDAP standards, common schema items used in this book, and the command-line syntax for OpenLDAP client tools.

Conventions Used in This Book

The following conventions are used in this book:

Italic
> Used for file, directory, user, and group names. It is also used for URLs and to emphasize new terms and concepts when they are introduced.

`Constant Width`
> Used for code examples, system output, parameters, directives, and attributes.

`Constant Width Italic`
> Used in examples for variable input or output (e.g., a filename).

`Constant Width Bold`
> Used in code examples for user input and for emphasis.

 This icon designates a note, which is an important aside to the nearby text.

 This icon designates a warning relating to the nearby text.

Comments and Questions

We at O'Reilly have tested and verified the information in this book to the best of our abilities, but you may find that features have changed (or even that we have made mistakes!). Please let us know about any errors you find, as well as your suggestions for future editions, by writing to:

O'Reilly & Associates, Inc.
1005 Gravenstein Highway North
Sebastopol, CA 95472
(800) 998-9938 (U.S. and Canada)

(707) 827-7000 (international/local)
(707) 829-0104 (fax)

You can also contact O'Reilly by email. To be put on the mailing list or request a catalog, send a message to:

info@oreilly.com

We have a web page for this book, which lists errata, examples, and any additional information. You can access this page at:

http://www.oreilly.com/catalog/ldapsa/

To comment or ask technical questions about this book, send email to:

bookquestions@oreilly.com

For more information about O'Reilly books, conferences, Resource Centers, and the O'Reilly Network, see the O'Reilly web site at:

http://www.oreilly.com/

Acknowledgments

At the end of every project, I am acutely aware that I could never have reached the end without the grace provided to me by God through my Savior, Jesus Christ. I hope He is proud of how I have spent my time. I am also very conscious of the patience bestowed upon me by my wife, Kristi, who is always there to listen when I need to talk and laugh when I need a smile. Thank you.

There is a long list of people who have helped make this book possible. I do not claim that this is a complete list. Mike Loukides has shown almost as much patience as my wife waiting on this book to be completed. I am in great debt to the technical reviewers who each provided comments on some version of this manuscript: Robbie Allen, David Blank-Edelman, Æleen Frisch, Robert Haskins, Luke Howard, Scott McDaniel, and Kurt Zeilenga. Thanks to Æleen for convincing me to do this (even if I complained more than once). I must also mention the various coffee shops, particularly the Books-A-Million in Auburn, AL, that have allowed me to consume far more than my fair share of caffeine and electricity.

Finally, a huge amount of recognition must be given to the developers who made various pieces of software available under open source and free software licenses. It is such an enjoyable experience to be able to send and receive feedback on problems, bugs, and solutions. Any other way would just be too painful.

## PART I

LDAP Basics

## CHAPTER 1

"Now where did I put that...?", or "What is a directory?"

I have a fairly good memory for numbers, phone numbers in particular. This fact amazes my wife. For those numbers I cannot recall to the exact digit, I have a dozen or so slots in my cell phone. However, as the company I worked for grew, so did the list of people with whom I needed to stay in contact. And I didn't just need phone numbers; I needed email and postal addresses as well. My cell phone's limited capabilities were no longer adequate for maintaining the necessary information.

So I eventually broke down and purchased a PDA. I was then able to store contact information for thousands of people. Still, two or three times a day I found myself searching the company's contact database for someone's number or address. And I still had to go to other databases (phone books, corporate client lists, and so on) when I needed to look up someone who worked for a different company.

Computer systems have exactly the same problem as humans—both require the capability to locate certain types of information easily, efficiently, and quickly. During the early days of the ARPAnet, a listing of the small community of hosts could be maintained by a central authority—SRI's Network Information Center (NIC). As TCP/IP became more widespread and more hosts were added to the ARPAnet, maintaining a centralized list of hosts became a pipe dream. New hosts were added to the network before everyone had even received the last, now outdated, copy of the famous *HOSTS.TXT* file. The only solution was to distribute the management of the host namespace. Thus began the Domain Name System (DNS), one of the most successful directory services ever implemented on the Internet.[*]

DNS is a good starting point for our overview of directory services. The global DNS shares many characteristics with a directory service. While directory services can take on many different forms, the following five characteristics hold true (at a minimum):

A directory service is highly optimized for reads. While this is not a restriction on the DNS model, for performance reasons many DNS servers cache the entire

---

[*] For more information on the Domain Name System and its roots, see *DNS and BIND*, by Paul Albitz and Cricket Liu (O'Reilly).

zone information in memory. Adding, modifying, or deleting an entry forces the server to reparse the zone files. Obviously, this is much more expensive than a simple DNS query.

A directory service implements a distributed model for storing information. DNS is managed by thousands of local administrators and is connected by root name servers managed by the InterNIC.

A directory service can extend the types of information it stores. Recent RFCs, such as RFC 2782, have extended the types of DNS records to include such things as server resource records (RRs).

A directory service has advanced search capabilities. DNS supports searches by any implemented record type (e.g., NS, MX, A, etc.).

A directory service has loosely consistent replication among directory servers. All popular DNS software packages support secondary DNS servers via periodic "zone transfers" that contain the latest copy of the DNS zone information.

The Lightweight Directory Access Protocol

Of course, you didn't buy this book to read about the Domain Name System. And it's not likely that you were looking for a general discussion of directory services. This book is about a particular kind of directory service—namely, a service for directories that implement the *Lightweight Directory Access Protocol* (LDAP). LDAP has become somewhat of a buzzword in contemporary IT shops. If you are like me, sometimes you just have to ask, "Why all the fuss?" The fuss is not so much about LDAP itself, but about the potential of LDAP to consolidate existing services into a single directory that can be accessed by LDAP clients from various vendors. These clients can be web browsers, email clients, mail servers, or any one of a myriad of other applications.

By consolidating information into a single directory, you are not simply pouring the contents of your multitude of smaller pots into a larger pot. By organizing your information well and thinking carefully about the common information needed by client applications, you can reduce data redundancy in your directories and therefore reduce the administrative overhead needed to maintain that data. Think about all the directory services that run on your network and consider how much information is duplicated. Perhaps hosts on your network use a DHCP server. This server has a certain amount of information about IP addresses, Ethernet addresses, hostnames, network topology, and so forth in its configuration files. Which other applications use the same or similar information and could share it if it were stored in a directory server? DNS comes immediately to mind, as does NIS. If you have networked printers as well, think about the amount of information that's replicated on each client of the printing system (for example, */etc/printcap* files).

Now consider the applications that use your user account information. The first ones that probably come to mind are authentication services: users need to type usernames and passwords to log in. Your mail server probably uses the same username information for mail routing, as well as for services such as mailing lists. There may also be online phone books that keep track of names, addresses, and phone numbers, as well as personnel systems that keep track of job classifications and pay scales.

Imagine the administrative savings that would result if all the redundant data on your network could be consolidated in a single location. What would it take to delete a user account? We all know what that takes now: you delete the user from */etc/passwd*, remove him by hand from any mailing lists, remove him from the company phone list, and so on. If you're clever, you've probably written a script or two to automate the process, but you're still manipulating the same information that's stored in several different places. What if there was a single directory that was the repository for all this information, and deleting a user was simply a matter of removing some records from this directory? Life would become much simpler. Likewise, what would it take to track host-related information? What would it be worth to you if you could minimize the possibility that machines and users use out-of-date information?

This sounds like a network administrator's utopia. However, I believe that as more and more client applications use LDAP directories, making an investment in setting up an LDAP server will have a huge payoff long-term. Realistically, we're not headed for a utopia. We're going to be responsible for more servers and more services, running on more platforms. The dividends of our LDAP investment come when we significantly reduce the number of directory technologies that we have to understand and administer. That is our goal.

What Is LDAP?

The best place to begin when explaining LDAP is to examine how it got its name. Let's start at the beginning. The latest incarnation of LDAP (Version 3) is defined in a set of nine documents outlined in RFC 3377. This list includes:

RFC 2251–2256
    The original core set of LDAPv3 RFCs

RFC 2829
    "Authentication Methods for LDAP"

RFC 2830
    "Lightweight Directory Access Protocol (v3): Extension for Transport Layer Security"

RFC 3377
    "Lightweight Directory Access Protocol (v3): Technical Specification"

Lightweight

Why is LDAP considered lightweight? Lightweight compared to what? (As we look at LDAP in more detail, you'll certainly be asking how something this complex could ever be considered lightweight.) To answer these questions, it is necessary to look at LDAP's origins. The roots of LDAP are closely tied to the X.500 directory service; LDAP was originally designed as a lighter desktop protocol used to gateway requests to X.500 servers. X.500 is actually a set of standards; anything approaching thorough coverage of X.500 is beyond the scope of this book.*

X.500 earned the title "heavyweight." It required the client and server to communicate using the Open Systems Interface (OSI) protocol stack. This seven-layered stack was a good academic exercise in designing a network protocol suite, but when compared to the TCP/IP protocol suite, it is akin to traveling the European train system with four fully loaded footlockers.†

LDAP is lightweight in comparison because it uses low overhead messages that are mapped directly onto the TCP layer (port 389 is the default) of the TCP/IP protocol stack.‡ Because X.500 was an application layer protocol (in terms of the OSI model), it carried far more baggage, as network headers were wrapped around the packet at each layer before it was finally transmitted on the network (see Figure 1-1).

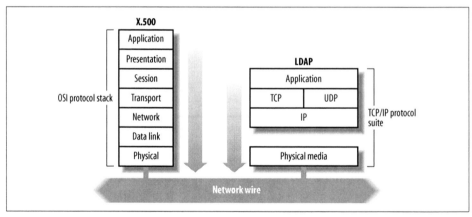

Figure 1-1. X.500 over OSI versus LDAP over TCP/IP

---

* *Understanding X.500—The Directory*, by David W. Chadwick, provides a good explanation of X.500 directories. While the book itself is out of print, an HTML version of it can be accessed from *http://www.salford. ac.uk/its024/X500.htm*.

† For a quick, general comparison of the OSI model and the TCP/IP protocol stack, see *Computer Networks*, by Andrew S. Tanenbaum (Prentice Hall).

‡ A connectionless version of LDAP that provided access via UDP was defined by an Internet-Draft produced by the LDAP Extension Working Group of the IETF. However, the current draft expired in November, 2001. You can access the group's web site at *http://www.ietf.org/html.charters/ldapext-charter.html*.

LDAP is also considered lightweight because it omits many X.500 operations that are rarely used. LDAPv3 has only nine core operations and provides a simpler model for programmers and administrators. Providing a smaller and simpler set of operations allows developers to focus on the semantics of their programs without having to understand rarely used features of the protocol. In this way, LDAP designers hoped to increase adoption by providing easier application development.

Directory

Network directory services are nothing new; we're all familiar with the rise of DNS. However, a directory service is often confused with a database. It is easy to understand why. Directory services and databases share a number of important characteristics, such as fast searches and an extendable schema. They differ in that a directory is designed to be read much more than it is written; in contrast, a database assumes that read and write operations occur with roughly the same frequency. The assumption that a directory is read often but written rarely means that certain features that are essential to a database, such as support for transactions and write locks, are not essential for a directory service such as LDAP.

At this point, it's important to make the distinction between LDAP and the backend used to store the persistent data. Remember that LDAP is just a protocol; we'll discuss what that means shortly, but essentially, it's a set of messages for accessing certain kinds of data. The protocol doesn't say anything about where the data is stored. A software vendor implementing an LDAP server is free to use whatever backend it desires, ranging from flat text files on one extreme to highly scalable, indexed relational databases on the other. So when I say that LDAP doesn't have support for transactions and other features of databases, I mean that the protocol doesn't have the messages that you would need to take advantage of these features (remember, it's lightweight) and doesn't require that the backend data store provide these features.

The point is that the client will never (and should never) see or even know about the backend storage mechanism (see Figure 1-2). For this reason, LDAP-compliant clients written by vendor A should interoperate with an LDAP-compliant server written by vendor Z. Standards can be a wonderful thing when followed.

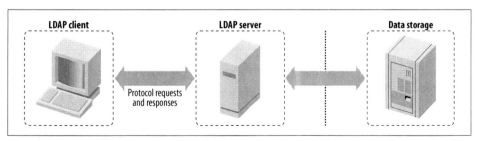

Figure 1-2. Relationship between an LDAP client, LDAP server, and data storage facility

It has been suggested that an LDAP server could be used as backend storage for a web server. All HTML and graphic files would be stored within the directory and could be queried by mutiple web servers. After all, a web server typically only reads files and sends them to clients; the files themselves change infrequently. While it's certainly possible to implement a web server that uses LDAP to access its backend storage, a special type of directory already exists that is better suited to meet the needs of serving files, namely a filesystem. So, for example, while an LDAP directory might not be a good location for storing spooled files in transit to a printer, using it to store printer configuration settings (e.g., */etc/printcap*) shared among clients would be a big win.

This brings up two good points about the intended function of LDAP:

1. LDAP is not a generalized replacement for specialized directories such as filesystems or DNS.

2. While storing certain types of binary information (e.g., JPEG photos) in directories can be useful, LDAP is not intended for storing arbitrary "blobs" (Binary Lumps of Bits).

What about storing individual application settings for roaming users on an LDAP server? It is a judgment call whether this is better served by a filesystem or a directory. For example, it is possible to store basic application settings for Netscape Communicator in LDAP. Such things as an address book, a bookmarks file, and personal preference settings are certainly appropriate for storage in a directory. However, using your directory as a location for browser cache files would violate rule #2.

Access Protocol

All of this talk of directory services makes it is easy to forget that LDAP is a protocol. It is not uncommon to hear someone refer to an LDAP server or LDAP tree. I have done so and will continue to do so. LDAP does provide a treelike view of data, and it is this treelike view to which people refer when speaking of an LDAP server.

This introduction won't go into the specifics of the actual protocol. It is enough to think of LDAP as the message-based, client/server protocol defined in RFC 2251. LDAP is asynchronous (although many development kits provide both blocking and nonblocking APIs), meaning that a client may issue multiple requests and that responses to those requests may arrive in an order different from that in which they were issued. Notice in Figure 1-3 that the client sends Requests 1 and 2 prior to receiving a response, and the response to Request 3 is returned before the response to Request 2.

More aspects of programming with LDAP operations will be covered in Chapter 10.

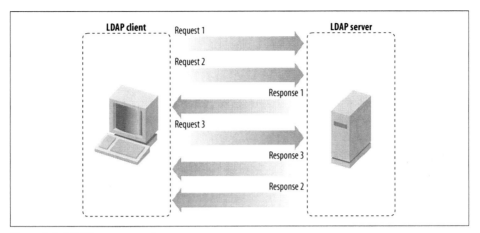

Figure 1-3. LDAP requests and responses

LDAP Models

LDAP models represent the services provided by a server, as seen by a client. They are abstract models that describe the various facets of an LDAP directory. RFC 2251 divides an LDAP directory into two components: the protocol model and the data model. However, in *Understanding and Deploying LDAP Directory Services*, by Timothy A. Howes, Mark C. Smith, and Gordon S. Good (MacMillan), four models are defined:

Information model

The information model provides the structures and data types necessary for building an LDAP directory tree. An entry is the basic unit in an LDAP directory. You can visualize an entry as either an interior or exterior node in the Directory Information Tree (DIT). An entry contains information about an instance of one or more objectClasses. These objectClasses have certain required or optional attributes. Attribute types have defined encoding and matching rules that govern such things as the type of data the attribute can hold and how to compare this data during a search. This information model will be covered extensively in the next chapter when we examine LDAP schema.

Naming model

The naming model defines how entries and data in the DIT are uniquely referenced. Each entry has an attribute that is unique among all siblings of a single parent. This unique attribute is called the relative distinguished name (RDN). You can uniquely identify any entry within a directory by following the RDNs of all the entries in the path from the desired node to the root of the tree. This string created by combining RDNs to form a unique name is called the node's distinguished name (DN).

In Figure 1-4, the directory entry outlined in the dashed square has an RDN of cn=gerald carter. Note that the attribute name as well as the value are included in the RDN. The DN for this node would be cn=gerald carter,ou=people, dc=plainjoe,dc=org.

Functional model

The functional model is the LDAP protocol itself. This protocol provides the means for accessing the data in the directory tree. Access is implemented by authentication operations (bindings), query operations (searches and reads), and update operations (writes).

Security model

The security model provides a mechanism for clients to prove their identity (authentication) and for the server to control an authenticated client's access to data (authorization). LDAPv3 provides several authentication methods not available in previous protocol versions. Some features, such as access control lists, have not been standardized yet, leaving vendors to their own devices.

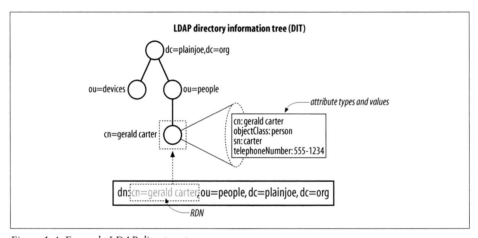

Figure 1-4. Example LDAP directory tree

At this high level, LDAP is relatively simple. It is a protocol for building highly distributed directories. In the next chapter, we will examine certain LDAP concepts such as schemas, referrals, and replication in much more depth.

## CHAPTER 2

LDAPv3 Overview

Chapter 1 should have helped you understand the characteristics of a directory in general, and an LDAP directory in particular. If you still feel a little uncomfortable about LDAP, relax. This chapter is designed to flesh out some of the details that we glossed over. Your immediate goal should be to understand the basic building blocks of any LDAPv3 directory server. In the next chapter, we will start building an LDAP directory.

LDIF

Most system administrators prefer to use plain-text files for server configuration information, as opposed to some binary store of bits. It is more comfortable to deal with data in vi, Emacs, or notepad than to dig though raw bits and bytes. Therefore, it seems fitting to begin an exploration of LDAP internals with a discussion of representing directory data in text form.

The LDAP Interchange Format (LDIF), defined in RFC 2849, is a standard text file format for storing LDAP configuration information and directory contents. In its most basic form, an LDIF file is:

- A collection of entries separated from each other by blank lines
- A mapping of attribute names to values
- A collection of directives that instruct the parser how to process the information

The first two characteristics provide exactly what is needed to describe the contents of an LDAP directory. We'll return to the third characteristic when we discuss modifying the information in the directory in Chapter 4.

LDIF files are often used to import new data into your directory or make changes to existing data. The data in the LDIF file must obey the schema rules of your LDAP directory. You can think of the schema as a data definition for your directory. Every item that is added or changed in the directory is checked against the schema for correctness. A *schema violation* occurs if the data does not correspond to the existing rules.

Figure 2-1 shows a simple directory information tree. Each entry in the directory is represented by an entry in the LDIF file. Let's begin with the topmost entry in the tree labeled with the distinguished name (DN) dc=plainjoe,dc=org:

```
# LDIF listing for the entry dn: dc=plainjoe,dc=org
dn: dc=plainjoe,dc=org
objectClass: domain
dc: plainjoe
```

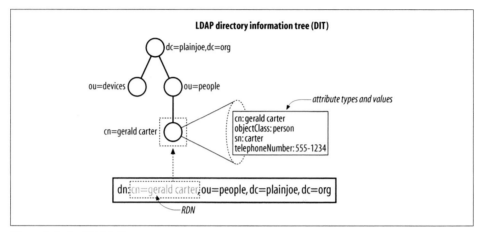

Figure 2-1. An LDAP directory tree

We can make a few observations about LDIF syntax on the basis of this short listing:

- Comments in an LDIF file begin with a pound character (#) at position one and continue to the end of the current line.

- Attributes are listed on the lefthand side of the colon (:), and values are presented on the righthand side. The colon character is separated from the value by a space.

- The dn attribute uniquely identifies the DN of the entry.

Distinguished Names and Relative Distinguished Names

It is important to realize that the full DN of an entry does not actually need to be stored as an attribute within that entry, even though this seems to be implied by the previous LDIF extract; it can be generated on the fly as needed. This is analogous to how a filesystem is organized. A file or directory does not store the absolute path to itself from the root of the filesystem. Think how hard it would be to move files if this were true.

If the DN is like the absolute path between the root of a filesystem and a file, a relative distinguished name (RDN) is like a filename. We've already seen that a DN is formed by stringing together the RDNs of every entity from the element in question to the root of the directory tree. In this sense, an RDN works similarly to a filename. However, unlike a filename, an RDN can be made up of multiple attributes. This is similar to a compound index in a relational database system in which two or more fields are used in combination to generate a unique index key.

While a multivalued RDN is not shown in our example, it is not hard to imagine. Suppose that there are two employees named Jane Smith in your company: one in the Sales Department and one in the Engineering Department. Now suppose the entries for these employees have a common parent. Neither the common name (cn) nor the organizational unit (ou) attribute is unique in its own right. However, both can be used in combination to generate a unique RDN. This would look like:

```
# Example of two entries with a multivalued RDN
dn: cn=Jane Smith+ou=Sales,dc=plainjoe,dc=org
cn: Jane Smith
ou: Sales
<...remainder of entry deleted...>

dn: cn=Jane Smith+ou=Engineering,dc=plainjoe,dc=org
cn: Jane Smith
ou: Engineering
<...remainder of entry deleted...>
```

For both of these entries, the first component of the DN is an RDN composed of two values: cn=Jane Smith+ou=Sales and cn=Jane Smith+ou=Engineering.

In the multivalued RDN, the plus character (+) separates the two attribute values used to form the RDN. What if one of the attributes used in the RDN contained the + character? To prevent the + character from being interpreted as a special character, we need to escape it using a backslash (\). The other special characters that require a backslash-escape if used within an attribute value are:

- A space or pound (#) character occurring at the beginning of the string
- A space occurring at the end of the string
- A comma (,), a plus character (+), a double quote ("), a backslash (\), angle brackets (< or >), or a semicolon (;)

Although multivalued RDNs have their place, using them excessively can become confusing, and can often be avoided by a better namespace design. In the previous example, it is obvious that the multivalued RDN could be avoided by creating different organizationalUnits (ou) in the directory for both Sales and Engineering, as illustrated in Figure 2-2. Using this strategy, the DN for the first entry would be cn=Jane Smith,ou=Sales,dc=plainjoe,dc=org. This design does not entirely eliminate the need for multivalued RDNs; we could still have two people named Jane Smith in the Engineering organization. But that will occur much less frequently than having two Jane Smiths in the company. Look for ways to organize namespaces to avoid multivalued RDNs as much as is possible and logical.

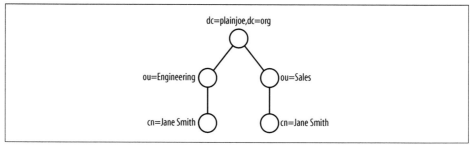

Figure 2-2. A namespace that represents Jane Smith with a unique, multivalued RDN

One final note about DNs. RFC 2253 defines a method of unambiguously representing a DN using a UTF-8 string representation. This normalization process boils down to:

- Removing all nonescaped whitespace surrounding the equal sign (=) in each RDN
- Making sure the appropriate characters are escaped
- Removing all nonescaped spaces surrounding the multi-value RDN join character (+)
- Removing all nonescaped trailing spaces on RDNs

Therefore, the normalized version of:

```
cn=gerald carter + ou=sales,  dc=plainjoe ,dc=org
```

would be:

```
cn=gerald carter+ou=sales,dc=plainjoe,dc=org
```

Without getting ahead of ourselves, I should mention that the string representation of a distinguished name is normally case-preserving, and the logic used to determine if two DNs are equal is usually a case-insensitive match. Therefore:

```
cn=Gerald Carter,ou=People,dc=plainjoe,dc=org
```

would be equivalent to:

```
cn=gerald carter,ou=people,dc=plainjoe,dc=org
```

However, this case-preserving, case-insensitive behavior is based upon the syntax and matching rules (see "What Is an Attribute?" later in this chapter) of the attribute type used in each relative component of the complete DN. So while DNs are often case-insensitive, do not assume that they will always be so.

Subsequent examples use the normalized versions of all DNs to prevent confusion, although I may tend to be lax on capitalization.

Back to Our Regularly Scheduled Program...

Going back to Figure 2-1, your next question is probably, "Where did the extra lines in the LDIF listing come from?" After all, the top entry in Figure 2-1 is simply dc=plainjoe,dc=org. But the LDIF lines corresponding to this entry also contain an objectClass: line and a dc: line. These extra lines provide additional information stored inside each entry. The next few sections answer the following questions:

- What is an attribute?
- What does the value of the objectClass attribute mean?
- What is the dc attribute?
- If dc=plainjoe,dc=org is the top entry in the directory, where is the entry for dc=org?

What Is an Attribute?

The concepts of attribute types and attribute syntax were mentioned briefly in the previous chapter. Attribute types and the associated syntax rules are similar to variable and data type declarations found in many programming languages. The comparison is not that big of a stretch. Attributes are used to hold values. Variables in programs perform a similar task—they store information.

When a variable is declared in a program, it is defined to be of a certain data type. This data type specifies what type of information can be stored in the variable, along with certain other rules, such as how to compare the variable's value to the data stored in another variable of the same type. For example, declaring a 16-bit integer variable in a program and then assigning it a value of 1,000,000 would make no sense (the maximum value represented by a signed 16-bit integer is 32,767). The data type of a 16-bit integer determines what data can be stored. The data type also determines how values of like type can be compared. Is 3 < 5? Yes, of course it is. How do you know? Because there exists a set of rules for comparing integers with other integers. The syntax of LDAP attribute types performs a similar function as the data type in these examples.

Unlike variables, however, LDAP attributes can be multivalued. Most procedural programming languages today enforce "store and replace" semantics of variable assignment, and so my analogy falls apart. That is, when you assign a new value to a variable, its old value is replaced. As you'll see, this isn't true for LDAP; assigning a new value to an attribute adds the value to the list of values the attribute already has. Here's the LDIF listing for the ou=devices,dc=plainjoe,dc=org entry from Figure 2-1; it demonstrates the purpose of multivalued attributes:

```
# LDIF listing for dn: ou=devices,dc=plainjoe,dc=org
dn: ou=devices,dc=plainjoe,dc=org
```

```
objectclass: organizationalUnit
ou: devices
telephoneNumber: +1 256 555-5446
telephoneNumber: +1 256 555-5447
description: Container for all network enabled
 devices existing within the plainjoe.org domain
```

 Note that the description attribute spans two lines. Line continuation in LDIF is implemented by leaving exactly one space at the beginning of a line. LDIF does not require a backslash (\) to continue one line to the next, as is common in many Unix configuration files.

The LDIF file lists two values for the telephoneNumber attribute. In real life, it's common for an entity to be reachable via two or more phone numbers. Be aware that some attributes can contain only a single value at any given time. Whether an attribute is single- or multivalued depends on the attribute's definition in the server's schema. Examples of single-valued attributes include an entry's country (c), display-able name (displayName), or a user's Unix numeric ID (uidNumber).

Attribute Syntax

An attribute type's definition lays the groundwork for answers to questions such as, "What type of values can be stored in this attribute?", "Can these two values be compared?", and, if so, "How should the comparison take place?"

Continuing with our telephoneNumber example, suppose you search the directory for the person who owns the phone number 555-5446. This may seem easy when you first think about it. However, RFC 2252 explains that a telephone number can contain characters other than digits (0–9) and a hyphen (-). A telephone number can include:

- a–z
- A–Z
- 0–9
- Various punctuation characters such as commas, periods, parentheses, hyphens, colons, question marks, and spaces

555.5446 or 555 5446 are also correct matches to 555-5446. What about the area code? Should we also use it in a comparison of phone numbers?

Attribute type definitions include matching rules that tell an LDAP server how to make comparisons—which, as we've seen, isn't as easy as it seems. In Figure 2-3, taken from RFC 2256, the telephoneNumber attribute has two associated matching rules. The telephoneNumberMatch rule is used for equality comparisons. While RFC 2552 defines telephoneNumberMatch as a whitespace-insensitive comparison only, this rule is often implemented to be case-insensitive as well. The telephoneNumberSubstringsMatch rule is used for partial telephone number matches—for example, when the search criteria includes wildcards, such as "555*5446".

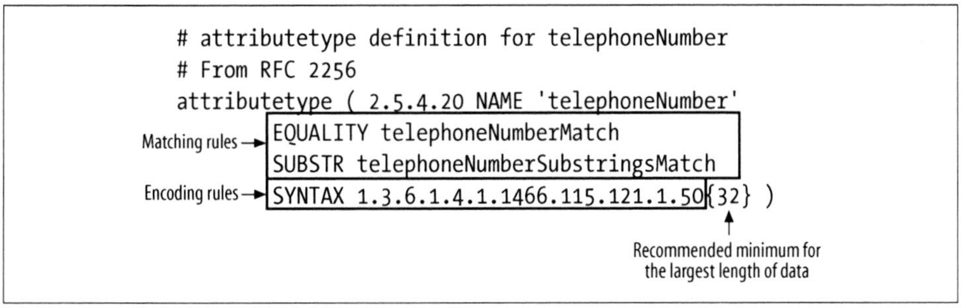

```
               # attributetype definition for telephoneNumber
               # From RFC 2256
               attributetype ( 2.5.4.20 NAME 'telephoneNumber'
Matching rules →  EQUALITY telephoneNumberMatch
               SUBSTR telephoneNumberSubstringsMatch
Encoding rules →  SYNTAX 1.3.6.1.4.1.1466.115.121.1.50{32} )

                                           Recommended minimum for
                                           the largest length of data
```

Figure 2-3. telephoneNumber attribute type definition

The SYNTAX keyword specifies the object identifier (OID) of the encoding rules used for storing and transmitting values of the attribute type. The number enclosed by curly braces ({ }) specifies the minimum recommended maximum length of the attribute's value that a server should support.

What Does the Value of the objectClass Attribute Mean?

All entries in an LDAP directory must have an objectClass attribute, and this attribute must have at least one value. Multiple values for the objectClass attribute are both possible and common given certain requirements, as you shall soon see. Each objectClass value acts as a template for the data to be stored in an entry. It defines a set of attributes that must be present in the entry and a set of optional attributes that may or may not be present.

Let's go back and reexamine the LDIF representation of the ou=devices,dc=plainjoe,dc=org entry:

```
# LDIF listing for dn: ou=devices,dc=plainjoe,dc=org
dn: ou=devices,dc=plainjoe,dc=org
objectclass: organizationalUnit
ou: devices
telephoneNumber: +1 256 555-5446
telephoneNumber: +1 256 555-5447
description: Container for all network enabled
  devices existing within the plainjoe.org domain
```

Object Identifiers (OIDs)

LDAPv3 uses OIDs such as those used in SNMP MIBs. SNMP OIDs are allocated by the Internet Assigned Numbers Authority (IANA) under the mgmt(2) branch of the number space displayed in Figure 2-4. Newly created LDAPv3 OIDs generally fall under the private(4), enterprise(1) branch of the tree. However, it is also common to see numbers under the joint-ISO-ccitt(2) branch of the number tree. OIDs beginning with 2.5.4 come from the user attribute specifications defined by X.500.

An OID is a string of dotted numbers that uniquely identifies items such as attributes, syntaxes, object classes, and extended controls. The allocation of enterprise numbers by IANA is similar to the central distribution of IP address blocks; once you have been assigned an enterprise number by the IANA, you can create your own OIDs underneath that number. Unlike the IP address space, there is no limit to the number of OIDs you can create because there's no limit to the length of an OID.

For example, assume that you were issued the enterprise number 55555. Therefore, all OIDs belonging to your branch of the OID tree would begin with 1.3.6.1.4.1.55555. How this subtree is divided is at your discretion. You may choose to allocate 1.3.6.1.4.1.55555.1 to department A and 1.3.6.1.4.1.55555.2 to department B. Each allocated branch of your OID is referred to as an arc. The local administrators of these departments could then subdivide their arcs according to the needs of their network.

OID assignments must be unique worldwide. If you ever need to make custom schema files for your directory (a common practice), go to *http://www.iana.org/cgi-bin/ enterprise.pl* and request a private enterprise number. The form is short and normally takes one to two weeks to be processed. Once you have your own enterprise number, you can create your own OIDs without worrying about conflicts with OIDs that have already been assigned. RFC 3383 describes some best practices for registering new LDAP values with IANA.

In this case, the entry's objectClass is an organizationalUnit. (The schema definition for this is illustrated by two different representations in Figure 2-5.) The listing on the right shows the actual definition of the objectClass from RFC 2256; the box on the left summarizes the required and optional attributes.

Here's how to understand an objectClass definition:

- An objectClass possesses an OID, just like attribute types, encoding syntaxes, and matching rules.
- The keyword MUST denotes a set of attributes that must be present in any instance of this object. In this case, "present" means "possesses at least one value."

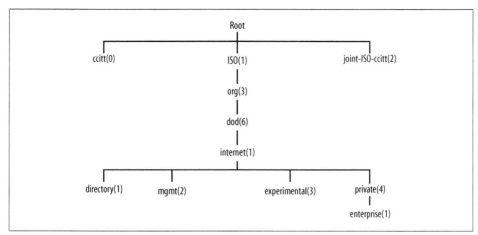

Figure 2-4. Private enterprise OID number space

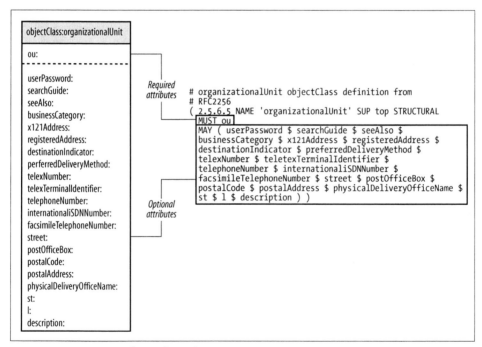

Figure 2-5. organizationalUnit object class

To represent a zero-length attribute value in LDIF syntax, the attribute name must be followed by a colon and zero or more spaces, and then a CR or CF/LF. For example, the following LDIF line stores a zero-length description:

```
description:<ENTER>
```

- The keyword MAY defines a set of attributes whose presence is optional in an instance of the object.

- The keyword SUP specifies the parent object from which this object was derived. A derived object possesses all the attribute type requirements of its parent. Attributes can be derived from other attributes as well, inheriting the syntax of its parent as well as matching rules, although the latter can be locally overridden by the new attribute. LDAP objects do not support multiple inheritance; they have a single parent object, like Java objects.

- It is possible for two object classes to have common attribute members. Because the attribute type namespace is flat for an entire schema, the telephoneNumber attribute belonging to an organizationalUnit is the same attribute type as the telephoneNumber belonging to some other object class, such as a person (which is covered later in this chapter).

Object Class Types

Three types of object class definitions are used in LDAP directory servers:

Structural object classes
> Represent a real-world object, such as a person or an organizationalUnit. Each entry within an LDAP directory must have exactly one structural object class listed in the objectClass attribute. According to the LDAP data model, once an entry's structural object class has been instantiated, it cannot be changed without deleting and re-adding the entire entry.

Auxiliary object classes
> Add certain characteristics to a structural class. These classes cannot be used on their own, but only to supplement an existing structural object. There is a special auxiliary object class referred to in RFC 2252 named extensibleObject, which an LDAP server may support. This object class implicitly includes all attributes defined in the server's schema as optional members.

Abstract object classes
> Act the same as their counterparts in object-oriented programming. These classes cannot be used directly, but only as ancestors of derived classes. The most common abstract class relating to LDAP (and X.500) that you will use is the top object class, which is the parent or ancestor of all LDAP object classes.

Note that the type of an object cannot be changed by a derived class.

What Is the dc Attribute?

Returning to our discussion of the topmost entry in Figure 2-1, we can now explain the meaning of the `domain` object class and the `dc` attribute. Here is the original LDIF listing for the entry:

```
# LDIF listing for the entry dn: dc=plainjoe,dc=org
dn: dc=plainjoe,dc=org
objectclass: domain
dc: plainjoe
```

The original recommendation for dividing the X.500 namespace was based on geographic and national regions. You frequently see this convention in LDAP directories as well, given the heritage that LDAP shares with X.500. For example, under X.500, the distinguished name for a directory server in the *plainjoe.org* domain might be:

```
dn: o=plainjoe,l=AL,c=US
```

Here, the `o` attribute is the `organizationName`, the `l` attribute is the locality of the organization, and the `c` attribute represents the country in which the organization exists. However, there is no central means of registering such names, and therefore no general way to refer to the naming context of a directory server. RFC 2247 introduced a system by which LDAP directory naming contexts can be piggybacked on top of an organization's existing DNS infrastructure. Because DNS domain names are guaranteed to be unique across the Internet and can be located easily, mapping an organization's domain name to an LDAP DN provides a simple way of determining the base suffix served by a directory and ensures that the naming context will be globally unique.

> A directory's naming context is the DN of its topmost entry. The naming context of the directory in our examples is `dc=plainjoe,dc=org`. This context is used by the LDAP server to determine whether it will be able to service a client request. For example, our directory server will return an error (or possibly a referral) to a client who attempts to look up the information in an entry named `cn=gerald carter,ou=people,dc=taco,dc=org` because the entry would be outside our naming context.
>
> However, the server would search the directory (and return no information) if the client attempts to look up `cn=gerald carter,ou=people,dc=taco,dc=plainjoe,dc=org`. In this case, the directory's naming context does match the rightmost substring of the requested entry's DN. The server just does not have any information on the entry.

To support a mapping between a DNS domain name and an LDAP directory namespace, RFC 2247 defines two objects, shown in Figures 2-6 and 2-7, for storing domain components. The `dcObject` is an auxiliary class to augment an existing entry containing organizational information (e.g., an `organizationalUnit`). The `domain` object class acts as a standalone container for both the organizational information and the domain name component (i.e., the dc attribute). The organizationalUnit and domain objects have many common attributes.

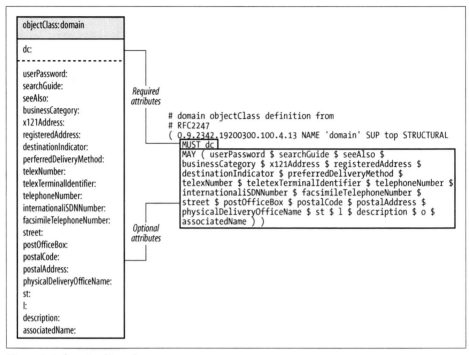

Figure 2-6. domain object class

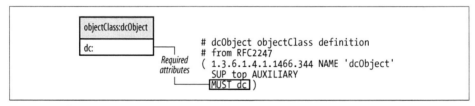

Figure 2-7. dcObject object class

Generating an LDAP DN to represent a DNS domain name is a simple process. An empty DN is used as a starting point. An RDN of dc=*domain component* is appended to the DN for each portion of the domain name. For example, the domain name *plainjoe.org* maps to our naming context of dc=plainjoe,dc=org.

Where Is dc=org?

As we saw in the previous section, dc=plainjoe,dc=org is the directory's naming context. If the directory's root entry was dc=org, with a child entry of `dc=plainjoe,dc=org`, then the naming context would have been `dc=org`. Our server would then unnecessarily respond to queries for any entry whose DN ended with `dc=org`, even though it only has knowledge of entries underneath `dc=plainjoe,dc=org`.

In this respect, designing an LDAP namespace is similar to designing a DNS hierarchy. Domain name servers for *plainjoe.org* have no need to service requests for the *.org* domain. These requests should be referred to the server that actually contains information about the requested hosts.

Schema References

One of the most frequent questions asked by newly designated LDAP administrators is, "What do all of these abbreviations mean?" Of course, the question refers to things such as `cn`, `c`, and `sn`. There is no single source of information describing all possible LDAPv3 attribute types and object classes, but there are a handful of online sites that can be consulted to cover the most common schema items:

RFC 3377 and related LDAPv3 standards (http://www.rfc-editor.org/)
> The documents outlined in RFC 3377 provide a list of references for researching related LDAPv3 and X.500 topics. RFC 2256 in particular describes a set of X.500 schema items used with LDAPv3 directory servers.

LDAP Schema Viewer (http://ldap.akbkhome.com/)
> This site, maintained by Alan Knowles, provides a nice means of browsing descriptions and dependencies among common LDAP attributes, object classes, and OIDs.

Object Identifiers Registry (http://www.alvestrand.no/objectid/)
> This site can be helpful in tracking down the owner of specific OID arcs.

Sun Microsystems Product Documentation (http://docs.sun.com)
> The SunOne Directory Server, formerly owned by Netscape Communications, includes a large set of reference documentation on various LDAP schema items. Even if you are not using the SunOne DS product, the schema reference can be helpful in understanding the meaning of various LDAP acronyms. Search the site for "LDAP schema reference" to locate the most recent versions of the product documentation.

Authentication

Why is authentication needed in an LDAP directory? Remember that LDAP is a connection-oriented, message-based protocol. The authentication process is used to establish the client's privileges for each session. All searches, queries, etc. are controlled by the authorization level of the authenticated user.

Figure 2-8 describes the person object class and gives you an idea of what other attributes are available for the cn=gerald carter entry in Figure 2-1. In particular, you will need to define a userPassword attribute value to further explore LDAP authentication.

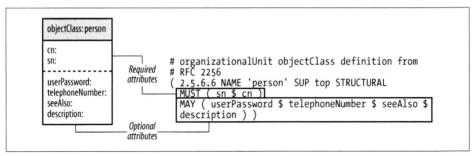

Figure 2-8. person objectClass

The LDIF representation for the expanded version cn=gerald carter is:

```
dn: cn=gerald carter,ou=people,dc=plainjoe,dc=org
objectClass: person
cn: gerald carter
sn: carter
telephoneNumber: 555-1234
userPassword: {MD5}Xr4ilOzQ4PCOq3aQOqbuaQ==
```

We have added an attribute named userPassword. This attribute stores a representation of the credentials necessary to authenticate a user. The prefix (in this case, {MD5}) describes how the credentials are encoded. The value in this case is simply the Base64 encoding of the MD5 hash of the word "secret."

RFC 2307 defines prefixes for several encryption algorithms. These are vendor-dependent, and you should consult your server's documentation to determine which are supported. Generating userPassword values will be covered in more detail in the context of various programming languages and APIs in later chapters. Some common encoding types are:

{CRYPT}

The password hash should be generated using the local system's crypt() function, which is normally included in the standard C library. The {CRYPT} prefix will be seen quite a bit in Chapter 6 when we discuss using LDAP as a replacement for NIS.

{MD5}

The password hash is the Base64 encoding of the MD5 digest of the user's password.

{SHA} *(Secure Hash Algorithm)*

The password hash is the Base64 encoding of the 160-bit SHA-1 hash (RFC 3174) of the user's password.

{SSHA} *(Salted Secure Hash Algorithm)*

This password-hashing algorithm developed by Netscape is a salted version of the previous SHA-1 mechanism. {SSHA} is the recommended scheme for securely storing password information in an LDAP directory.

The act of being authenticated by an LDAP directory is called binding. Most users are accustomed to providing a username and password pair when logging onto a system. When authenticating an LDAP client, the username is specified as a DN—in our example, cn=gerald carter,ou=people,dc=plainjoe,dc=org. The credentials used to authenticate this entry are given by the value of the userPassword attribute.

The LDAPv3 specifications define several mechanisms for authenticating clients:

- Anonymous Authentication
- Simple Authentication
- Simple Authentication over SSL/TLS
- Simple Authentication and Security Layer (SASL)

Anonymous Authentication

Anonymous Authentication is the process of binding to the directory using an empty DN and password. This form of authentication is very common; it's frequently used by client applications (for example, email clients searching an address book).

Simple Authentication

For Simple Authentication, the login name in the form of a DN is sent with a password in clear text to the LDAP server. The server then attempts to match this password with the userPassword value, or with some other predefined attribute that is contained in the entry for the specified DN. If the password is stored in a hashed format, the server must generate the hash of the transmitted password and compare it to the stored version. However, the original password has been transmitted over the network in the clear. If both passwords (or password hashes) match, the client is successfully authenticated. While this authentication method is supported by virtually all existing LDAP servers (including LDAPv2 servers), its major drawback is its dependency on the client transmitting clear-text values across the network.

Simple Authentication Over SSL/TLS

If sending usernames and passwords over the network is not particularly tasty to you, perhaps wrapping the information in an encrypted transport layer will make it more palatable. LDAP can negotiate an encrypted transport layer prior to performing any bind operations. Thus, all user information is kept secure (as well as anything else transmitted during the session).

There are two means of using SSL/TLS with LDAPv3:

- LDAP over SSL (LDAPS - tcp/636) is well supported by many LDAP servers, both commercial and open source. Although frequently used, it has been deprecated in favor of the StartTLS LDAP extended operation.

- RFC 2830 introduced an LDAPv3 extended operation for negotiating TLS over the standard tcp/389 port. This operation, which is known as StartTLS, allows a server to support both encrypted and nonencrypted sessions on the same port, depending on the clients' requests.

With the exception of the transport layer security negotiation, the binding process is the same as for Simple Authentication.

 Designers of LDAPv3 defined two pieces of functionality, Extended Operations and Controls, to allow for additions to the original protocol without requiring a new version to be standardized. LDAP Controls apply only to individual requests and responses, similar to the way an adjective extends a noun. Depending on the client's needs, if a server does not support a specified Control, the request may fail, or the Control may simply be ignored and the request will continue normally. An Extended Operation is the equivalent of defining a new word that must be understood by both the client and server.

Simple Authentication and Security Layer (SASL)

SASL is an extensible security scheme defined in RFC 2222 that can be used to add additional authentication mechanisms to connection-oriented protocols such as IMAP and LDAP. In essence, SASL supports a pluggable authentication scheme by allowing a client and server to negotiate the authentication mechanism prior to the transmission of any user credentials.

In addition to negotiating an authentication mechanism, the communicating hosts may also negotiate a security layer (such as SSL/TLS) that will be used to encrypt all data during the session. The negotiation of transport layer security within SASL is not related either to the StartTLS Extended Operation or to LDAPS.

RFC 2222 defines the several authentication schemes for SASL, including:

- Kerberos v4 (`KERBEROS_V4`)
- The Generic Security Service Application Program Interface, Version 2 (`GSSAPI`), which is defined in RFC 2078

- The S/Key mechanism (SKEY), which is a one-time password scheme based on the MD5 message digest algorithm

- The External (EXTERNAL) mechanism, which allows an application to make use of a user's credentials provided by a lower protocol layer, such as authentication provided by SSL/TLS

In addition to these, RFC 2831 has added an SASL/DIGEST-MD5 mechanism. This mechanism is compatible with HTTP/1.1 Digest Access Authentication.

During the binding process, the client asks the server to authenticate its request using a particular SASL plug-in. The client and server then perform any extra steps necessary to validate the user's credentials. Once a success or failure condition has been reached, the server returns a response to the client's bind request as usual, and LDAP communication continues normally.

Distributed Directories

At this point we have completed examining the simple directory of Figure 2-1. Since we have covered the basics, let's expand Figure 2-1 to create a distributed directory. In a distributed directory, different hosts possess different portions of the directory tree.

Figure 2-9 illustrates how the directory would look if the people ou were housed on a separate host. There are many reasons for distributing the directory tree across multiple hosts. These can include, but are not limited to:

Performance
> Perhaps one section of the directory tree is heavily used. Placing this branch on a host by itself lets clients access the remaining subtrees more quickly.

Geographic location
> Are all the clients that access a particular branch of the directory in one location? If so, it would make more sense to place this section of the directory closer to the client hosts that require it. In this way, trips across a possibly slow WAN link can be avoided.

Administrative boundaries
> It is sometimes easier to delegate administrative control of a directory branch by placing the branch on a server controlled by the group responsible for the information in that branch. In this way, the server operators can have full access for duties such as replication and backups without interfering with a larger, more public server.

To divide the directory tree between the two servers in Figure 2-9, you must configure two links between the main directory server and the server that holds people ou. To do so, create the superior and subordinate knowledge reference links as shown.

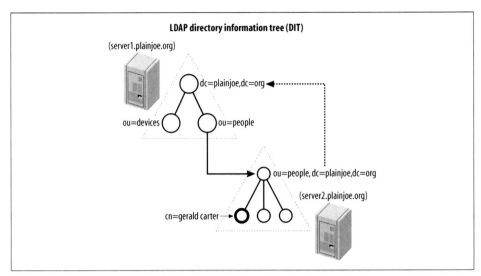

Figure 2-9. Building a distributed directory

A subordinate knowledge link, often called simply a *reference*, logically connects a node within a directory tree to the naming context of another server. Most often, the naming context of the second server is a continuation of the directory. In this example, the people ou in the main directory tree has no children because all queries of entries in the ou=people,dc=plainjoe,dc=org tree should be served by the second server. The entry ou=people,dc=plainjoe,dc=org on the main directory server is now a placeholder that contains the referral to the actual directory server for this entry. Figure 2-10 shows the definition for the the referral object class defined in RFC 3296.

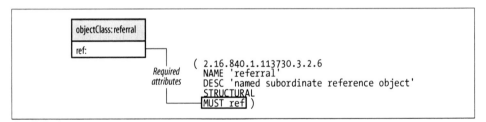

Figure 2-10. The referral object class

 LDAPv2 servers based on the original University of Michigan LDAP server supported an experimental means of using referrals that is incompatible with the standardized referrals included in LDAPv3.

The referral object contains only a single required attribute, ref. This attribute holds the URI that points to the host that contains the subtree. The format of this URI is defined in RFC 2255 as:

```
ldap://[host:port]/[/dn[?attribute][?scope][?filter][?extensions]]
```

This syntax will make more sense when we have covered LDAP search parameters in Chapter 4. For our purposes, the most common URI used as a ref value looks like:

```
ldap://[host:port]/dn
```

For example, the LDIF listing for the new people ou entry is:

```
# LDIF listing for the entry ou=people,dc=plainjoe,dc=org
dn: ou=people,dc=plainjoe,dc=org
objectClass: referral
ref: ldap://server2.plainjoe.org/ou=people,dc=plainjoe,dc=org
```

Configuring the superior knowledge reference link, also called simply a *referral* but not to be confused with the referral object class, from the second server back to the main directory is a vendor-dependent operation, so it is difficult to tell you exactly what to expect. However, the purpose is to define an LDAP URI (just like the one used as the ref attribute value) that should be returned to clients who attempt to search or query entries outside of the naming context of the subordinate server. In the example discussed here, server2 would be configured to return ldap://server1.plainjoe.org/dc=plainjoe,dc=org to all clients who attempt to go outside of ou=people,dc=plainjoe,dc=org.

Who should follow the referral link? There are two possible answers:

- The server follows and resolves any referrals that it runs into during an LDAP operation. The client receives only the result and never knows that the referral happened. This is known as "chaining" and is similar to a recursive DNS server. Chaining has not been standardized. If you are interested, you should consult the documentation for your server to determine whether chaining is supported.

- The client follows links for itself. The LDAP client library normally follows the link, but the URI can be handed to the calling application, which is then responsible for following the link itself. This method is supported by all LDAPv3-compliant clients and servers.

 There is one more mechanism for redirecting a client. An *alias* is a symbolic link in the directory pointing from one entry to another (possibly on a different server). Aliases can be used only on an entry, not on individual attributes. There may be specific situations that require the use of aliases, but these are likely to be few. For this reason, aliases are not stressed beyond the discussion here.

Continuing Standardization

LDAP is continuing to evolve as a protocol. There are currently two working groups within the IETF to help shepherd this process:

- The LDAP Duplication/Replication/Update Protocols (LDUP) working group focuses on data replication and consistency in LDAP directories. More information on the group's current activities can be found at *http://ietf.org/html.charters/ldup-charter.html*.

- The LDAPv3 Revision (LDAPbis) working group directs its efforts toward attempting to clarify parts of the original LDAPv3 specifications. This does not include work on a Version 4 of the LDAP protocol. More information on the LDAPbis working group can be found at *http://ietf.org/html.charters/ldapbis-charter.html*.

While not related to standardization processes, the LDAPzone web site (*http://www.ldapzone.com*) does provide a nice collection of LDAP-related topics, forums, and downloads.

## CHAPTER 3

OpenLDAP

While reading this book, you may find yourself feeling a little like a sky diver who has just jumped out of an airplane. As you approach the ground, things come more into focus. As you squint and try to make out the color of that house far below, you suddenly realize that you are plummeting closer and closer toward the very thing you are trying to observe.

Conceptual ideas need concrete implementations in order to solidify our understanding of them. A directory access protocol is of no use without an actual implementation that allows us to put the protocol to work to solve real information problems on a network. This chapter introduces OpenLDAP, a popular, open source LDAPv3-compliant server. There are a number of popular commercial products, including Sun Microsystem's SunOne directory server (formerly owned by Netscape), Novell's eDirectory (formerly referred to as NDS), and Microsoft's Active Directory, although this directory encompasses much more than just LDAP.

Why are we using the OpenLDAP* server instead of one from another vendor? OpenLDAP is attractive for several reasons:

- The OpenLDAP source code is available for download from *http://www.openldap.org/* under the OpenLDAP Public License. Source code can provide a great deal of information to supplement existing (or absent) documentation.

- OpenLDAP 2 is compliant with the core LDAPv3 specifications.

- OpenLDAP is available for multiple platforms, including Linux, Solaris, Mac OS 10.2, and Windows (in its various incarnations). For more information regarding OpenLDAP on Mac OS 10.2, see *http://www.padl.com//Articles/AdvancedOpenDirectoryConf.html*.

- The OpenLDAP project is a continuation of the original University of Michigan LDAP server. The relationship between Michigan's LDAP server and many

---

* The "Open" in OpenLDAP refers to the open engineering process and community used to create OpenLDAP software.

modern, commercial LDAP servers can be compared to the relationship between modern web browsers and the original NCSA Mosaic code base.

The examples presented in this chapter configure OpenLDAP on a Unix-based server. Therefore, they use standard Unix command-line tools such as *tar*, *gzip*, and *make*.

Obtaining the OpenLDAP Distribution

The OpenLDAP project does not make binary distributions of its software available. The reason for this has a lot to do with the number of dependencies it has on other packages. Many Linux vendors include precompiled versions of OpenLDAP with their distributions. Still, we'll discuss how to compile the OpenLDAP source code distribution; you'll need to build OpenLDAP to stay up to date, and studying the build process gives you a chance to learn more about the LDAP protocol.

 Symas Corporation also provides some precompiled OpenLDAP packages (including requisite software components) for Solaris and HP-UX at *http://www.symas.com/*.

The latest version of OpenLDAP can be obtained from *http://www.OpenLDAP.org/software/download/*. There are two major incarnations of OpenLDAP. The older 1.2 releases are essentially enhancements or small bug fixes to the original University of Michigan code base and implement only LDAPv2. The OpenLDAP 2 branch is an LDAPv3-compliant implementation.

There are several advantages of LDAPv3 over the previous version, such as:

- The ability to refer clients to other LDAP servers for information. The LDAPv2 RFCs contained no provision for returning a referral to a client. While the University of Michigan server supported an experimental implementation of referrals, the concept was not standardized until the LDAPv3 specifications. Standardization made interoperability between servers and clients from different vendors possible, something that was missing under LDAPv2.

- The ability to publish the server's schema via LDAP operations, which makes it easier for clients to learn the server's schema before performing searches. The only way to determine the schema supported by an LDAPv2 server was to examine the server's configuration files. Publishing the server's schema as entries within the directory allows for such things as real-time updates via standard LDAP operations. (Note that LDAPv3 does not require dynamic updates.)

- Internationalization support through the use of UTF-8 characters in strings (RFC 2253) and language tags for attribute descriptions (RFC 2596).

- Improved security and flexibility for authentication credentials and data via SASL and SSL/TLS. LDAPv2 supported only simple binds or Kerberos 4 authentication.

- Support for protocol extensions as a mechanism to enhance existing operations or add new commands without requiring that a new revision of the LDAP protocol be defined.

The OpenLDAP 2 release is an LDAPv3 server. However, LDAPv2 clients are not going away anytime soon. Therefore, OpenLDAP 2 and the majority of other LDAP servers can support both LDAPv2 and v3 clients.*

Software Requirements

The examples presented in this book for building the client tools and server components are based on the latest OpenLDAP 2.1 release available at the current time (Version 2.1.8). As with any piece of software, version numbers and dependencies change. Make sure to consult the documentation included with future OpenLDAP releases before building your server.

Our OpenLDAP server will require several external software packages:

- Support for POSIX threads, either by the operating system or an external library.

- SSL/TLS libraries (such as the OpenSSL package, which is available from *http://www.openssl.org/*).

- A database manager library that supports DBM type storage facilities. The current library of choice is the Berkeley DB 4.1 package from Sleepycat Software (*http://www.sleepycat.com/*).

- Release 2.1 of the SASL libraries from Carnegie Mellon University (*http://asg.web.cmu.edu/sasl/sasl-library.html*).

Threads

If your server's operating system supports threads, OpenLDAP 2 can take advantage of this feature. This support works fine out of the box on most current Linux systems, Solaris, and several other platforms.

If you run into problems related to POSIX thread support, your first option is to check the OpenLDAP.org web site for installation notes specific to your platform. You may also wish to visit *http://www.gnu.ai.mit.edu/software/pth/related.html* for a list of known POSIX thread libraries for Unix systems. It is possible to disable thread support in the OpenLDAP server, *slapd*, by specifying the *--disable-threads* option in

---

* Most people are referring to the University of Michigan LDAP client and server implementation when using the term LDAPv2. LDAPv2 as specified in the original RFCs has been moved to historic status.

the OpenLDAP configure script prior to compiling. However, the replication helper daemon, *slurpd*, which is covered in Chapter 5, requires thread support.

SSL/TLS Libraries

RFC 2246 describes TLS 1.0, which resembles SSL 3.0. The StartTLS extended operation defined in RFC 2830 allows LDAP clients and servers to negotiate a TLS session at any point during a conversation (even prior to authenticating the client). To enable support for this extended operation or the LDAPS protocol, you need to obtain and install the latest version of the OpenSSL libraries. These can be downloaded from the OpenSSL Project at *http://www.openssl.org/*.

Building and installing the OpenSSL libraries is straightforward. Just remember that, as of release 0.9.6g, shared libraries are not built by default. To build shared libraries, pass the *shared* option to the OpenSSL build script. The *--openssldir* option is used to define the install directory:

```
$ ./config shared --openssldir=/usr/local
```

Then follow with the obligatory:

```
$ make
$ /bin/su -c "make install"
```

to install the development libraries and tools in */usr/local/*.

Database Backend Modules

In order to build a standalone OpenLDAP server, it is necessary to provide libraries for some type of database manager (DBM). OpenLDAP presently supports two categories of local DB storage. The first, referred to as *ldbm*, can use either the GNU Database Manager from the Free Software Foundation (*http://www.fsf.org/*) or the BerkeleyDB package from Sleepycat software (*http://www.sleepycat.com/*). The second database type introduced in OpenLDAP 2.1, called *bdb*, has been customized to use only the Berkeley DB 4 libraries. The newer *bdb* backend type is preferred to the *ldbm* interface for servers that maintain local copies of data, such as those we will build in this book.

To obtain and install the Berkeley DB 4.1 libraries, begin by downloading the source code from *http://www.sleepycat.com/download.html*. Next, extract the source code to a temporary directory such as */usr/local/src/*. This example uses the release 4.1.24:

```
$ cd /usr/local/src/
$ gzip -dc {path-to-download-directory}/db-4.1.24.tar.gz | tar xvf -
```

The instructions for building the software on Unix-like systems are linked from the beginning page of the software's documentation in *db-<version>/docs/index.html*. For most purposes, this boils down to:

```
$ cd db-version/build_unix
$ ../dist/configure --prefix=/usr/local/
```

```
$ make
$ /bin/su -c "make install"
```

You can choose an installation directory other than */usr/local/* as long as you remember to take any necessary steps to ensure that the libraries and development files can be found by both the Cyrus SASL libraries and OpenLDAP when compiling these packages.

Once the process is completed, verify that the file *libdb-4.1.so* exists in the *lib/* directory below the installation root (e.g., */usr/local/lib/*).

SASL Libraries

Chapter 2 introduced the concept of pluggable authentication mechanisms. While the SASL libraries are not required to build OpenLDAP 2, the resulting LDAP server will not be completely LDAPv3-compliant if SASL is absent.

The Computing Services Department at Carnegie-Mellon University has made a set of SASL libraries available for download under a BSD-like license. The latest version can be found at *ftp://ftp.andrew.cmu.edu/pub/cyrus-mail/*. The cyrus-sasl libraries v2.1 support several SASL mechanisms, including:

ANONYMOUS
CRAM-MD5
DIGEST-MD5
GSSAPI (MIT Kerberos 5 or Heimdal Kerberos 5)
KERBEROS_V4
PLAIN

 To support the Kerberos plug-ins, you must obtain libraries from either Heimdal Kerberos (*http://www.pdc.kth.se/heimdal/*) or the MIT Kerberos distribution (*http://web.mit.edu/kerberos/www/*).

Understanding SASL is somewhat of an undertaking. You don't need to install the SASL libraries if you plan to support only simple (clear-text) binds and simple binds over SSL/TLS. The most common reasons for requiring SASL integration with LDAP are Kerberos authentication and integration with other SASL-enabled applications, such as Sendmail or CMU's Cyrus IMAPD server.

For the sake of flexibility, we will build the server with SASL support. I recommend reading the SASL System Administrator's HOWTO (*sysadmin.html*) included as part of the CMU distribution. This document gives some general setup and configuration information. You may also wish to review the "GSSAPI Tutorial" mentioned in the HOWTO and the Programmer's Guide. All of these are included in the Cyrus SASL distribution under the *doc/* directory. You may also wish to refer to RFC 2222 for a

---

general overview of SASL. The *sample/* subdirectory also includes a program for testing the SASL libraries. Chapter 9 includes examples of using the GSSAPI SASL mechanism when exploring interoperability with Microsoft's Active Directory.

Building the SASL distribution requires only a few familar steps. In most environments, the following commands will install the libraries and development files in */usr/local/*:

```
$ gzip -dc cyrus-sasl-2.1.9.tar.gz | tar xf -
$ cd cyrus-sasl-2.1.9
$ ./configure
$ make
$ /bin/su -c "make install && \
   ln -s /usr/local/lib/sasl2 /usr/lib/sasl2"
```

The symbolic link is needed because the SASL library will look for installed mechanisms in */usr/lib/sasl2/* (as described in the cyrus-sasl documentation).

Compiling OpenLDAP 2

Once the necessary software libraries have been installed and correctly configured, compiling and installing OpenLDAP becomes a matter defining the appropriate options for the *configure* script and executing the *make* command. For the sake of simplicity, all examples in this book assume that the root directory for the OpenLDAP installation is */usr/local*, which is the default.

Most of the configuration options are set to reasonable defaults or will be set appropriately by the *configure* script itself. I've already mentioned the *--disable-threads* option, which you can use if you don't want thread support. You should also be aware of the *--enable-wrappers* option, which uses the tcp_wrappers libraries for restricting access via the standard */etc/hosts.allow* and */etc/hosts.deny*. In order to use this option, the *tcpd.h* header file and *libwrap.a* library must be installed on a local system.

 For more information on tcp_wrappers, refer to the hosts_access(5) manpage or Wietse Venema's tcp_wrappers web page, which is located at *ftp://ftp.porcupine.org/pub/security/index.html*.

After extracting the source files using the command:

```
$ gzip -dc openldap-2.1.8.tar.gz | tar xvf -
```

go into the newly created directory and execute the *./configure* script, defining any options you wish to enable or disable. For example:

```
$ cd openldap-2.1.8/
$ ./configure --enable-wrappers
```

Be sure to examine the output that follows this command to verify that the correct DBM libraries were located and any other options you defined were correctly configured. Once you are satisfied with the configuration process, building the OpenLDAP clients and servers is a four-step process:

```
$ make depend
$ make
$ make test
$ /bin/su -c "make install"
```

Here are some things to check if you have any problems:

- On systems that support it, the *ldd* tool can be used to verify that the LDAP server binary, *slapd*, is linked with the correct shared libraries. For example, if *libsasl.so* cannot be located but is installed in */usr/local/lib/*, check your system's documentation for adding directories to the library search path. Under Linux, add the directory to */etc/ld.so.conf* and rerun *ldconfig -v*; under Solaris (or Linux), set the LD_LIBRARY_PATH environment variable.

- Verify that DNS resolution for your host is configured correctly. In particular, reverse DNS resolution is important. Problems with DNS resolution can make it appear that the OpenLDAP server is not responding.

- Verify that the network interface on the host is configured and functioning properly. I experience this problem quite often when using my laptop as a test server.

OpenLDAP Clients and Servers

The OpenLDAP package includes clients, servers, and development libraries. Table 3-1 gives an overview of the utilities that come with the package. All pathnames are relative to the installation location, which defaults to */usr/local*.

Table 3-1. Installed components included with OpenLDAP

Name	Description
libexec/slapd	The LDAP server.
libexec/slurpd	The LDAP replication helper.
bin/ldapadd *bin/ldapmodify* *bin/ldapdelete* *bin/ldapmodrdn*	Command-line tools for adding, modifying, and deleting entries on an LDAP server. These commands support both LDAPv2 and LDAPv3.
bin/ldapsearch *bin/ldapcompare*	Command-line utilities for searching for an LDAP directory or testing a compare operation on a specific attribute held by an entry.
bin/ldappasswd	A tool for changing the password attribute in LDAP entries. This tool is the LDAP equivalent of */bin/passwd*.
sbin/slapadd *sbin/slapcat* *sbin/slapindex*	Tools for manipulating the local backend data store used by the *slapd* daemon.

Table 3-1. Installed components included with OpenLDAP (continued)

Name	Description
sbin/slappasswd	A simple utility to generate password hashes suitable for use in *slapd.conf*.
lib/libldap* *lib/liblber** *include/ldap*.h* *include/lber*.h*	The OpenLDAP client SDK.

The slapd.conf Configuration File

The *slapd.conf* file is the central source of configuration information for the OpenLDAP standalone server (*slapd*), the replication helper daemon (*slurpd*), and related tools, such as *slapcat* and *slapadd*. As a general rule, the OpenLDAP client tools such as *ldapmodify* and *ldapsearch* use *ldap.conf* (not *slapd.conf*) for default settings.

In the tradition of Unix configuration files, *slapd.conf* is an ASCII file with the following rules:

- Blank lines and lines beginning with a pound sign (#) are ignored.
- Parameters and associated values are separated by whitespace characters (space or tab).
- A line with a blank space in the first column is considered to be a continuation of the previous one. There is no need for a line continuation character such as a backslash (\).

For general needs, the *slapd.conf* file used by OpenLDAP 2 can be broken into two sections. The first section contains parameters that affect the overall behavior of the OpenLDAP servers (for example, the level of information sent to log files). The second section is composed of parameters that relate to a particular database backend used by the *slapd* daemon. It is possible to define some default settings for these in the global section of *slapd.conf*. However, any value specified in the database section will override default settings.

Here's a partial listing that shows how these two sections look:

```
# /usr/local/etc/openldap/slapd.conf

# Global section

## Global parameters removed for brevity's sake, for now...

#######################################################
# Database #1 - Berkeley DB
database        bdb

## Database parameters and directives would go here.

#######################################################
```

```
# Database #2 - Berkeley DB
database        bdb

## Database parameters and directives would go here.

## And so on...
```

The global section starts at the beginning of the file and continues until the first database directive. We will revisit the few parameters listed here in a few moments.

The start of a database backend section is marked by the database parameter; the section continues until the beginning of the next database section or the end of the file. It is possible to define multiple databases that are served by a single installation of *slapd*. Each one is logically independent, and the associated database files will be stored separately.

 For security reasons, the *slapd.conf* file should be readable and writable only by the user who runs the *slapd* daemon, which is normally the superuser. A working server's *slapd.conf* often contains sensitive information that should be restricted from unauthorized viewing.

Schema Files

The first step in configuring your LDAP server is to decide which schema the directory should support. It's not easy to answer this question in a few lines. We'll start our example with the bare minimum.

OpenLDAP 2 includes several popular schema files to be used at the administrator's discretion. The needs of the applications that will use the directory determine which schema you use. All the attributeType and objectClass definitions required for a bare-bones server are included in the file *core.schema*. Some of these attributeTypes and objectClasses are:

- Attributes for storing the timestamp of the last update on an entry
- Attributes for representing name, locations, etc.
- Objects to represent an organization or person
- Objects to represent DNS domain names
- And so on...

By default, this file is located in the directory */usr/local/etc/openldap/schema/* after installation. In the configuration file, the include parameter specifies schemas to be included by the server. Here's how the file looks for a minimal configuration:

```
# /usr/local/etc/openldap/slapd.conf

# Global section

## Include the minimum schema required.
include      /usr/local/etc/openldap/schema/core.schema
```

```
#######################################################
## Database sections omitted
```

 I won't discuss the details of what is contained in *core.schema* yet. I'll delay this discussion until adequate time can be spent on the syntax of the file. If you would like a head start, reading RFC 2252 will provide the necessary knowledge for understanding the majority of OpenLDAP's schema files.

There are several schema files included with a default OpenLDAP 2.1 installation:

corba.schema

A schema for storing Corba objects in an LDAP directory, as described in RFC 2714.

core.schema

OpenLDAP's required core schema. This schema defines basic LDAPv3 attributes and objects described in RFCs 2251–2256.

cosine.schema

A schema for supporting the COSINE and X.500 directory pilots. Based on RFC 1274.

inetorgperson.schema

The schema that defines the inetOrgPerson object class and its associated attributes defined in RFC 2798. This object is frequently used to store contact information for people.

java.schema

A schema defined in RFC 2713 for storing a Java serialized object, a Java marshalled object, a remote Java object, or a JNDI reference in an LDAP directory.

misc.schema

A schema that defines a small group of miscellaneous objects and attributes. Currently, this file contains the schema necessary to implement LDAP-based mail routing in Sendmail 8.10+.

nis.schema

A schema that defines attributes and objects necessary for using LDAP with the Network Information Service (NIS) as described in RFC 2307 (see Chapter 6).

openldap.schema

Miscellaneous objects used by the OpenLDAP project. Provided for information purposes only.

The client applications that you want to support may require you to include schema files in addition to *core.schema*. Make sure you are aware of dependencies between schema files. Dependencies are normally described at the beginning of the file. For example, many applications require you to include the inetOrgPerson object class, which is frequently used to store contact information. The beginning of the *inetorgperson.schema* file tells you that you must also include *cosine.schema*.

Logging

The next group of parameters that you frequently find in the global section of *slapd.conf* control where *slapd* logs information during execution, as well as how much information is actually written to the log. Here's our configuration file with logging added:

```
# /usr/local/etc/openldap/slapd.conf

# Global section

## Include the minimum schema required.
include     /usr/local/etc/openldap/schema/core.schema

## Added logging parameters
loglevel    296
pidfile     /usr/local/var/slapd.pid
argsfile    /usr/local/var/slapd.args


########################################################
## Database sections omitted
```

The first new parameter is `loglevel`. This directive accepts an integer representing the types of information that should be recorded in the system logs. It is helpful to think of `loglevel` as a set of bit flags that can be logically ORed together. The flags are listed in Table 3-2. In this example, the logging level is set to 296, which equals 8 + 32 + 256. Table 3-2 tells us that this value causes *slapd* to log the following information:

8
> Connection management

32
> Search filter processing

256
> Statistics for connection, operations, and results

Table 3-2. OpenLDAP logging levels

Level	Information recorded
−1	All logging information
0	No Logging information
1	Trace function calls
2	Packet-handling debugging information
4	Heavy trace debugging
8	Connection management

Table 3-2. OpenLDAP logging levels (continued)

Level	Information recorded
16	Packets sent and received
32	Search filter processing
64	Configuration file processing
128	Access control list processing
256	Statistics for connection, operations, and results
512	Statistics for results returned to clients
1024	Communication with shell backends
2048	Print entry parsing debug information

All debugging information is logged using the LOG_LEVEL4 syslog facility. Therefore, to instruct *slapd* to write log entries to a separate log file, add the following line to */etc/syslog.conf* and instruct the *syslogd* daemon to reread its configuration file by sending it a hangup (*kill -HUP*) signal:

```
local4.debug           /var/log/slapd.log
```

The syntax of *syslog.conf* on your system may be slightly different, so you should consult the *syslog.conf* manpage for details.

 Some *syslogd* daemons require that the specified logging file exists before they write information to the log. If you think you have set up syslog correctly, but no data is being collected and your file doesn't exist, try creating the logging file with the touch command.

The remaining two parameters introduced in this section can be summed up in a sentence or two:

pidfile *filename*
> This parameter specifies the absolute location of a file that will contain the process ID of the currently running master *slapd* process.

argsfile *filename*
> This parameter specifies the absolute path to a file containing the command-line parameters used by the currently running master *slapd*. This parameter is processed only if *slapd* is started without the debug command-line argument.

SASL Options

When I first introduced the topic of installing the Cyrus SASL libraries, I said that SASL is not needed if only simple binds will be used to access the directory. However, it's often useful to allow a combination of simple binds and SASL mechanisms for user connections. For example, we might want to allow most users (who are only allowed to look up data) to authenticate via a simple bind, while requiring administrators (who are allowed to change data) to authenticate via SASL. So let's see how to configure the directory server to require the use of SASL for certain administrative accounts, while still allowing simple binds (possibly over TLS) for most clients.

slapd.conf has three SASL-related global options. These are:

```
sasl-host hostname
sasl-realm string
sasl-secprops properties
```

`sasl-host` is the fully qualified domain name of the host used for SASL authentication. For local authentication mechanisms such as DIGEST-MD5, this will be the host and domain name of the *slapd* server. `sasl-realm` is the SASL domain used for authentication. If you are unsure of this value, use *sasldblistusers* to dump the */etc/sasldb* database and obtain the realm name to use.

The third parameter, `sasl-secprops`, allows you to define various conditions that affect SASL security properties. The possible values for this parameter are given in Table 3-3. Note that it is legal to use multiple values in combination. The default security properties are noanonymous and noplain.

Table 3-3. sasl-secprops parameter values and descriptions

Flag	Description
None	Clears the default security properties (noplain, noanonymous).
noplain	Disables mechanisms vulnerable to passive attacks, such as viewing network packets to examine passwords.
noactive	Disables mechanisms vulnerable to active attacks.
nodict	Disables mechanisms that are vulnerable to dictionary-based password attacks.
noanonymous	Disables mechanisms that support anonymous login.
forwardsec	Requires forward secrecy between sessions.
passcred	Requires mechanisms that pass client credentials.
minssf=factor	Defines the minimum security strength enforced. Possible values include: 0 (no protection), 1 (integrity protection only), 56 (allow DES encryption), 112 (allow 3DES or other string encryption methods), and 128 (allow RC4, Blowfish, or other encryption algorithms of this class).
maxssf=factor	Defines the maximum security strength setting. The possible values are identical to those of minssf.
maxbufsize=size	Defines the maximum size of the security layer receive buffer. A value of 0 disables the security layer. The default value is the maximum of INT_MAX (i.e., 65536).

To fully understand the `sasl-secprops` parameter, you must also understand the effects of the various cyrus-sasl plug-ins. Table 3-4 summarizes the available mechanisms and property flags.

Table 3-4. SASL authentication mechanism security properties

SASL mechanism	Security property flags	maxssf
ANONYMOUS	NOPLAIN	0
CRAM-MD5	NOPLAIN NOANONYMOUS	0
DIGEST-MD5	NOPLAIN NOANONYMOUS	128 if compiled with RC4; 112 if compiled with DES; 0 if compiled with neither RC4 nor DES
GSSAPI	NOPLAIN NOACTIVE NOANONYMOUS	56
KERBEROS_V4	NOPLAIN NOACTIVE NOANONYMOUS	56
LOGIN	NOANONYMOUS	0
PLAIN	NOANONYMOUS	0
SCRAM-MD5	NONE	0
SRP	NOPLAIN	0

Consider if you had added the following line to the global section of your current *slapd.conf*:

```
## No PLAIN or ANONYMOUS mechanisms; use DES encrpytion
sasl-secprops     noplain,noanonymous,minssf=56
```

Comparing the value of sasl-secprops with the mechanisms listed in Table 3-4 shows that your server will allow only the following mechanisms for authentication:

> DIGEST-MD5
> GSSAPI
> KERBEROS_4

This configuration assumes that all of these SASL plug-ins have been installed as well. Also remember that configuring these SASL parameters does not require that an SASL mechanism must always be used for authentication.

SSL/TLS Options

Like the SASL parameters, *slapd.conf* offers several options for configuring settings related to SSL and TLS. These parameters include:

```
TLSCipherSuite cipher-suite-specification
TLSCertificateFile filename
TLSCertificateKeyFile filename
```

The TLSCipherSuite parameter allows you to specify which ciphers the server will accept. It also specifies a preference order for the ciphers. The value for TLSCipherSuite should be a colon-separated list of cipher suites. The explanation of available cipher suites is lengthy, so I won't reproduce it; refer to the *ciphers(1)* manpage distributed with OpenSSL. Here are a few common options; the order of preference is from left to right:

```
RC4:DES:EXPORT40
HIGH:MEDIUM
3DES:SHA1:+SSL2
```

The next two parameters, TLSCertificateFile and TLSCertificateKeyFile, inform *slapd* of the location of the server's certificate and the associated private key. This will be used to implement both LDAP over SSL (LDAPS) and the StartTLS extended operation. However, you have yet to create a certificate for your server.

Generating the server's certificate

The *CA.pl* Perl script, installed in */usr/local/misc/* as part of the OpenSSL installation, provides a nice wrapper around the *openssl* tool and its command-line arguments. To use this script, *openssl* must be located in the current search path.

Crypto 101

In my own work configuring OpenSSL and the services that use these libraries, I have found the documentation a little sparse. If you are interested in learning more about SSL, cryptography, or digital certificates, the following sources are a good place to start:

- "An Introduction to SSL," *http://developer.netscape.com/docs/manuals/security/sslin/content.htm*.
- T. Dierks, et al., "The TLS Protocol Version 1.0", RFC2246, January 1999.
- C. Kaufman, et al., *Network Security: PRIVATE Communication in a PUBLIC World* (Prentice Hall).
- Peter Gutmann's "Godzilla Crypto Tutorials Slides," *http://www.cs.auckland.ac.nz/~pgut001/*.
- Bruce Schneier, *Applied Cryptography: Protocols, Algorithms, and Source Code in C* (John Wiley & Sons).
- John Viéga, et al., *Network Security with OpenSSL* (O'Reilly).

The *CA.pl* script greatly simplifies the creation of server certificates. In order to create a new certificate, use the *-newcert* command-line option and answer the questions as prompted. Here's how to use *CA.pl* to create a new certificate:

```
$ /usr/local/misc/CA.pl -newcert
Enter PEM pass phrase:test
Verifying password - Enter PEM pass phrase:test
-----
```

```
You are about to be asked to enter information that will be incorporated into your
certificate request.
What you are about to enter is what is called a Distinguished Name or a DN.
There are quite a few fields but you can leave some blank
For some fields there will be a default value,
If you enter '.', the field will be left blank.
-----
Country Name (2 letter code) [GB]:US
State or Province Name (full name) [Berkshire]:Alabama
Locality Name (eg, city) [Newbury]:Somewhere
Organization Name (eg, company) [My Company Ltd]:PlaineJoe Dot Org
Organizational Unit Name (eg, section) [ ]:IT
Common Name (eg, your name or your server's hostname) [ ]:pogo.plainjoe.org
Email Address [ ]:jerry@plainjoe.org
Certificate (and private key) is in newreq.pem
```

This command creates a file named *newreq.pem* that contains a password-protected
private key and a self-signed certificate. Here are the contents of *newreq.pem*:

```
-----BEGIN RSA PRIVATE KEY-----
Proc-Type: 4,ENCRYPTED
DEK-Info: DES-EDE3-CBC,D8851189E7EA85CE

ImZpOfzqhNhNa6MRQBtYxjPbWmHw+3XxVAowO1FJyFQRQhuRDqrUia1IW7Tikb4d
rvjbv8T1+SN9vRGWBpz3nAERnS6uEnzPu201b9X413uXaF8OTYYId7OUalG5mjqr
GGOoHaYwbmvAIRyhq3zhqCnBgscZOl5DCXGTwOT1TeqaTfD8BpRE4ES+FOdlKjRf
yXuXmLrTgOC9ITokzRj4XtuOnJfQ5LKouooeI43FHqFBFV4Jw5IIKOuAg/tkinez
VqVesaV707PLqdlYNAVx26z/nPwbbAT2JY4fqemBzjBJPDN6Tr/QncYgbMcG+H5/
7z7mBmOWq7nCpgFSwV1KgvtDIOjqZmGSpTLbZ/pY+JUT3iPsRAaL5XHDZDM6pFOl
R7OePd3Z5sUcg1TJlnuPYejyTi1OM/hoKrNnjM+4bTY8St14zAaMV15G/3GGJueO
jeJkBZba8UpQ539yPfuPINueJFG+QipDUnHWVHSWIGhqiKVZxPTZWCZrgHx7UbYw
fQVORGQ6ddu6vYNiODYXUnN3YtvDO2OkbiGVl53OXlYv5hOydqdWRhA1hfR8SKAG
fnt1OV9yjC/OK2mj+nMNOu5kHMfA+Q6hw7mvWAsR/2ldX+/QTA8n1oRi7U4zySUL
iaAycSQl/yFHeHBhjOqFzKhvJU9Ux1A/lDzmFZ/vPGsSCvyv3GD1IzK1wvbUgxKE
3DzA1OuuUCl36HYTEgeFG2DqHPxzjhtqPyGgTG4xmB3dOndMys4VxeWB3Y+3vy3I
B6faH3/UKv1S6Fhj6xzxODjlLLt2zVOobi3F67QBXEvDO8FCYtLIww==
-----END RSA PRIVATE KEY-----
-----BEGIN CERTIFICATE-----
MIIDsDCCAxmgAwIBAgIBADANBgkqhkiG9w0BAQQFADCBnTELMAkGA1UEBhMCVVMx
EDAOBgNVBAgTBOFsYWJhbWExEjAQBgNVBAcTCVNvbWV3aGVyZTEaMBgGA1UEChMR
UGxhaW5lSm9lIERvdCBPcmcxCzAJBgNVBAsTAklUMRwwGgYDVQQDExNnYXJpJpb24u
cGxhaW5qb2Uub3JnMSEwHwYJKoZIhvcNAQkBFhJqZXJyeUBwbGFpbmpvZS5vcmcw
HhcNMDIxMTE2MjIOMzA5WhcNMDMxMTE2MjIOMzA9WjCBnTELMAkGA1UEBhMCVVMx
EDAOBgNVBAgTBOFsYWJhbWExEjAQBgNVBAcTCVNvbWV3aGVyZTEaMBgGA1UEChMR
UGxhaW5lSm9lIERvdCBPcmcxCzAJBgNVBAsTAklUMRwwGgYDVQQDExNnYXJiJpb24u
cGxhaW5qb2Uub3JnMSEwHwYJKoZIhvcNAQkBFhJqZXJyeUBwbGFpbmpvZS5vcmcw
gZ8wDQYJKoZIhvcNAQEBBQADgY0AMIGJAoGBALVOpZLKCwqioakJtgKrO+DScZ9h
C/nLcOxw9t6RUHlWSD9aGC9rMaMGrxG5YqI+dEuhbGWhnVo37IsMlHC+oJsXwY/2
r/RQT5dk1jyC4qt+2r4mGGC/QbCXOGRjTOgn3obB57OXZ19qBCfYwIXOtYncIXOP
OfUwFVRG5frBL5QDAgMBAAGjgfOwgfowHQYDVR0OBBYEFPVRTbSjVJ4v4pObON0k
oJk8YZIGMIHKBgNVHSMEgcIwgb+AFPVRTbSjVJ4v4pObON0koJk8YZIGoYGjpIGg
MIGdMQswCQYDVQQGEwJVUzEQMA4GA1UECBMHQWxhYmFtYTESMBAGA1UEBxMJU29t
ZXdoZXJlMRowGAYDVQQKExFQbGFpbmVKb2UgRG90IE9yZzELMAkGA1UECxMCSVQx
HDAaBgNVBAMTE2dhcmlvbi5wbGFpbmpvZS5vcmcxITAfBgkqhkiG9w0BCQEWEmpl
```

cnJ5QHBsYWluam9lLm9yZ4IBADAMBgNVHRMEBTADAQH/MAOGCSqGSIb3DQEBBAUA
A4GBAIM+ySiITRXb/d1qcO/XUQSKdU3IXqPgS8jY3U12Bll/kCZFcZxjksg6xBib
91Y/bonSEisJG74zn/Ots3sjsr3QKZp5xFcYCyK3IYjaqnFeAOh+eUp54vLpmQZX
e4QaeTkg/8MnS3vFvWoxfo4Z1Zu/wWhp9WMRRwIVAR99Ppps
-----END CERTIFICATE-----

Notice that the *CA.pl* script places a private key in the same file as the public certificate. You must remove the password for the private key unless you always want to start the OpenLDAP server manually. It is extremely important to protect this key carefully. Public key cryptography is no good if the private key is readily available to anyone.

Because this private key is password protected, it will require some modification before integrating it into the server's setup. The following command removes the password from the private key and places the modified version of the key in a separate file:

```
$ openssl rsa -in newreq.pem -out newkey.pem
read RSA key
Enter PEM pass phrase:test
writing RSA key
```

The *newkey.pem* file can be renamed to a filename of your choosing. Something like *slapd-key.pem* would be appropriate. Make sure that the new file is safely secured using the appropriate filesystem permissions (i.e., rw-------).

Finally, using your favorite text editor, remove the original private key from *newreq.pem*. I'll rename the certificate file to *slapd-cert.pem* for the remaining examples in this chapter. At this point, we have the following files:

slapd-key.pem
    LDAP server's private key

slapd-cert.pem
    LDAP server's public certificate

Here are the TLS configuration parameters in the context of *slapd.conf*:

```
# /usr/local/etc/openldap/slapd.conf

# Global section

## Include the minimum schema required.
include     /usr/local/etc/openldap/schema/core.schema

## Added logging parameters
loglevel    296
pidfile     /usr/local/var/slapd.pid
argsfile    /usr/local/var/slapd.args

## TLS options for slapd
TLSCipherSuite          HIGH
TLSCertificateFile      /etc/local/slapd-cert.pem
TLSCertificateKeyFile   /etc/local/slapd-key.pem
```

```
#######################################################
## Database sections omitted
```

More Security-Related Parameters

There are also five other security-related global options to be covered prior to continuing on to the database section. These are:

```
security
require
allow
disallow
password-hash
```

The security parameter allows us to specify general security strength factors. Table 3-5 lists the options and values for the security parameter. All of these options take an integer value specifying the strength factor; the integer must be one of the values used for the minssf and maxssf parameters described in Table 3-3.

Table 3-5. Possible values for the slapd.conf security parameter

Value	Description
sasl	Defines the SASL security strength factor.
ssf	Defines the overall security strength factor.
tls	Defines the security strength factor to the SSL/TLS security layer.
transport	Defines the security strength provided by the underlying transport layer. Eventually, this option will be used to choose between multiple secure transport layer protocols, such as TLS and IPSEC.
update_sasl update_ssf update_tls update_transport	Define the security strength of the various layers when performing update operations on the directory.

For example, we can require very strong authentication and transport layer security when performing updates by adding the following line to the global section of *slapd.conf*:

```
## Require strong authentication and transport layer security for update operations.
## NOTE: This is just an example and will not be added to our final slapd.conf.
security    update_sasl=128,update_tls=128
```

To take full advantage of the security parameter, you must disable simple binds and use only SASL mechanisms for authentication. See the disallow parameter in this section for details of how this can be done.

The require parameter differs from the security parameter by allowing an administrator to define general conditions that must be met to provide access to the directory. This setting may be done globally or on a per-database basis. The require parameter accepts a comma-separated list of the strings described in Table 3-6.

Table 3-6. Values for the require parameter

Value	Description
none	Clears all requirements.
authc	Requires client authentication prior to directory access (i.e., no anonymous access).
bind	Requires the client to issue a bind request, possibly an anonymous bind, prior to directory operations.
LDAPv3	Requires the client to use Version 3 of the LDAP protocol for directory access. By default, OpenLDAP supports both LDAPv2 and v3 clients.
SASL strong	Require the client to use strong (SASL) authentication in order to be granted access to the directory. Currently, these two options are identical.

The effect of some of the require settings can be obtained by other means as well. For example, if anonymous users should have no access to directory information, OpenLDAP provides access control lists within a database that can restrict access in a much more flexible way.

The allow (and complementary disallow) parameters provide another means of enabling and disabling certain features. Currently, the allow parameter supports only two options:

none
> This is the default setting.

tls_2_anon
> Allows TLS to force the current session to anonymous status.

The disallow parameter, however, offers many more options. These include:

bind_v2
> Disables LDAPv2 bind requests

bind_anon
> Disables anonymous binds

bind_anon_cred
> Disables anonymous credentials when the DN is empty

bind_anon_dn
> Disables anonymous binds when the DN is nonempty

bind_simple
> Disables simple binds

bind_krbv4
> Disables Kerberos 4 bind requests

tls_authc
> Disables StartTLS if the client is authenticated

Finally, the password-hash parameter defines the default password encryption scheme used to store values in the userPassword attribute. This setting can be overridden on

an individual attribute basis by prefixing the password with the appropriate directive. The default encryption scheme is {SSHA}. Other possibilities include:

```
{SHA}
{SMD5}
{MD5}
{CRYPT}
{CLEARTEXT}
```

The security parameters and examples presented here are enough for our needs.
Refer to the *openssl(1)* manpage for more information on OpenSSL tools and configuration.

After covering these final parameters, you can complete the global section of your
slapd.conf:

```
# /usr/local/etc/openldap/slapd.conf

# Global section

## Include the minimum schema required.
include     /usr/local/etc/openldap/schema/core.schema

## Added logging parameters
loglevel    296
pidfile     /usr/local/var/slapd.pid
argsfile    /usr/local/var/slapd.args

## TLS options for slapd
TLSCipherSuite          HIGH
TLSCertificateFile      /etc/local/slapd-cert.pem
TLSCertificateKeyFile   /etc/local/slapd-key.pem

## Misc security settings
password-hash    {SSHA}


#######################################################
## Database sections omitted
```

Serving Up Data

Following the global section of *slapd.conf* will be one or more database sections, each
defining a directory partition. A database section begins with the database directive
and continues until the next occurrence of the database directive or the end of the
file. This parameter has several possible values:

bdb

This backend has been specifically written to take advantage of the Berkley DB 4
database manager. This backend makes extensive use of indexing and caching to

speed up performance; it is the recommended backend used on an OpenLDAP server.

ldbm

An ldbm database is implemented via either the GNU Database Manager or the Sleepycat Berkeley DB software package. This backend is the older implementation of the bdb backend. The details of this backend are described in the *slapd-ldbm(5)* manpage.

passwd

The passwd backend is a quick and dirty means of providing a directory interface to the system *passwd(5)* file. It has only one configuration parameter: the file directive, which defines the location of the password file (if different from */etc/passwd*) used to respond to directory queries. The details of this backend are described in the *slapd-passwd(5)* manpage.

shell

The shell backend directive allows the use of alternative (and external) databases. This directive lets you specify external programs that are called for each of the LDAPv3 core operations. The details of this backend are described in the *slapd-shell(5)* manpage.

The first step in writing a database section is defining the type of backend. The examples in the remainder of this book almost exclusively use the bdb database value.

```
## Begin a new database section.
database     bdb
```

The next item is to define the directory partition's naming context. The naming context allows *slapd* to serve multiple, potentially disconnected partitions from a single server. Each partition has a unique naming context that identifies the root entry in the tree. The following example defines the naming context of the database to correspond with the local domain name, a practice recommended by RFC 2247 ("Using Domains in LDAP/X.500 Distinguished Names"):

```
## Define the beginning of example database.
database     bdb

## Define the root suffix you serve.
suffix          "dc=plainjoe,dc=org"
```

Each LDAP directory can have a root DN (*rootdn*), which is similar to the superuser account on Unix systems. When authenticated, this DN is authorized to do whatever the user desires; access control restrictions do not apply. For this reason, some administrators prefer not to configure a root DN at all, or at least remove it once the directory has been sufficiently populated to hand over control to existing user accounts.

The naming of the root DN is arbitrary, although the cn values of "admin" and "Manager" have become common choices. The root DN also requires a corresponding root password (rootpw), which can be stored in clear text or encrypted form using one of the prefixes accepted by the password-hash parameter. OpenLDAP 2 provides the *slappasswd(8c)* utility for generating {CRYPT}, {MD5}, {SMD5}, {SSHA}, and {SHA} passwords. Do not place the root password in plain text regardless of what the permissions on *slapd.conf* are. Even if the password is encrypted, it is extremely important not to allow unauthorized users to view *slapd.conf*.

```
## Define a root DN for superuser privileges.
rootdn      "cn=Manager,dc=plainjoe,dc=org"

## Define the password used with rootdn. This is a salted secure hash of the phrase
## "secret."
rootpw          {SSHA}2aksIaicAvwc+DhCrXUFlhgWsbBJPLxy
```

You aren't required to define a root password. If no rootpw directive is present, the rootdn is authenticated using the server's default authentication method (e.g., SASL). OpenLDAP 2.1 uses a DN representation of an SASL identify. The general syntax is:

```
uid=name,[cn=realm],cn=SASL Mechanism,cn=auth
```

The cn=*realm* portion on the DN is omitted if the mechanism does not support the concept of realms or if the one specified is the default realm for the server. If your OpenLDAP server existed within the PLAINJOE.ORG realm and you chose to use a Kerberos 5 principal named *ldapadmin@PLAINJOE.ORG* as the rootdn, it would appear as:

```
rootdn "uid=ldapadmin,cn=gssapi,cn=auth"
```

The next two parameters should be left to their default values:

lastmod
> This parameter determines whether *slapd* will maintain the operational attributes modifiersName, modifyTimestamp, creatorsName, and createTimestamp for all entries defined in *core.schema*. The default behavior is to maintain the information for all entries. The option accepts a value of off or on. Disabling this parameter means that client-side caching of information is not possible because no marker exists to test whether an entry has been updated.

readonly
> The readonly parameter allows a server to disable all update access, including update access by the rootdn. Directory data is writable by default, assuming that there are no access control lists in place. Under some circumstances, such as backing up the data, you may want to prevent the directory from accepting modifications. Like the lastmod parameter, the readonly options also accept the values off or on.

bdb backend-specific parameters

The database parameters discussed up to this point are applicable to OpenLDAP's various database backends in general. This section examines several parameters that are used only by the *bdb* database.

The directory and mode parameters define the physical location and filesystem permissions of the created database files. These parameters are necessary because, when using an ldbm backend, *slapd* manages the data store itself. In the following configuration file, the directory and mode parameters tell *slapd* and the other LDAP tools how to locate and store the database files for this partition. The files are stored in the directory */var/ldap/plainjoe.org/* and created with read/write permission (0600) for the owner only (the account under which the *slapd* daemon runs).

```
## Define the beginning of example database.
database        bdb

## Define the root suffix you serve.
suffix          "dc=plainjoe,dc=org"

## Define a root DN for superuser privileges.
rootdn          "cn=Manager,dc=plainjoe,dc=org"

## Define the password used with rootdn. This is the Base64-encoded MD5 hash of
## "secret."
rootpw          {SSHA}2aksIaicAvwc+DhCrXUFlhgWsbBJPLxy

## Directory containing the database files
directory       /var/ldap/plainjoe.org

## Files should be created rw for the owner **only**.
mode            0600
```

 It's a good idea to maintain tight security on the physical database files even if the directory server is a closed box (i.e., no users can log into the server and run a shell). It is easier to manage the server when the only way to access the backend storage is via *slapd* itself.

The index parameter specifies the attributes on which *slapd* should maintain indexes. These indexes are used to optimize searches, similar to the indexes used by a relational database management system. *slapd* supports four types of indexes. However, not all attributes support all four index types. Each index type corresponds to one of the matching rules defined in the directory schema.

approx (approximate)
    Indexes the information for an approximate, or phonetic, match of an attribute's value.

eq (equality)

> Indexes the information necessary to perform an exact match of an attribute value. The match may be case-sensitive or whitespace-sensitive, depending on the matching rules defined in the attribute's syntax.

pres (presence)

> Indexes the information necessary to determine if an attribute has any value at all. If an attribute does not possess a value, then the attribute is not present in the directory entry.

sub (substring)

> Indexes the information necessary to perform a simple substring match on attribute values.

There can be multiple index definitions for the same database—and even multiple attributes or index types—on the same line. Each attribute or index type should be separated by a comma; use whitespace to separate the attribute list from the list of index types. Here's how to define an equality and presence index on the cn attribute:

```
## Maintain presence and equality searches on the cn and uid attributes.
index          cn          pres,eq
```

Which indexes should be maintained depends on the client applications that the server will support and the types of searches that those applications will perform. The best way to determine which indexes to maintain is to include the search processing debug output (*loglevel 32*) in the server's log file.

 OpenLDAP 2 requires an equality index on the objectClass attribute for performance reasons.

```
## Must be maintained for performance reasons
index          objectClass          eq
```

I cannot stress the use of proper indexes enough. Misconfigured indexes are probably the number one reason administrators experience performance problems with OpenLDAP servers. Many of the applications and scenarios presented later in the book focus on functionality and not necessarily performance. This should not be construed as lessening the importance of properly indexing the attributes used freqently in searches. It simply means that I assume you have learned your lesson about indexes here and can fill in the blanks later.

While an indexed database offers many performance benefits over flat text files, these benefits can be increased by caching entries and indexes in memory to prevent disk I/O in response to common searches. The cachesize parameter allows you to tune caching according to the needs of the directory.

The cachesize parameter defines the number of entries that should be cached in memory. The default is to cache 1,000 entries. If your total directory size is less than 1,000 entries, there is no need to modify this setting. If, however, your directory contains 1,000,000 entries, a cache size of 100,000 would not be unusual.

When setting parameters to integer values in *slapd.conf*, make sure to remove commas from the number. For example, 100,000 should be entered as 100000.

Here is what the database section looks like so far:

```
## Define the beginning of example database.
database        bdb

## Define the root suffix you serve.
suffix          "dc=plainjoe,dc=org"

## Define a root DN for superuser privileges. This is the Base64-encoded MD5 hash of
## "secret."
rootdn          "cn=Manager,dc=plainjoe,dc=org"

## Define the password used with rootdn.
rootpw          {SSHA}2aksIaicAvwc+DhCrXUFlhgWsbBJPLxy

## Directory containing the database files
directory       /var/ldap/plainjoe.org

## Files should be created rw for the owner **only**.
mode            0600

## Indexes to maintain
index           objectClass     eq
index           cn              pres,eq

## db tuning parameters; cache 2,000 entries in memory
cachesize       2000
```

Access Control Lists (ACLs)

The Directory ACLs provided by OpenLDAP are simple in their syntax, yet very flexible and powerful in their implementation. The basic idea is to define *Who* has *Access* to *What?* The most frequent forms of "Who" include:

*

Matches any connected user, including anonymous connection

self

The DN of the currently connected user, assuming he has been successfully authenticated by a previous bind request

anonymous

Nonauthenticated user connections

users

Authenticated user connections

Regular expression

Matches a DN or an SASL identity

Remember that the login name used to specify a user for authentication takes the form of a DN (e.g., dn="cn=gerald carter,ou=people,dc=plainjoe,dc=org") or an SASL identify (e.g., dn="uid=jerry,cn=gssapi,cn=auth"). The self value is used as a shortcut for the DN of the authenticated user of the current session. The examples later in this section will help clarify this concept.

The notion of an access level is a new concept. Table 3-7 summarizes the various access privileges. Higher levels possess all of the capabilities of the lower levels. For example, compare access implies auth access, and write access implies read, search, compare, and auth.

Table 3-7. Summary of access levels from most (top) to least (bottom)

Access level	Permission granted
write	Access to update attribute values (e.g., Change this telephoneNumber to 555-2345).
read	Access to read search results (e.g., Show me all the entries with a telephoneNumber of 555*).
search	Access to apply search filters (e.g., Are there any entries with a telephoneNumber of 555*).
compare	Access to compare attributes (e.g., Is your telephoneNumber 555-1234?).
auth	Access to bind (authenticate). This requires that the client send a username in the form of a DN and some type of credentials to prove his or her identity.
none	No access.

The simplest way to control access is to define a default level of authorization. A global *slapd.conf* parameter defines the default access given to a user in the absence of a more explicit rule. For example, adding the following lines to the global section of *slapd.conf* gives all users search access unless an explicit ACL says otherwise:

```
## Give users search access when no other ACL applies.
defaultaccess    search
```

Finally, the "What" defines the entry and attributes to which the ACL should apply. It is composed of three basic parts, all of which are optional.

- A regular expression defining the DN of the proposed target of the ACL. The actual syntax is dn.*targetstyle*=*regex*, in which *targetstyle* is one of base, subtree, one, or children, and *regex* is a regular expression representing a DN. The *targetstyle*, which defaults to subtree, is used to broaden or narrow the scope of the ACL. If, for example, the *targetstyle* is set to one, the ACL applies only to children immediately below the defined DN. Very rarely does this setting need be changed from its default. The *regex* follows normal regular expression rules, with the addition that the DN must be in normalized form. The most common error is to add extra whitespace between components of the DN—for example, you can't add a space after the comma in dc=plainjoe,dc=org.

- An LDAP search filter that conforms to RFC 2254. (More on LDAP searches will be covered in the next chapter.) The syntax for specifying a filter is filter=*ldapFilter*.

- A comma-separated list of attribute names taking the form attrs=*attributeList*. If this item is not present, the ACL applies to all attributes held by the entry that matches the DN regular expression pattern.

If none of these components are present, a single asterisk (*) is used as a placeholder (for "What") to include everything.

Now that we've looked at the parts of an ACL, let's see how to put an ACL together. It is easiest to understand the syntax of an ACL by examining some practical uses. The following ACL grants read access to everyone:

```
# Simple ACL granting read access to the world
access to *
    by * read
```

The space at the beginning of the second line indicates that this is a continuation of the previous line. This control list could have been written on a single line, but the multiline style is more readable for complex ACLs.

This next example restricts access to the userPassword attribute; any user can access the attribute, but can access it only for authentication purposes. Users can't read or write this attribute.

```
# Restrict userPassword to be used for authentication only.
access to attrs=userPassword
    by * auth
```

If a user should be allowed to modify her own password in the directory, the ACL would need to be rewritten as follows:

```
# Restrict userPassword to be used for authentication only, but allow users to modify
# their own passwords.
access to attrs=userPassword
    by self write
    by * auth
```

Once authenticated, a user can write her own password. Anyone is allowed to use passwords for authentication purposes.

ACLs are evaluated on a "first match wins" basis. An ACL listed first takes precedence over ACLs mentioned later. This means that more restrictive ACLs should be listed prior to more general ones. Consider what behavior would result from the following two ACLs. What sort of access would be granted to the userPassword attribute?

```
# Simple ACL granting read access to the world
access to *
    by * read

# Restrict userPassword to be used for authentication only, but allow users to modify
# their own passwords.
access to attrs=userPassword
    by self write
    by * auth
```

The previous ACLs grant all users (anonymous and authenticated) read access to userPassword. This clearly isn't a policy you would want. To achieve the desired effect of restricting read privileges to this attribute, the ACLs should be ordered as follows:

```
# Restrict userPassword to be used for authentication only, but allow users to modify
# their own passwords.
access to attrs=userPassword
     by self write
     by * auth

# Simple ACL granting read access to the world
access to *
     by * read
```

For the next example, assume that the following conditions are met:

- Administrative user accounts are located beneath the DN ou=admins,ou=eng, dc=plainjoe,dc=org.
- Normal user accounts are located beneath ou=users,ou=eng,dc=plainjoe,dc=org.
- Normal users should not be able to view passwords of other users.
- A user should be able to modify his password.
- Administrative users should be able to modify any user's password.

We can model these rules with the following ACL:

```
# Set control on the userPassword attribute.
access to dn=".*,ou=eng,dc=plainjoe,dc=org"
  attrs=userPassword
  by self write
  by * auth
  by dn=".*,ou=admins,ou=eng,dc=plainjoe,dc=org" write
```

ACLs can very often be written in more than one equivalent form. The following access rule is functionally identical to the one just presented:

```
# Set control on the userPassword attribute.
access to dn.children="ou=eng,dc=plainjoe,dc=org"
  attrs=userPassword
  by self write
  by * auth
  by dn.children="ou=admins,ou=eng,dc=plainjoe,dc=org" write
```

These examples are only a few possibilities of what can be done. We will continue to explore ACLs as a means of securing our server as we add more information into the directory in later chapters.

## CHAPTER 4

OpenLDAP: Building a Company White Pages

The previous chapter discussed how to install OpenLDAP and provided an overview of the *slapd* configuration file, *slapd.conf*. However, we have yet to launch the server, let alone add any data to the directory. Using the *slapd.conf* from Chapter 3 as a starting point, this chapter shows you how to create a company directory for storing employee contact information, including postal addresses, email addresses, and phone numbers.

A Starting Point

Here is the *slapd* configuration file developed in Chapter 3. We will change some of the entries in this listing as things progress.

```
# /usr/local/etc/openldap/slapd.conf

# Global section

## Include the minimum schema required.
include         /usr/local/etc/openldap/schema/core.schema

## Added logging parameters
loglevel        296
pidfile         /usr/local/var/slapd.pid
argsfile        /usr/local/var/slapd.args

## TLS options for slapd
TLSCipherSuite          HIGH
TLSCertificateFile      /etc/local/slapd-cert.pem
TLSCertificateKeyFile   /etc/local/slapd-key.pem

## Misc security settings
password-hash           {SSHA}

#######################################################
## Define the beginning of example database.
database        bdb
```

```
## Define the root suffix you serve.
suffix              "dc=plainjoe,dc=org"

## Define a root DN for superuser privileges.
rootdn              "cn=Manager,dc=plainjoe,dc=org"

## Define the password used with rootdn. This is the base64-encoded MD5 hash of
## "secret."
rootpw              {SSHA}2aksIaicAvwc+DhCrXUFlhgWsbBJPLxy

## Directory containing the database files
directory           /var/ldap/plainjoe.org

## Files should be created rw for the owner **only**.
mode                0600

## Indexes to maintain
index               objectClass         eq
index               cn                  pres,eq

## db tuning parameters; cache 2,000 entries in memory
cachesize           2000

# Simple ACL granting read access to the world
access to *
    by * read
```

Defining the Schema

The first step in implementing a directory is determining what information to store in the directory. The naming context of your server has already been defined as:

```
dc=plainjoe,dc=org
```

Store contact information for employees in the people organizational unit:

```
ou=people,dc=plainjoe,dc=org
```

There are several ways to identify the data that should be placed in an employee's entry. Information stored in an existing Human Resources database can provide a good starting point. Of course, you may not want to place all of this information in your directory. As a general rule, I prefer not to put information in a directory if that data probably won't be used. If it turns out that the data is actually necessary, you can always add it later. Eliminating unnecessary data at the start means that there's less to worry about when you start thinking about protecting the directory against unauthorized access.

An alternative to starting with an existing database is to determine which employee attributes you wish to make available and define a schema to match that list. The reverse also works: you can select a standard schema and use the attributes already defined. I prefer this approach because it makes it easy to change from one server vendor to another. Widely used, standard schemas are more likely to be supported by a wide range of vendors. Custom, in-house schemas may need to be redesigned to adapt to a new vendor (or even a new version from the same vendor).

For your directory, the inetOrgPerson schema defined in RFC 2798 is more than adequate. From "Schema Files" in Chapter 3, we know that this object class and associated attributes are defined in OpenLDAP's *inetorgperson.schema* file. As shown in Figure 4-1, an inetOrgPerson is a descendant of the organizationalPerson, which was itself derived from the person object class.

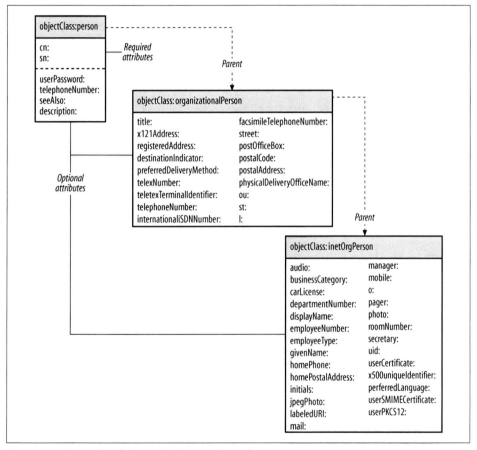

Figure 4-1. Hierarchy of the inetOrgPerson object class

The union of these object classes defines the set of required and optional attributes that are available. This means that the only required attributes in an inetOrgPerson object are the cn and sn attributes derived from the person object class.

From this point on, diagrams of an object class will not include RFC 2252–style schema definitions. If you wish to study the exact syntax of any object class, refer to the schema files included with OpenLDAP or the relevant RFC (or Internet-Draft).

Your directory will use the cn attribute as the RDN for each entry. Remember that the RDN of an entry must be unique among siblings of a common parent. In larger organizations, two people may have the same first and last name. In these cases, using a more specific value for the cn, such as including a middle name (or initial), can alleviate name collisions.

Another way to reduce the number of name collisions is to redesign the directory layout to reduce the total number of user entries sharing a common parent. In other words, group employees in some type of logical container, such as a departmental organizational unit. Figure 4-2 illustrates how this design avoids namespace conflicts. In this directory the "John Arbuckle" in sales is different from the "John Arbuckle" in engineering because the entries possess different parent nodes.

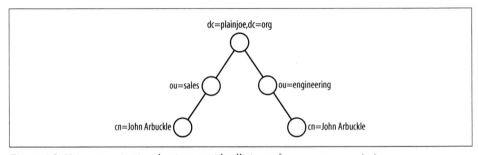

Figure 4-2. Using organizational unit to avoid collisions of common names (cn)

For our example, going with a single container of ou=people is fine; furthermore, our employee base is small enough to use an employee's common name (cn) without fear of conflict. Figure 4-3 shows the directory namespace developed so far.

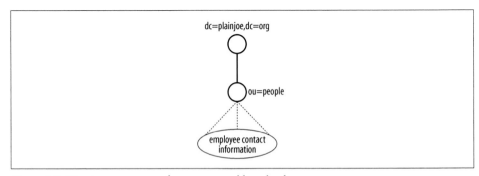

Figure 4-3. Directory namespace for company address book

Here is an employee entry that contains the attributes needed for our directory. Notice that the two required attributes outlined in Figure 4-1, cn and sn, are present in addition to several optional attributes.

```
## LDIF entry for employee "Gerald W. Carter"
dn: cn=Gerald W. Carter,ou=people,dc=plainjoe,dc=org
objectClass: inetOrgPerson
cn: Gerald W. Carter
sn: Carter
mail: jerry@plainjoe.org
mail: gcarter@valinux.com
labeledURI: http://www.plainjoe.org/
roomNumber: 1234 Dudley Hall
departmentNumber: Engineering
telephoneNumber: 222-555-2345
pager: 222-555-6789
mobile: 222-555-1011
```

Deep or Wide?

Is it better to maintain a shallow (and wide) tree or a deep (and narrow) directory? The best structure for your directory depends on two factors.

First, how likely is it for a change to force an entry (in our case, a person) to be moved from one organizational unit to another? The answer to this question is based on a solid understanding of your organization and its needs. Deeper directory trees imply that an entry must meet more requirements in order to be placed in a certain container. For example, rather than placing all employees under the ou=people, using characteristics such as departments, job description, and geographic location makes for a more defined grouping. However, if these characteristics are likely to change frequently, you will only be creating more work for yourself in the long term. It is also good to note that deep directories require longer DNs to reference entries. This can become an annoyance over time.

Second, does the implementation of your LDAP directory server favor one design over another? For OpenLDAP, this answer depends on your needs. The determining factor will be the number of updates, or writes, that will be made to the directory. To update an entry, the *slapd* server obtains a lock on the parent entry for the requesting client. Now suppose that you have a very shallow directory tree with 10,000 entries under a single parent. If many updates occur at the same time, the contention for the lock on the parent entry will be very high. The end result will be slower updates because processes will block waiting for the lock.

A deeper tree means that you can often make searches more efficient by giving a more detailed search base. For more information on designing LDAP namespaces, you may wish to read Howes, et al., *Understanding and Deploying LDAP Directory Services* (MacMillan Technical Press).

Updating slapd.conf

Once the schema has been selected, the next step is to modify *slapd.conf* to support the selected attribute types and object classes. In order to support the inetOrgPerson object class, you must include *inetorgperson.schema*, *core.schema*, and *cosine.schema* in *slapd.conf*. The comments that begin *inetorgperson.schema* outline the dependency on the COSINE schema. Here are the modifications to the global section of *slapd.conf*:

```
# /usr/local/etc/openldap/slapd.conf

# Global section

## Include the minimum schema required.
include         /usr/local/etc/openldap/schema/core.schema

## Added to support the inetOrgPerson object.
include         /usr/local/etc/openldap/schema/cosine.schema
include         /usr/local/etc/openldap/schema/inetorgperson.schema

## Added logging parameters
...
```

The database section is currently in working condition, so only a few changes are needed. To better support searches for employees, you should modify the set of indexes to include a more complete list of attributes. In addition to creating an index for the cn attribute, you'll also index the surname (sn) and email address (mail) attributes. In addition to the equality (*eq*) index, you'll add a substring (*sub*) index to support searches such as "All employees whose last names begin with C." Finally, you will add an equality index for the departmentNumber attribute so that users can search for employees within a given department. This index would not be necessary if the directory were laid out as shown in Figure 4-2 because the same effect could be achieved by beginning the search at the department ou. Here are the changes to the database section:

```
## Indexes to maintain
index         objectClass        eq
index         cn,sn,mail         eq,sub
index         departmentNumber   eq
...
```

At this point, it's a good idea to verify that the location specified by the directory parameter exists and has the proper permissions. In our example, that directory is */var/ldap/plainjoe.org*. If this directory does not exist, the following two commands ensure that the filesystem is ready to store data:

```
root# mkdir -p /var/ldap/plainjoe.org
root# chmod 700 /var/ldap/plainjoe.org
```

Starting slapd

Once the final tweaks have been added to the configuration file, the next step is to start the *slapd* daemon by executing the following command as root:

```
root# /usr/local/libexec/slapd
```

Use the *ps* command to verify that *slapd* is running. On a Linux system, the output should appear similar to:

```
$ ps -ef | grep slapd
root    8235    1  0 12:37 ?   00:00:00 /usr/local/libexec/slapd
root    8241 8235  0 12:37 ?   00:00:00 /usr/local/libexec/slapd
root    8242 8241  0 12:37 ?   00:00:00 /usr/local/libexec/slapd
```

On Linux and IRIX, multiple threads of a process will show up as individual entries in the output from *ps*. On Solaris, *slapd* will be displayed as a single process.

Stopping the OpenLDAP server requires that the daemon have a chance to flush modified directory data to disk. The best way to do this is to send the parent *slapd* process an INT signal, as shown here (the *pidfile* location was defined in the server's configuration file):

```
root# kill -INT 'cat /var/run/slapd.pid'
```

Shutting down *slapd* by more drastic means, such as *kill -9*, can result in data corruption and should be avoided at all costs.

In the absence of any command-line options, *slapd*'s behavior is governed by compile-time defaults or options defined in the *slapd.conf* file. At times, it is necessary to override some of these settings via the command line. Table 4-1 lists the available *slapd* options.

Table 4-1. Command-line options for the slapd server

Option	Description
-d integer	Specifies the log level to use for logging information. This option causes *slapd* to log all information to standard output on the controlling terminal; it can be very helpful for quick server debugging sessions. The integer value specified should be a combination of the logging levels associated with the `loglevel` parameter in *slapd.conf*.
-f filename	Uses a configuration file other than the compile-time default (*slapd.conf*).
-h URI_list	Specifies a space-separated list of LDAP URIs that the *slapd* daemon should serve. The most common URIs are `ldap:///` (LDAP on port 389; the default), `ldaps:///` (LDAP over SSL on port 636), and `ldapi:///` (LDAP over IPC).
-l syslog-local-user	Specifies the local user of the syslog facility. The default value is LOCAL4. Possible values range from LOCAL0 to LOCAL7. This option may not be supported on all systems. Check the *syslog(8)* manpage to verify the existence of the local-user syslog facility.
-n name	Defines the service name used when logging messages to syslog. This is for convenience only and defaults to the string `slapd`.
-r directory	Specifies a *chroot(1)* jail directory to be used by *slapd*.

Table 4-1. Command-line options for the slapd server (continued)

Option	Description
-s syslog-level	Defines a syslog level other than the default level to log all syslog messages. Refer to the *syslog.conf(5)* manpage for available levels on your system.
-u username -g groupname	Specify the effective user or group ID for *slapd*.

Of course, starting *slapd* from the command line is something you do only while testing. In practice, it would be started by one of the system's boot time initialization scripts—either *rc.local* for BSD systems, or one of the */etc/rc.d/rc?.d/* (or */etc/init.d/*) scripts for System V hosts. You should refer to the *init(8)* manpage for a brief description of run levels and which levels are used (and for what functions) on your system. On most Linux systems, the *slapd* daemon should be launched at run levels 3 and 5. Run level 5 is basically the same as run level 3 with the addition of X11.

Adding the Initial Directory Entries

A directory without data isn't of much use. There are two ways to add information to your directory; which method to use depends on the directory's state. First, *slapadd* and the other *slap** commands were presented in Chapter 3 as database maintenance tools. They allow an administrator to import entries directly into the database files and export the entire directory as an LDIF file. They work directly with the database, and don't interact with *slapd* at all. Second, the OpenLDAP distribution includes a number of tools, such as *ldapmodify*, that can update a live directory using the LDAPv3 network operations. These tools access the directory through the server.

What are the advantages and disadvantages of these approaches? The offline tools can be much faster; furthermore, there are circumstances when you can't start the server without first adding data (for example, when restoring the directory's contents from a backup). The disadvantage of the offline tools, of course, is that they must be run locally on the server.

In contrast to the offline tools, the LDAP client utilities are more flexible and allow a directory administrator greater control by forcing user authentication and by using access control lists on directory entries. A good rule of thumb is that the *slap** tools are used for getting your LDAP server online, and the *ldap** tools are for day-to-day administration of the directory.

OpenLDAP 2.1 removed the restriction that *slapd* must not be running before any of the *slap** tools can be used. However, OpenLDAP 2.0 caches data in memory, so using the *slap** tools while the directory is running can present an inconsistent view of the directory at best, and corrupt data at worst.

The tools for offline manipulation of directory information are *slapadd*, *slapcat*, *slapindex*, and *slappasswd* (covered in Chapter 3). The *slapadd* tool determines which files and indexes to update based on the *slapd.conf* file. Because it is possible for a given configuration file to define more than one database partition, *slapadd* provides options for specifying a database partition by either the directory suffix (*-b suffix*) or the numbered occurrence (*-n integer*) in *slapd.conf*. Referring to a particular database using a numbered instance is confusing and error-prone. It is far more intuitive to refer to the same database by using the directory suffix. Note that the *-b* and *-n* options are mutually exclusive. A summary of the various *slapadd* command-line options is provided in Table 4-2.

Table 4-2. Summary of slapadd command-line arguments

Option	Description
-c	Continues processing input in the event of errors.
-b suffix -n integer	Specify which database in the configuration file to use by the directory's suffix (-b) or by its location (-n) in the *slapd.conf* file (the first database listed is numbered 0). These options are mutually exclusive.
-d integer	Specifies which debugging information to log. See the loglevel parameter in *slapd.conf* for a listing of log levels.
-f filename	Specifies which configuration file to read.
-l filename	Specifies the LDIF file to use for input. In the absence of this option, *slapadd* reads data from standard input.
-v	Enables verbose mode. In this mode, *slapd* prints some additional messages on standard output.

The *slapcat* utility dumps the contents of an entire directory (including persistent operational attributes such as modifyTimeStamp) in LDIF format. The command-line options for *slapcat* are identical to the options for *slapadd* (Table 4-2), except that the *-l* switch specifies an output filename instead of an input filename. In the absence of this switch, *slapcat* writes all entries to standard output. *slapcat* can provide a useful means of backing up the directory. Unlike the actual DBM datafiles, which are machine- and version-dependent, LDIF is very portable and allows easier editing in case of corrupted data. I don't mean to discourage you from backing up the DBM files, but you could do worse than backing up the directory in both forms.

The *slapindex* command can be used to regenerate the indexes for a bdb backend. This might be necessary if a new index was added to *slapd.conf* after the directory was populated with entries. The *slapindex* tool shares the same command-line options as *slapadd*, with the exception of *-l*. The *-l* option isn't used for *slapindex* because neither an input nor an output file is needed.

To start populating your directory, create a file containing the LDIF entries of the top-level nodes. These LDIF entries build the root node and the people organizational unit.

```
## Build the root node.
dn: dc=plainjoe,dc=org
```

```
dc: plainjoe
objectClass: dcObject
objectClass: organizationalUnit
ou: PlainJoe Dot Org

## Build the people ou.
dn: ou=people,dc=plainjoe,dc=org
ou: people
objectClass: organizationalUnit
```

Assuming that these entries are stored in a file named */tmp/top.ldif*, you can add them to the directory by executing:

```
root# slapadd -v -l /tmp/top.ldif
added: "dc=plainjoe,dc=org" (00000001)
added: "ou=people,dc=plainjoe,dc=org" (00000002)
```

The output indicates that the entries were added successfully.

Verifying the Directory's Contents

Next, you will bring the directory online so that you can use it in conjunction with *ldapsearch*, *ldapmodify*, and the other tools for working on a live directory:

```
root# /usr/local/libexec/slapd
```

After the directory server has started, you can use *ldapsearch* to query the server. *ldapsearch* allows you to dig through your directory, test for the existence of data, and test whether access control has been set up correctly.

OpenLDAP's *ldapsearch* began life as a simple wrapper for the LDAP search operation. The list of search possibilities is lengthy; I won't cover it until Chapter 5. For now, I will focus on very simple searches that assure you the directory is up and running correctly. In its simplest form, a query requires the following information:

- The LDAP server's hostname or IP address
- The credentials (i.e., user DN and password) to use to bind to the host
- The search base in the form of a DN
- The scope of the directory to search
- A search filter
- A list of attributes to return

We'll start with a "Show me everything" search. Here, you ask the directory to return all entries that have a value for the objectClass attribute (which is all entries).

```
$ ldapsearch -x -b "dc=plainjoe,dc=org" "(objectclass=*)"
version: 2

#
# filter: (objectclass=*)
# requesting: ALL
#
```

```
# plainjoe,dc=org
dn: dc=plainjoe,dc=org
dc: plainjoe.org
objectClass: dcObject
objectClass: organizationalUnit
ou: PlainJoe Dot Org

# people,dc=plainjoe,dc=org
dn: ou=people,dc=plainjoe,dc=org
ou: people
objectClass: organizationalUnit

# Search result
search: 2
result: 0 Success

# numResponses: 3
# numEntries: 2
```

The ldapsearch options used here are:

-x

> Instructs *ldapsearch* to perform a simple bind (i.e., do not use SASL for authentication).

-b dc=plainjoe,dc=org

> Defines the DN dc=plainjoe,dc=org as the search's base suffix. This DN specifies the point at which the search begins. Therefore, it must be a DN that is held by the LDAP server. All entries located higher in the tree will be ignored.

(objectclass=*)

> The search filter. If you are familiar with filename globbing, or just general wildcard patterns, this filter should be familiar. RFC 2254 defines ways to represent an LDAP search filter as a string. The syntax of filters is covered in Chapter 5. For now, it's sufficient to know that this filter matches any value of the objectClass attribute.

The surprising thing about this command is that it doesn't explicitly contain most of the items that I said were necessary for any search. In fact, the only two items that we can clearly see are the search base and the search filter. What's going on? Let's look at the missing items one at a time:

The LDAP server's hostname (or IP address)

> *ldapsearch* queries the local host if the server isn't specified explicitly. The -h *hostname* option specifies the hostname or IP address. In this case, though, you're running the server locally, so you don't need it.

Credentials used to bind to the directory

> The ACL defined in *slapd.conf* gave read permission to all users. Therefore, you don't need to authenticate to perform this search. When authentication is

required, the -D *DN* and -w *password* options specify the login DN and password to be used.

The search scope

By default, *ldapsearch* queries the server for all entries contained in the subtree of the root node defined by the *-b* option. Other possibilities include searching only the immediate children of the base suffix entry or searching this entry alone. The search scope (*-s*) option can be used to specify either sub, base, or one.

A list of attributes to return

By default, *slapd* returns all nonoperational attributes. On a complex directory, you might get an extremely long list of attributes for every entry in the directory. To limit the result to a few specific attributes, list the attributes you want on the command line, separated by commas. Operational attributes such as modifyTimestamp and modifiersName are not returned unless specifically asked for by name or by using the plus character (+) as the attribute list in the search.

The default values for many LDAP client parameters can be controlled via the system-wide *ldap.conf* configuration file (located in the same directory as *slapd.conf*) or the user-specific version in *$HOME/.ldaprc*. For more details, refer to the *ldap.conf(5)* manpage. Our examples explicitly list all parameters required by the command-line tools unless the compile-time defaults can be used, which was the case in the previous *ldapsearch* listing.

Tables 4-3 and 4-4 list all the options and arguments for *ldapsearch*. Don't worry about understanding them all now.

Table 4-3. Command-line options common to ldapsearch, ldapadd, ldapdelete, ldapmodify, and ldapmodrdn

Option	Description
-d integer	Specifies what debugging information to log. See the loglevel *slapd.conf* parameter for a listing of log levels.
-D binddn	Specifies the DN to use for binding to the LDAP server.
-e [!]ctrl[=ctrlparam]	Defines an LDAP control to be used on the current operation. See also the *-M* option for the manageDSAit control.
-f filename	Specifies the file containing the LDIF entries to be used in the operations.
-H URI	Defines the LDAP URI to be used in the connection request.
-I	Enables the SASL "interactive" mode. By default, the client prompts for information only when necessary.
-k	Enables Kerberos 4 authentication.
-K	Enables only the first step of the Kerberos 4 bind for authentication.
-M *-MM*	Enable the Manager DSA IT control. This option is necessary when modifying an entry that is a referral or an alias. *-MM* requires that the Manager DSA IT control be supported by the server.
-n	Does not perform the search; just displays what would be done.

Table 4-3. Command-line options common to ldapsearch, ldapadd, ldapdelete, ldapmodify, and ldapmodrdn (continued)

Option	Description
-O security_properties	Defines the SASL security properties for authentication. See previous information on the sasl-secprops parameter in *slapd.conf*.
-P [2|3]	Defines which protocol version to use in the connection (Version 2 or 3). The default is LDAPv3.
-Q	Suppresses SASL-related messages such as the authentication mechanism use, username, and realm.
-R sasl_realm	Defines the realm to be used by the SASL authentication mechanism.
-U username	Defines the username to be used by the SASL authentication mechanism.
-v	Enables verbose mode.
-w password	Specifies the password to be used for authentication.
-W	Instructs the client to prompt for the password.
-x	Enables simple authentication. The default is to use SASL authentication.
-X id	Defines the SASL authorization identity. The identity has the form dn:*dn* or u:*user*. The default is to use the same authorization identity as the authenticated user.
-y passwdfile	Instructs the *ldap* tool to read the password for a simple bind from the given filename.
-Y sasl_mechanism	Instructs the client as to which SASL mechanism should be used. The bind request will fail if the server does not support the chosen mechanism.
-Z -ZZ	Issue a StartTLS request. Use of -*ZZ* makes the support of this request mandatory for a successful connection.

Table 4-4. Command-line options specific to ldapsearch

Option	Description
-a [never|always|search|find]	Specifies how to handle aliases when located during a search. Possible values include never (the default), always, search, or find.
-A	For any entries found, returns the attribute names but not their values.
-b basedn	Defines the base DN for the directory search.
-F prefix	Defines the URL prefix for filenames. The default is to use the value stored in $LDAP_FILE_URI_PREFIX.
-l limit	Defines a time limit (in seconds) for the server in the search.
-L -LL -LLL	Print the resulting output in LDIFv1 format. -*LL* causes the result to be printed in LDIF format without comments. -*LLL* prints the resulting output in LDIF format without comments or version information.
-s [sub|base|one]	Defines the scope of the search to be base, one, or sub (the default).
-S attribute	Causes the *ldapsearch* client to sort the results by the value of *attribute*.
-t -tt	Write binary values to files in a temporary directory defined by the -*T* option. -*tt* specifies that all values should be written to files in a temporary directory defined by the -*T* option.
-T directory	Defines the directory used to store the resulting output files. The default is the directory specified by $LDAP_TMPDIR.

Table 4-4. Command-line options specific to ldapsearch (continued)

Option	Description
-u	Includes user-friendly entry names in the output.
-z limit	Specifies the maximum number of entries to return

Updating What Is Already There

Eventually, the information stored in a directory will need to be updated or deleted. While a directory isn't designed to be updated as frequently as a database, there are very few applications in which the data never changes. This section covers how to update the data in the directory using *ldapmodify*. The name *ldapmodify* is a little misleading; this utility can add new entries and delete or update existing entries using some of the advanced features of LDIF for its input language.

The following LDIF listing defines two entries that we will add to our directory:

```
## filename: /tmp/users.ldif

## LDIF entry for "Gerald W. Carter"
dn: cn=Gerald W. Carter,ou=people,dc=plainjoe,dc=org
cn: Gerald W. Carter
sn: Carter
mail: jerry@plainjoe.org
mail: gcarter@valinux.com
labeledURI: http://www.plainjoe.org/
roomNumber: 1234 Dudley Hall
departmentNumber: Engineering
telephoneNumber: 222-555-2345
pager: 222-555-6789
mobile: 222-555-1011
objectclass: inetOrgPerson

## LDIF entry for "Jerry Carter"
dn: cn=Jerry Carter,ou=people,dc=plainjoe,dc=org
cn: Jerry Carter
sn: Carter
mail: carter@nowhere.net
telephoneNumber: 555-123-1234
objectclass: inetOrgPerson
```

The following command shows how to add these entries to the directory while it is running. Because write privileges are required to add new entries, *ldapmodify* binds to the directory using the credentials from the rootdn and rootpw *slapd.conf* parameters.

```
$ ldapmodify -D "cn=Manager,dc=plainjoe,dc=org" -w secret \
> -x -a -f /tmp/users.ldif
adding new entry "cn=Gerald W. Carter,ou=people,dc=plainjoe,dc=org"

adding new entry "cn=Jerry Carter,ou=people,dc=plainjoe,dc=org"
```

The output indicates that both entries were added successfully. The *-D*, *-w*, and *-x* options to *ldapmodify* should be familiar; they specify the DN to use for the modification, specify the password for the modification, and request simple authentication, respectively. This leaves only two new options to discuss:

-a

Entries are to be added to the directory. The default for *ldapmodify* is to update existing information.

-f filename

Reads the new entries from the given filename. By default, *ldapmodify* reads from standard input.

If *ldapmodify* returns an error message such as the following, try enabling verbose messages via the *-v* command-line switch:

```
ldap_add: Invalid syntax
additional info: value contains invalid data
```

There are two common causes of this error message. You may have forgotten to include all the necessary schema files in *slapd.conf*, or you may have extra whitespace at the end of line in the LDIF file. The *set list* command in vi can help you track down extra whitespace.

Refer again to Table 4-3 for a list of the common options for all of these *ldap* client tools. Table 4-5 lists those options specific to *ldapmodify* and *ldapadd*. Note that *ldapadd* and *ldapmodify* are the same executable; *ldapadd* is only a hard link to *ldapmodify*. The commands differ only in their default behavior, which depends on the name by which the program was invoked.

Table 4-5. Command-line options specific to ldapadd and ldapmodify

Option	Description
-a	Adds entries. This option is the default for *ldapadd*.
-r	Replaces (or modifies) entries and values. This is the default for *ldapmodify*.
-F	Forces all change records to be used from the input.

Now let's see how a modification works. Suppose you want to add a URL to the entry for cn=Jerry Carter,ou=people,dc=plainjoe,dc=org. To add a URL, use the labeledURI attribute:

```
labeledURI: http://www.plainjoe.org/~jerry/
```

In addition, you should delete the *gcarter@valinux.com* email address for "Gerald W. Carter" because it has become invalid. You can place both changes in a single LDIF file:

```
## /tmp/update.ldif

## Add a web page location to Jerry Carter.
dn: cn=Jerry Carter,ou=people,dc=plainjoe,dc=org
```

```
changetype: modify
add: labeledURI
labeledURI: http://www.plainjoe.org/~jerry/

## Remove an email address from Gerald W. Carter.
dn: cn=Gerald W. Carter,ou=people,dc=plainjoe,dc=org
changetype: modify
delete: mail
mail: gcarter@valinux.com
```

The changetype keyword in the LDIF file is the key to modifying existing entries. This keyword can accept the following values:

add

Adds the entry to the directory.

delete

Deletes the entry from the directory.

modify

Modifies the attributes of an entry. With this keyword, you can both add and delete attribute values.

modrdn

Changes the RDN of an entry.

moddn

Changes the DN of an entry.

This LDIF file tells *ldapmodify* what changes to make. We'll invoke *ldapmodify* with the verbose (-*v*) option so you can follow the update operations more closely. The -*a* option isn't needed because you're not adding new entries.

```
$ ldapmodify -D "cn=Manager,dc=plainjoe,dc=org" -w secret
> -x -v -f /tmp/update.ldif
ldap_initialize( <DEFAULT> )
add labeledURI:
        http://www.plainjoe.org/~jerry/
modifying entry "cn=Jerry Carter,ou=people,dc=plainjoe,dc=org"
modify complete

delete mail:
        gcarter@valinux.com
modifying entry "cn=Gerald W. Carter,ou=people,dc=plainjoe,dc=org"
modify complete
```

Notice that the LDIF file is parsed sequentially from the top. Therefore, later LDIF entries can modify entries created previously in the file. You can also create an LDIF file with entries having different changetype values. For example, the following LDIF file adds an entry for user Peabody Soup, adds a new telephoneNumber to Jerry Carter's entry, and finally deletes the previously created entry for Peabody Soup.

```
## /tmp/changetypes.ldif

## Add entry for Peabody Soup.
dn: cn=Peabody Soup,ou=people,dc=plainjoe,dc=org
changetype: add
cn: Peabody Soup
sn: Soup
objectclass: inetOrgPerson

## Add new telephoneNumber for Jerry Carter.
dn: cn=Jerry Carter,ou=people,dc=plainjoe,dc=org
changetype: modify
delete: telephoneNumber
telephoneNumber: 555-123-1234
-
add: telephoneNumber
telephoneNumber: 234-555-6789

## Remove the entry for Peabody Soup.
dn: cn=Peabody Soup,ou=people,dc=plainjoe,dc=org
changetype: delete
```

A couple of facts about this LDIF file are worth mentioning:

- Entries are separated by a blank line, as noted earlier.

- Multiple changes to a single entry using the modify changetype are separated by a single dash (-) on a line by itself. These should be handled as a single change by the server. Either all the changes for this DN take effect or none are applied.

The modify changetype supports add and delete keywords for adding and deleting attribute values. In order to delete the value of an attribute, the delete: must immediately be followed by an *attributetype:value* pair. It's necessary to specify the value you're deleting because some attributes can hold multiple values. Specifying which value to remove eliminates any ambiguity about what you want to do. When the last value of an attribute is removed from an entry, that attribute is no longer present in the entry.

Here's how to apply this second set of changes to the directory. Again, we've specified the -v option to see how *ldapmodify* processes the LDIF file.

```
$ ldapmodify -D "cn=Manager,dc=plainjoe,dc=org" -w secret -x -v -f
/tmp/changetype.ldif
ldap_initialize( <DEFAULT> )
add cn:
        Peabody Soup
add sn:
        Soup
add objectclass:
        inetOrgPerson
adding new entry "cn=Peabody Soup,ou=people,dc=plainjoe,dc=org"
modify complete
```

```
delete telephoneNumber:
      555-123-1234
add telephoneNumber:
      234-555-6789
modifying entry "cn=Jerry Carter,ou=people,dc=plainjoe,dc=org"
modify complete

deleting entry "cn=Peabody Soup,ou=people,dc=plainjoe,dc=org"
delete complete
```

Modifying the RDN of an entry takes a little more thought than adding an entry or changing an attribute of an entry. If the entry is not a leaf node, changing its RDN orphans the children in the directory because the DN of their parent has changed. You should make sure that you don't leave orphaned nodes in the directory—you should move the nodes with their parent or give them a new parent. With that in mind, let's think about how to change the RDN of the entry:

```
dn: cn=Jerry Carter,ou=people,dc=plainjoe,dc=org
```

from cn: Jerry Carter to cn: Gerry Carter. Here's the LDIF file that makes the changes:

```
## /tmp/modrdn.ldif

## Change the RDN from "Jerry Carter" to "Gerry Carter."
dn: cn=Jerry Carter,ou=people,dc=plainjoe,dc=org
changetype: modrdn
newrdn: cn=Gerry Carter
deleteoldrdn: 1
```

You can also use the *ldapmodrdn* command to perform the same task:

```
$ ldapmodrdn \
> "cn=Jerry Carter,ou=people,dc=plainjoe,dc=org" \
> "cn=Gerry Carter"
```

Not counting the DN of the entry to be changed and the new RDN value, the *ldapmodrdn* tool has three command-line options besides those common to the other OpenLDAP client tools (Table 4-3). These additional options are listed in Table 4-6.

Table 4-6. Command-line options specific to ldapmodrdn

Option	Description
-c	Instructs *ldapmodrdn* to continue if errors occur. By default, it terminates if there is an error.
-r	Removes the old RDN value. The default behavior is to add another RDN value and leave the old value intact. The default behavior makes it easier to modify a directory without leaving orphaned entries.
-s new_superior_node	Defines the new superior, or parent, entry under which the renamed entry should be located.

If an entire subtree of the directory needs to be moved, a better solution may be to export the subtree to an LDIF file, modify all occurrences of the changed attribute in all the DNs, and finally re-add the subtree to the new location. Once the information has been entered correctly into a location, you can then use a recursive *ldapdelete* to remove the old subtree.

ldapdelete possesses all of the command-line options common to *ldapsearch* and *ldapmodify*. The only new option is *-r* (recursive), which deletes all entries below the one specified on the command line, in addition to the named entry. Note that this deletion is not atomic; entries are deleted individually. The following command deletes the entire ou=people subtree:

```
$ ldapdelete -D "cn=Manager,dc=plainjoe,dc=org" -w secret -x \
> -r -v "ou=people,dc=plainjoe,dc=org"

ldap_initialize( <DEFAULT> )
deleting entry "ou=people,dc=plainjoe,dc=org"
deleting children of: ou=people,dc=plainjoe,dc=org
deleting children of: cn=Gerald W. Carter,ou=people,dc=plainjoe,dc=org
    removing cn=Gerald W. Carter,ou=people,dc=plainjoe,dc=org
    cn=Gerald W. Carter,ou=people,dc=plainjoe,dc=org removed
deleting children of: cn=Gerry Carter,ou=people,dc=plainjoe,dc=org
    removing cn=Gerry Carter,ou=people,dc=plainjoe,dc=org
    cn=Gerry Carter,ou=people,dc=plainjoe,dc=org removed
Delete Result: Success (0)
```

Now that you have a working directory, a good exercise would be to experiment with various ACLs to restrict access to certain attributes. This exercise will also help you become more comfortable with the tools presented in this chapter. Use the *slapcat* tool to dump the directory to an LDIF file and start over from scratch until you are comfortable with adding, deleting, and modifying entries. The next chapter explores creating a distributed directory, replicating information to multiple servers, more searching techniques, and some advanced ACL configurations.

Graphical Editors

Working with command-line tools and LDIF files is constructive, but certainly not convenient. There are a number of graphical editors and browsers for LDAP that make it easier to see what you're doing. I won't discuss any of these in detail, but I'll give you some pointers to some tools that are worth looking at:

GQ (http://biot.com/gq/)
   GQ is a GTK+-based LDAPv3 client capable of browsing the subSchema entry on LDAPv3 servers. It is distributed under the GNU GPL and includes features such as:

   - Support for browsing or searching LDAP servers
   - Support for editing and deleting directory entries

- Support for creating template entries based on existing ones
- Support for exporting subtrees or an entire directory to an LDIF file
- Support for multiple server profiles
- SASL authentication

Java LDAP Browser/Editor (http://www.iit.edu/~gawojar/ldap/)
This is an editor written in Java using the JNDI class libraries. It supports:

- LDAPv2 and v3 servers, including SSL connections
- Editing attribute values
- Searching for specific entries
- Exporting and importing data using LDIF files
- Creating template entries
- Utilizing multiple server profiles

Softerra LDAP Browser (http://www.ldapbrowser.com/)
The Softerra LDAP Browser is a freely available, Win32-based browser and editor for Windows 98/NT/2000 clients. The browser has the following qualities:

- Support for a familiar Windows Explorer–like interface
- Support for LDAPv2 and v3
- Support for SSL connections for v3 sessions
- Support for multiple server profiles, similar to the GQ editor
- Support for exporting entries and subtrees to an LDIF file

## CHAPTER 5

Replication, Referrals, Searching, and SASL Explained

The previous chapters have prepared the foundation for understanding and building an LDAP-based directory server. This chapter presents some of the more advanced features provided by LDAP and shows how to use these features in your directory service. As such, this chapter ties up a lot of loose ends that have been left hanging by the previous discussions.

More Than One Copy Is "a Good Thing"

We begin by exploring directory replication. This feature hasn't been standardized yet; our example focuses on the OpenLDAP project. The concepts and principles that I will present are applicable to all LDAP directories, but the examples themselves are specific to OpenLDAP.

Because LDAP replication is vendor-specific at the moment, it is not possible to replicate data from one vendor's server to another vendor's server. It is possible to achieve cross-vendor replication by using tricks such as parsing a change log, but these tricks are themselves vendor-dependent.

> The LDAP Duplication/Replication/Update Protocols (LDUP) Working Group of the IETF attempted to define a standardized replication protocol that would allow for interoperability between all LDAPv3-compliant servers. However, there appears to be more demand for an LDAP client update protocol (LCUP) that would allow clients to synchronize a local cache of a directory as well as be notified of updates. Details of the group's progress can be found at *http://www.ietf.org/html.charters/ldup-charter.html*.

A frequently asked question is: "When should I install a replica for all or part of my directory?" The answer depends heavily on your particular environment. Here are a few symptoms that indicate the need for directory replicas:

- If one application makes heavy use of the directory and slows down the server's response to other client applications, you may want to consider installing a replica and dedicating the second server solely to the application that is causing the congestion.

- If the directory server does not have enough CPU power to handle the number of requests it is receiving, installing a replica can improve response time. You may also wish to install several read-only replicas and use some means of load balancing, such as round-robin DNS or a virtual server software package. Before taking this route, make sure that the limiting factor is CPU and not other finite resources such as memory or disk I/O.

- If a group of clients is located on the other side of a slow network link, installing a local replica (i.e., a replica that is close to the clients making the request) will decrease traffic over the link and improve response time for the remote clients.

- If the directory server cannot be taken offline for backups, consider implementing a read-only replica to provide service while the master server is taken down for backups or normal maintenance.

- If your directory is a critical part of the services provided by your network, using replicas can help provide failover and redundancy.

Once the questions of "When?" and "Why?" have been answered, the next question is "How?" The OpenLDAP project uses the original design for replication that was implemented by the University of Michigan's LDAP server. This design uses a secondary daemon (*slurpd*) to process a change log written by the standalone LDAP server (*slapd*). *slurpd* then forwards the changes to the replica's local *slapd* instance using normal LDAP modify commands. Figure 5-1 displays the relationship between *slapd* and *slurpd* on the master directory server and the replica.

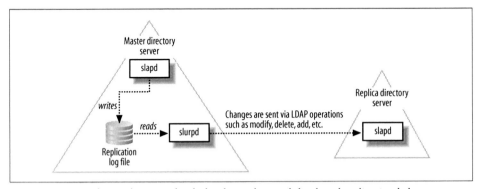

Figure 5-1. Dependencies between slapd, the change log, and the slurpd replication helper

Building slurpd

When you built the OpenLDAP package in Chapter 3, you didn't build the *slurpd* binary. To build *slurpd*, you must pass the command-line option *--enable-slurpd* to the *configure* script. Note that thread support is required for *slurpd*; there is no non-threaded version.

After running *./configure* with the *--enable-slurpd* option, executing *make* creates the server in the *servers/slurpd/* subdirectory of the OpenLDAP source code tree. This binary can then be copied to the same location as *slapd*. You can copy *slurpd* to the appropriate location by hand or by running *make install*. All of the examples in this chapter assume that *slurpd* has been installed in the default location of */usr/local/libexec/*.

Replication in a Nutshell

Before implementing replication in a directory, you must have a working LDAP master server. The directory server built in previous chapters will be used as a starting point. Once the master *slapd* server has been created, implementing a replica server can be accomplished by following these steps:

1. Stop the master server's *slapd* daemon.
2. Reconfigure the master server's *slapd.conf* to enable replication to the new slave server.
3. Copy the database from the master server to the replica.
4. Configure the replica server's *slapd.conf*.
5. Start the replica server's *slapd* process
6. Start the master server's *slapd* process.
7. Start the master server's *slurpd* process.

This quick list glosses over a few details, such as how to configure a server to send updates and how to configure a server to accept updates from a master server. Let's start with step 2 (if step 1 is not obvious, refer to Chapter 4 for a refresher on starting and stopping *slapd*).

Configuring the Master Server

To configure your master server to log changes that can be processed by the *slurpd* helper daemon, you need to add two directives to the database section of *slapd.conf*. It is possible to give *slurpd* its own configuration file using the *-f* command-line option, but because of the producer/consumer relationship between *slapd* and *slurpd*, the most common setup is to use a single configuration file for both daemons. Here's the database configuration developed in the previous chapter:

```
## -- master slapd --
#######################################################
## Define the beginning of example database.
database        bdb

## Define the root suffix you serve.
suffix          "dc=plainjoe,dc=org"

## Define a root DN for superuser privileges.
rootdn          "cn=Manager,dc=plainjoe,dc=org"

## Define the password used with rootdn. This is the Base64-encoded MD5 hash of
## "secret."
rootpw          {SSHA}2aksIaicAvwc+DhCrXUFlhgWsbBJPLxy

## Directory containing the database files
directory       /var/ldap/plainjoe.org

## Files should be created rw for the owner **only**.
mode            0600

## Indexes to maintain
index           objectClass     eq
index           cn              pres,eq

## db tuning parameters; cache 2,000 entries in memory
cachesize       2000

# Simple ACL granting read access to the world
access to *
     by * read
```

First, you need to add the name of the log file in which *slapd* will record all LDAP modifications. This is specified using the replogfile parameter.

```
## -- master slapd --
# Specify the location of the file to append changes to.
replogfile      /var/ldap/slapd.replog
```

> The *slurpd* daemon will use only the first instance of the replogfile parameter in a configuration file. On a server that is configured to hold multiple databases, all of these partitions must use a single replogfile value. The best way to do this is to define the replogfile parameter in the configuration file's global section. In this way, the value will be used for all databases defined later in *slapd.conf*. The alternative is to start a separate *slurpd* instance, each with its own configuration file, for each database section.

The second parameter you need to add informs *slurpd* where to send the changes. You add this parameter, replica, just below the replogfile directive.

```
## -- master slapd --
# Set the hostname and bind credentials used to propagate the changes in the
# replogfile.
```

```
replica       host=replica1.plainjoe.org:389
              suffix="dc=plainjoe,dc=org"
              binddn="cn=replica,dc=plainjoe,dc=org"
              credentials=MyPass
              bindmethod=simple
              tls=yes
```

replica specifies the host and port to which the data should be sent, the portion of the partition to be replicated, the DN to use when binding to the replicated server, any credentials that are acquired, and information about the binding method and protocols. Note that the binddn used in the replica directive must possess write access to the slave server. The most common binddn to use is the the rootdn specified in the replica's *slapd.conf*. However, any DN that has the appropriate level of access (possibly granted by ACLs on the directory) will work. The credentials parameter specifies the password used for simple binds and SASL binds to the slave server. The bindmethod option for the replica directive accepts one of the following two values: simple or sasl. Examples using SASL accounts with OpenLDAP will be presented later in this chapter.

In our example, the slave server *replica1.plainjoe.org* must be listening on the default LDAP port of 389. TLS is enabled (tls=yes) to protect the privacy of information as it is replicated. Because the LDAP connection will be made on port 389, it is essential that the slave server support the StartTLS extended command to ensure secure replication. Regardless of how careful you are about securing the data in your directory, if you are replicating the directory to a slave server over an insecure link and do not use some type of transport layer security such as TLS or IPSec, all of your efforts will be in vain.

Configuring the Replica Server

The first step in creating a replica is to initialize its database with a current copy of the directory from the master server. There are two ways to accomplish this:

* Copy the master's database files to the replica.
* Export the master's database to an LDIF file and reimport the entries into the replica.

There are a few restrictions to keep in mind when copying the actual database files from the master to the slave server:

* Both hosts must have the same (or compatible) versions of the DBM libraries.
* In most cases, both hosts must use the same byte ordering (little-endian versus big-endian).
* Some methods of copying DBM sparse files, such as using *cp*, will fill in the holes, resulting in much larger files on the replica host.

For these reasons, a more general way to transfer the master's database is to export the database to an LDIF file using *slapcat*. The file can then be imported into the replica's directory using the *slapadd* command. Using the *slapd.conf* file from your directory, the following commands initialize the replica's directory:

```
root@master# slapcat -b "dc=plainjoe,dc=org" -l contents.ldif

...copy contents.ldif to the slave server...

root@replica1# slapadd -l contents.ldif
```

In this example, specifying the base suffix with the *-b* option is not necessary because your server contains only one partition. Had there been more than one database section in *slapd.conf*, the base suffix would have specified which partition to dump. Specifying a base suffix isn't necessary when you import the file into the replica because *slapadd* parses the configuration file and places the data into the first database to match the base suffix of the LDIF entries.

Once the data has been copied to the slave server, it is time to update the replica's *slapd.conf* to accept updates from the master server. The global section of the replica's configuration file will be identical to the master server's. However, certain pieces of information, such as the server's public certificate, should be unique to the slave. The database section of the slave's *slapd.conf* will also be identical, minus the replication parameters and with an appropriate local rootdn and rootpw. For the purposes of this chapter, the slave's database section contains the following rootdn and rootpw:

```
## -- slave slapd --
## replica's administrative DN
rootdn     "cn=replica,dc=plainjoe,dc=org"

## Salted Secure Hash version of MyPass
rootpw     {SSHA}SMKnFPO435G+QstIzNGb4RGjTOKLz2TV
```

To make the server act as a slave, you must add two parameters to the configuration. Just as the master must know where to send updates, the slave server must know who is authorized to make these changes. This is done by defining an updatedn:

```
## -- slave slapd --
## Define the DN that will be used by the master slurpd to replicate data. Normally,
## this is the rootdn of the slave server or, at the minimum, a DN that is allowed
## write access to all entries via an ACL.
updatedn       "cn=replica,dc=plainjoe,dc=org"
```

Because a slave server contains only replicated data and OpenLDAP currently supports only a single master replication system (i.e., updates must be made on the master directory server), the slave server requires an LDAP URL (updateref) that points cli-

---

ents to the master directory server. The slave refers clients to the master when clients send modification requests. Here's the appropriate addition to the database section of the replica's *slapd.conf*:

```
## -- slave slapd --
## Specify the LDAP URL of the master server, which can accept update requests.
updateref    ldap://pogo.plainjoe.org
```

 Development versions of OpenLDAP support an experimental implementation of a multimaster replication protocol. Multimaster replication means that changes to the directory can be accepted at any replica: the replica propagates the changes to all servers containing copies of the partition. Multimaster replication is not covered in this book.

This completes step 4 of the configuration process. Steps 5 and 6 are to launch the master and slave's *slapd* processes using the procedure described in earlier chapters.

slurpd's replogfile

As Figure 5-1 illustrates, the *slurpd* daemon processes the change log written by *slapd*. The replication log uses a format similar to the LDIF examples used throughout this book. After reading the replogfile, *slurpd* copies the entry to its own replay log. The location of the *slurpd.replog* file can be controlled using the -*t* command-line option when starting *slurpd*. In a default installation, *slurpd.replog* will be stored in */usr/local/var/openldap-slurp/replica/*.

The following log entry in the replogfile was generated when the email address for cn=Jerry Carter,ou=people,dc=plainjoe,dc=org was changed to jcarter@nowhere. com:

```
replica: pogo.plainjoe.org
time: 975434259
dn: cn=jerry carter,ou=People,dc=plainjoe,dc=org
changetype: modify
replace: mail
mail: jcarter@nowhere.com
-
replace: entryCSN
entryCSN: 2002110403:55:49Z#0x0001#0#0000
-
replace: modifiersName
modifiersName: cn=Manager,dc=plainjoe,dc=org
-
replace: modifyTimestamp
modifyTimestamp: 20001128175739Z
-
```

While only one attribute value was changed, the replication log entry updates four attributes: mail (as expected), plus modifiersName, modifyTimestamp, and entryCSN.

These last three attributes, two of which are described in RFC 2251, are maintained by the LDAP server and cannot be modified by clients.

The log entry also specifies two additional values not used in normal LDIF entries. The replica directive defines the host to which the change should be propagated. There can be multiple replica lines if a partition will be synchronized to several directory slaves. The time parameter defines the timestamp of the entry in seconds since 1970 GMT. *slurpd* maintains the timestamp of the most recently read change, which prevents it from reparsing entries it has already processed. This state information is stored in a status file named *slurpd.status* in the same directory as the *slurpd.replog* file.

slurpd reads entries in the replication log file one at a time and propagates the changes using basic LDAP commands (e.g., *add*, *modify*, *delete*, *modrdn*, etc.). If a change cannot be made, *slurpd* writes the entry and reason for the failure to a reject log named *<hostname:port>.rej* in the same directory as the *slurpd.replog* file. It's the administrator's responsibility to read this log and figure out how to handle changes that were not made. There are many possible reasons for failure—for example, a conflict between the schemas on the master and slave servers, access control entries that aren't set up appropriately, etc.

Certain errors, such as a network problem in the connection from the server to the slave, cause *slurpd* to requeue a modification. However, any entry written to the reject log cannot be replicated in its current state. These entries will require manual intervention on a case-by-case basis. If the update resulted in an object schema violation, perhaps one of the schema files was left out of the configuration file. If the replica arrived in a state inconsistent with the directory master, attempting to add an entry that already existed would also result in an error. These types of circumstances can be very data-specific, and the examples given here represent only a few of the possible causes. In any case, the appropriate response to an error isn't to try to update the slave by hand; rather, you should figure out why the update can't take place automatically, and fix the appropriate configuration file.

Our setup will utilize *slurpd* as a daemon that monitors the replication log file and propagates changes periodically. However, it can also operate as a command-line tool to process a single change log and exit. This is referred to as "one shot" mode, and it's invaluable for dealing with rejected entries. A complete list of command-line options used when starting *slurpd* is given in Table 5-1.

Table 5-1. Command-line options for slurpd

Option	Description
-d integer	Specifies the debugging information to be written to the log. See the discussion of the loglevel *slapd.conf* parameter for more information on the debugging flags.
-f "config filename"	Specifies the location and filename of the *slapd.conf* file to be used.

Table 5-1. Command-line options for slurpd (continued)

Option	Description
-r replogfile	Specifies the location and filename of the replication log to be processed. The -r switch is often used in conjunction with the *slurpd's* one-shot mode to process a particular file.
-o	Executes *slurpd* in one-shot mode to process a single replication log and exit.
-t directory	Specifies the directory to be used for temporary files such as lock and status files. The default is to store the files in */usr/local/var/openldap-slurp/replica/*.
-k "srvtab file"	Specifies the location of the *srvtab* file when using LDAPv2 Kerberos 4 binds to a slave *slapd* server.

To complete the configuration of your directory replica, you must start the *slurpd* daemon on the master server. To do so, execute *slurpd* as root from a shell prompt:

```
root@master# /usr/local/libexec/slurpd
```

From this point on, any changes made to the master directory will be replicated to the slave server. In current 2.x versions, the *slurpd* thread responsible for monitoring the replication log checks every three seconds for updates and propagates these updates as necessary. This interval is not configurable from the command line nor from *slapd.conf*. However, if less frequent updates are required, *slurpd* could be run manually using the -o argument to process the replication log when desired.

Using a Replica in a Backup Plan

Backing up a directory that must be available 24 hours a day can require special arrangements. By using replication, a slave server can act as a backup server.

Even if the backup plan relies on offline storage, a directory replica can be very helpful. If you stop the *slurpd* daemon on the master server, the replica server contains a read-only copy of the directory at that point in time. Of course, the master *slapd* continues to write changes to the *replogfile*. You can now use *slapcat* on the slave to dump the database files to LDIF while *slapd* is running because data is guaranteed not to change in mid-backup. Once the backup is complete, restarting *slurpd* ensures that all changes made to the master while the replica was being backed up will be propagated, bringing the slave in sync with the current state of the directory.

Distributing the Directory

The scenarios presented thus far have all assumed that the entire directory consists of a single partition on one server. In the real world, this may not always suffice. There are many reasons (which I touched on in Chapter 2) for splitting a directory into two or more partitions, which may reside on multiple servers.

Let's assume that, according to Figure 5-2, the top level of your directory server (dc=plainjoe,dc=org) is maintained by one department, and the server containing host information (ou=hosts,dc=plainjoe,dc=org) is managed by another. How can these two directories be combined into one logical DIT?

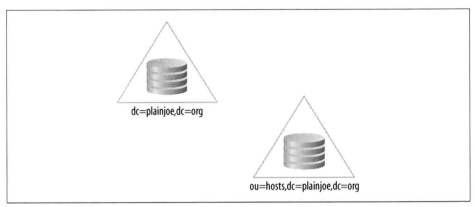

Figure 5-2. Two separate directory partitions held by different servers

The definition for the ou=hosts partition held by the second server is very similar to the database section we have been using so far. The main changes are to the suffix served by the backend (ou=hosts,dc=plainjoe,dc=org) and the directory in which the BerkeleyDB files are stored (*/var/ldap/hosts/*). The rootdn (cn=Manager,ou=hosts,dc=plainjoe,dc=org) must also be updated due to the requirement that it must exist within the partition's naming context.

```
###########################################################
## Partition on second server holding ou=hosts
database        bdb

## Define the root suffix you serve.
suffix          "ou=hosts,dc=plainjoe,dc=org"

## Define a root DN for superuser privileges.
rootdn          "cn=Manager,ou=hosts,dc=plainjoe,dc=org"

## Define the password used with rootdn. This is the Base64-encoded MD5 hash of
## "secret."
rootpw          {SSHA}2aksIaicAvwc+DhCrXUFlhgWsbBJPLxy

## Directory containing the database files
directory       /var/ldap/hosts

## Files should be created rw for the owner **only**.
mode            0600

## Indexes to maintain
index           objectClass     eq
index           cn              pres,eq
```

```
## db tuning parameters; cache 2,000 entries in memory
cachesize        2000

# Simple ACL granting read access to the world
access to *
    by * read
```

Chapter 2 described a distributed directory implemented by superior knowledge references (referrals) that point from the root of a subtree to the server of the larger directory, and subordinate knowledge references (references) that point from a node in the larger directory to the subtree, or partition, to which it should be attached. In terms of Figure 5-2, these knowledge references would link the dc=plainjoe,dc=org partition to ou=hosts,dc=plainjoe,dc=org, as shown in Figure 5-3.

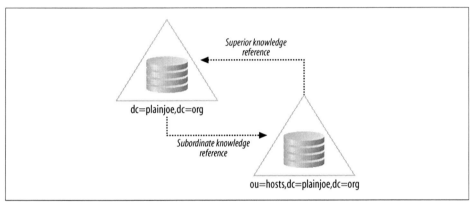

Figure 5-3. Connecting the two partitions using a referral and a reference

These connecting links allow a client to request a search that starts at any node in the directory and continues down through the directory tree, traversing all the directory's partitions. In this case, the search reference URI is returned to the client, which then has the option of continuing the search using the new server and the new base suffix.

The *slapd.conf* for the server holding the ou=hosts tree possesses a global section identical to your existing server, with one exception. OpenLDAP uses the referral global parameter to define an LDAP URI for the server's superior knowledge reference. This feature is implemented as a global, server-wide parameter as opposed to a database-specific directive because a superior knowledge reference refers the client to a server that has knowledge that the server receiving the request does not possess. Normally, this superior server would be higher in the directory tree, but OpenLDAP does not enforce this rule. If the ou=hosts partition is held by a server separate from one containing the top-level naming context, the referral parameter would look similar to the following:

```
## slapd.conf for ou=hosts (ldap2.plainjoe.org)
##
```

```
## <Preceding portion of global section omitted>
## ...
## Define the URL (only host:port) for the host that clients should contact in the
## event that you cannot service their requests.
referral      ldap://master.plainjoe.org:389/
```

Subordinate knowledge references are implemented as entries within the directory itself. These entries use the referral structural object class defined in RFC 3296. This class contains a single required attribute named ref, which holds the LDAP URI for the root of the subtree. So to connect the top-level partition in Figure 5-3 to the people organizational unit, you must create the referral entry to the directory. Assuming that the ou=hosts naming context is held by a server named *ldap2.plainjoe.org*, this *ldapadd* example reads the new entry from standard input:

```
$ ldapadd -H ldap://localhost/ -D "cn=Manager,dc=plainjoe,dc=org" \
> -w secret -x << EOR
> dn: ou=hosts,dc=plainjoe,dc=org
> ou: people
> objectClass: extensibleObject
> objectClass: referral
> ref: ldap://ldap2.plainjoe.org/ou=hosts,dc=plainjoe,dc=org
> EOR
adding new entry "ou=hosts,dc=plainjoe,dc=org"
```

 The OpenLDAP server implements the ManagerDSAIT LDAP control defined in the RFC 3088. This control enables a client to access the actual attribute values (including the ref attribute) in a referral entry without having the server return the referral itself. If a need arises to update a referral entry, enable this control by using the -M (or -MM) command-line option to *ldapmodify*.

Next, create a sample in the ou=hosts tree *ldap2.plainjoe.org* for later use:

```
$ ldapadd -H ldap://ldap2.plainjoe.org/ \
> -D "cn=Manager,ou=hosts,dc=plainjoe,dc=org" \
> -w secret -x << EOR
> dn: ou=hosts,dc=plainjoe,dc=org
> objectclass: organizationalUnit
> ou: hosts
> description: Container for host information in plainjoe.org domain
> EOR
adding new entry "ou=hosts,dc=plainjoe,dc=org"
```

The next section will show you how to handle these search references when querying the directory using *ldapsearch*.

Advanced Searching Options

Chapter 4 presented LDAP searches as a means of verifying the correctness of your directory. That's obviously a very limited use of the search capability: a directory isn't much use if you can't search it. Given our limited goals in the previous chapter, we didn't do justice to the topic of search filters. It's now time to take a more thorough look at the topic of filters.[*]

In its commonly used form, an LDAP search filter has the following syntax:

```
( attribute filterOperator value )
```

The *attribute* is the actual name of the attribute type. The *filterOperator* is one of:

=   For equality matches

~=   For approximate matches

<=   For less than comparisons

>=   For greater than comparisons

If you deal only with string comparisons, you may only need the equality operator.

The *value* portion can be either an absolute value, such as carter or 555-1234, or a pattern using the asterisk (*) character as a wildcard. Here are some wildcard searches:

(cn=*carter)
> Finds all entries whose cn attribute ends in "carter" (not just those with a last name of Carter)

(telephoneNumber=555*)
> Finds all telephone numbers beginning with 555

You can combine single filters like these using the following Boolean operators:

&   Logical AND

| Logical OR

!   Logical NOT

LDAP search filters use prefix notation for joining search conditions. Therefore, to search for users with a surname (sn) of "smith" or "jones," you can build the following filter:

```
(|(sn=smith)(sn=jones))
```

The sn attribute uses a case-insensitive matching rule, so it doesn't matter whether you use "Smith," "smith," or "SMITH" in the filter (or in the directory itself). To look for people with a last name of "smith" or "jones" and a first name beginning with "John," the search would be modified to look like:

```
(&(|(sn=smith)(sn=jones))(cn=john*))
```

Note that the (cn=john*) search filter matches any cn that begins with "john": it matches cn=john doe as well as cn=johnathon doe.

---

[*] For the full details of representing LDAP searches using strings, read RFC 2254.

Following Referrals with ldapsearch

By default, the *ldapsearch* tool shipped with OpenLDAP 2 prints information about referral objects but does not automatically follow them. For example, let's use *ldapsearch* to list all entries in your directory that possess an ou attribute:

```
$ ldapsearch -H ldap://localhost/ -LL -x \
> -b "dc=plainjoe,dc=org"  "(ou=*)" ou

# plainjoe.org
dn: dc=plainjoe,dc=org
ou: PlainJoe Dot Org

# people, plainjoe.org
dn: ou=people,dc=plainjoe,dc=org
ou: people

# Search reference
# refldap://ldap2.plainjoe.org/ou=hosts,dc=plainjoe,dc=org??sub
```

Note that *ldapsearch* returned the referral value, but not the entries below the ou=hosts,dc=plainjoe,dc=org naming context. This information is obviously useful when you're trying to debug a directory tree that is distributed between several servers, but it's not what you want if you only intend to look up information. To follow the search referral, give the *-C* (chase referrals) option when you invoke *ldapsearch*:

```
$ ldapsearch -H ldap://localhost/ -LL -x \
> -b "dc=plainjoe,dc=org"  "(ou=*)" ou

# plainjoe.org
dn: dc=plainjoe,dc=org
ou: PlainJoe Dot Org

# people, plainjoe.org
dn: ou=people,dc=plainjoe,dc=org
ou: people

# hosts, plainjoe.org
dn: ou=hosts,dc=plainjoe,dc=org
ou: hosts
```

Limiting Your Searches

A production directory can easily grow to thousands or millions of entries—and with such large directories, searches with filters such as (objectclass=*) can put quite a strain on the directory server and generate more output than you want to deal with. Therefore, *ldapsearch* lets you define limits for both the client and the server that control the amount of time a search is allowed to take and the number of entries it is allowed to return. Table 5-2 lists the *ldapsearch* parameters that limit the resources required by any search.

Table 5-2. Command-line parameters for defining search limits in ldapsearch

Parameter	Description
-l integer	Specifies the number of seconds in real time to wait for a response to a search request. A value of 0 removes the `timelimit` default in *ldap.conf*.
-z integer	Defines the maximum number of entries to be retrieved as a result of a successful search request. A value of 0 removes the limits set by the `sizelimit` option in *ldap.conf*.

You can also specify limits on the server, in the *slapd.conf* file. Table 5-3 lists the global parameters that limit searches.

Table 5-3. OpenLDAP 2 slapd.conf global search limit parameters

Parameter	Description
`sizelimit` *integer*	Defines the maximum number of entries that the server will return to a client when responding to a search request. The default value is 500 entries.
`timelimit` *integer*	Specifies the maximum number of seconds in real time to be spent when responding to a search request. The default limit is 1 hour (3,600 seconds).

Determining a Server's Capabilities

Chapter 2 alluded to two new LDAPv3 features: the subschemaSubentry and the rootDSE objects. Both of these objects allow clients to find out information about a previously unknown directory server.

The rootDSE object contains information about features such as the server naming context, implemented SASL mechanisms, and supported LDAP extensions and controls. LDAPv3 requires that the rootDSE has an empty DN. To list the rootDSE, perform a base-level search using a DN of "". OpenLDAP will provide only values held by the rootDSE if the search requests that operational attributes be returned, so the + character is appended to the search request.

```
$ ldapsearch -x -s base -b "" "(objectclass=*)" +

dn:
structuralObjectClass: OpenLDAProotDSE
namingContexts: dc=plainjoe,dc=org
supportedControl: 2.16.840.1.113730.3.4.2
supportedControl: 1.3.6.1.4.1.4203.1.10.2
supportedControl: 1.2.826.0.1.334810.2.3
supportedExtension: 1.3.6.1.4.1.4203.1.11.3
supportedExtension: 1.3.6.1.4.1.4203.1.11.1
supportedExtension: 1.3.6.1.4.1.1466.20037
```

```
supportedFeatures: 1.3.6.1.4.1.4203.1.5.1
supportedFeatures: 1.3.6.1.4.1.4203.1.5.2
supportedFeatures: 1.3.6.1.4.1.4203.1.5.3
supportedFeatures: 1.3.6.1.4.1.4203.1.5.4
supportedFeatures: 1.3.6.1.4.1.4203.1.5.5
supportedLDAPVersion: 3
supportedSASLMechanisms: GSSAPI
supportedSASLMechanisms: DIGEST-MD5
supportedSASLMechanisms: CRAM-MD5
subschemaSubentry: cn=Subschema
```

This list can change over time and will vary from server to server. Our example shows us that this server supports:

- StartTLS (OID 1.3.6.1.4.1.1466.20037) and two other extended operations
- ManageDsaIT (OID 2.16.840.1.113730.3.4.2) and two other LDAP controls
- LDAPv3 operations only
- The GSSAPI, DIGEST-MD5, and CRAM-MD5 SASL mechanisms
- A single naming context of "dc=plainjoe,dc=org"

There may be additional attributes and values, depending on the LDAP server.

The SubSchemaSubentry attribute specifies the base search suffix for querying the schema supported by the server. This means that clients can verify that the server supports a given matching rule, attribute type, or object class prior to performing an operation that depends on a certain characteristic. The output from the following *ldapsearch* command shows the kind of information that is in the SubSchemaSubentry tree. Since this tree contains many entries, I've shortened it for convenience.

```
$ ldapsearch -D "cn=Manager,dc=plainjoe,dc=org"
> -w n0pass -x -s base -b "cn=SubSchema" \
> "(objectclass=*)" +
ldapSyntaxes: ( 1.3.6.1.4.1.1466.115.121.1.26 DESC 'IA5 String' )
...
matchingRules: ( 2.5.13.2 NAME 'caseIgnoreMatch' SYNTAX
1.3.6.1.4.1.1466.115.121.1.15 )
...
attributeTypes: ( 0.9.2342.19200300.100.1.42 NAME ( 'pager' 'pagerTelephoneNumber' )
EQUALITY telephoneNumberMatch SUBSTR telephoneNumberSubstringsMatch SYNTAX
1.3.6.1.4.1.1466.115.121.1.50 )
...
objectClasses: ( 2.5.6.6 NAME 'person' SUP top STRUCTURAL MUST ( sn $ cn ) MAY
( userPassword $ telephoneNumber $ seeAlso $ description ) )
...
```

 You can't modify the schema supported by an OpenLDAP directory server by modifying entries contained in the cn=SubSchema tree.

Creating Custom Schema Files for slapd

There are times when the standard schema files distributed with your LDAP server don't meet the needs of your application. Creating a custom schema file for OpenLDAP is a simple process:

- Assign a unique OID for all new attribute types and object classes.
- Create the schema file and include it in *slapd.conf*.

It's also possible to create alternate schema syntaxes and matching rules, but implementing them is beyond the scope of this book; typically, they require implementing a plug-in for the directory server or modifying the server's source code. For more information on this process, you should consult the OpenLDAP source code or your vendor's documentation for other directory servers.

Chapter 2 described how to obtain a private enterprise number from IANA (see the form at *http://www.iana.org/cgi-bin/enterprise.pl* and RFC 3383). When creating new attributes or object classes, it is a good idea to use an OID that is guaranteed to be unique, whether or not the schema will ever be used outside of your organization. The best way to guarantee that the OID is unique is to obtain a private enterprise number and place all your definitions under that number.

For example, suppose that an LDAP client application requires a new object class based on person. This new object class should contain all of the attributes possessed by the person object, with the addition of the userPassword and mail attributes.

In order to create this new object, I have allocated the OID arc of 1.3.6.1.4.1.7165.1.1.1 for the new object classes:

```
iso (1)
  org (3)
    dod (6)
      internet (1)
        private (4)
          enterprise (1)
            SAMBA.org (7165)
              plainjoe.org (1)
                O'Reilly LDAP Book(1)
```

The private enterprise number 7165 has been issued by IANA for use by the Samba developers, the 7165.1 arc has been allocated to the plainjoe.org domain, and 7165.1.1 has been set aside for this book; I can't touch the numbers above 7165.1 in the tree, but I have complete freedom to assign numbers below it as I see fit. I've chosen to allocate 7165.1.1.1 to ldap object classes that I create and 7165.1.1.2 for new attributes. I could put my new objects directly under plainjoe.org, but that might cause problems if I want to create other kinds of objects (for example, private SNMP MIBs):

```
SAMBA.org (7165)
  plainjoe.org (1)
```

```
O'Reilly LDAP Book(1)
|-- objectclasses  (1)
|-- attributeTypes (2)
```

Let's call the new object plainjoePerson. Add the following definition to a custom schema file named *plainjoe.schema*; you'll use this file for all custom objects that you define.

```
## objectclass definition for 'plainjoePerson' depends on core.schema.
objectclass ( 1.3.6.1.4.1.7165.1.1.1.1 NAME 'plainjoePerson'
     SUP person STRUCTURAL
     MUST (userPassword $ mail) )
```

LDAP's object inheritance allows this new object to reuse the existing characteristics of person; you need to add only the new required attributes. If new attributes are defined as well, they must be defined prior to their use in the plainjoePerson object. The new object has to be defined as STRUCTURAL since it is derived from a structural class.

New attributes can be defined in the same way or even be derived from existing attributes. RFC 2252 should be considered required reading in this case, as it describes the various LDAPv3 syntaxes and matching rules. For example, you could create a new attribute named plainjoePath to store a single, case-sensitive pathname by defining the following in *plainjoe.schema*:

```
## Store a case-sensitive path to a directory.
attributetype( 1.3.6.1.4.1.7165.1.1.2.1  NAME 'plainjoePath'
    DESC 'A directory on disk'
    SUBSTR caseExactIA5SubstringsMatch
    EQUALITY caseExactIA5Match
    SYNTAX 1.3.6.1.4.1.1466.115.121.1.26 SINGLE-VALUE )
```

 Servers other than OpenLDAP may use a different schema syntax for representing object classes. You should refer to your directory server's vendor documentation for more details. General LDAPv3 schema syntax is described in RFC 2252.

Finally, you need to add an include line in *slapd.conf* for your new schema file:

```
# /usr/local/etc/openldap/slapd.conf

# Global section

## Include the minimum schema required.
include    /usr/local/etc/openldap/schema/core.schema

## **NEW**
## Include support for special plainjoe objects.
include    /usr/local/etc/openldap/schema/plainjoe.schema
```

After restarting *slapd*, you can now add objects of the type plainjoePerson or include the plainjoePath in entries that use the extensibleObject class.

SASL and OpenLDAP

The final section of this chapter explores how to replace the simple authentication used in your current directory server with SASL mechanisms. You will be using the GSSAPI mechanism for Kerberos 5 authentication (RFCs 1510, 2743, and 2478). The examples assume that a Kerberos realm named *PLAINJOE.ORG* has already been established and that a service principal named *ldapadmin* has been created. If you are unclear on the details of Kerberos 5, a good place to start would be *Kerberos: A Network Authentication System*, by Brian Tung (Addison-Wesley), or *The Moron's Guide to Kerberos*, located at *http://www.isi.edu/gost/brian/security/kerberos.html*.

So far, the rootdn and rootpw values used in *slapd.conf* have appeared similar to:

```
rootdn        "cn=Manager,dc=plainjoe,dc=org"
rootpw        {SSHA}2aksIaicAvwc+DhCrXUFlhgWsbBJPLxy
```

In OpenLDAP 2.1, an SASL ID can be converted to a distinguished name and used for authentication or authorization wherever a normal DN would be appropriate. This includes operations such as defining the updatedn used for replication or the binddn used by a client in a search request. There's one important exception to this rule: don't use an SASL ID as the DN of an entry in the directory. To summarize from Chapter 3, an SASL ID converted to a DN appears as:

```
uid=name[,realm=realm],cn=mechanism,cn=auth
```

To illustrate how to use SASL as the authentication mechanism, we'll replace the rootdn in our master server's *slapd.conf* with the Kerberos 5 principal *ldapadmin*. Following the conversion algorithm just discussed, the new rootdn in *slapd.conf* will be:

```
## New SASL-based rootdn
rootdn        "uid=ldapadmin,cn=gssapi,cn=auth"
```

The rootpw entry can be deleted because authentication for the new rootdn will be done using the SASL GSSAPI mechanism. The OpenLDAP server must possess a valid keytab file containing the key for decrypting tickets transmitted with client requests.* Moreover, our tests will assume that the server is configured to use the default realm of *PLAINJOE.ORG*.

Once the configuration change has been made, restart *slapd*. You can then verify that the change has been made correctly by using the *ldapadd* command to add an entry; the rootdn is currently the only DN allowed to write to the directory.

To run this test, create a file with an LDIF entry; we'll use the following LDIF entry, stored in */tmp/test.ldif*:

```
## Test user to verify that the new rootdn is OK.
dn: cn=test user,ou=people,dc=plainjoe,dc=org
cn: test user
```

---

* More information on generating keytab files can be found on the *kadmin(8)* manpage.

```
sn: test
objectclass: person
```

To add this entry to the directory, invoke *ldapadd* with some additional arguments:

```
$ kinit ldapadmin@PLAINJOE.ORG
Password for ldapadmin@PLAINJOE.ORG: password
$ klist
Ticket cache: FILE:/tmp/krb5cc_780
Default principal: ldapadmin@PLAINJOE.ORG

Valid starting      Expires             Service principal
11/28/02 19:20:15   11/29/02 05:20:15   krbtgt/PLAINJOE.ORG@PLAINJOE.ORG

$ ldapmodify -a -H ldap://master.plainjoe.org/ \
> -f testuser.ldif
SASL/GSSAPI authentication started
SASL username: ldapadmin@PLAINJOE.ORG
SASL SSF: 56
SASL installing layers
adding new entry "cn=test user,ou=people,dc=plainjoe,dc=org"

$ klist
Ticket cache: FILE:/tmp/krb5cc_780
Default principal: ldapadmin@PLAINJOE.ORG

Valid starting      Expires             Service principal
11/28/02 19:20:15   11/29/02 05:20:15   krbtgt/PLAINJOE.ORG@PLAINJOE.ORG
11/28/02 19:23:34   11/29/02 05:20:15   ldap/garion.plainjoe.org@PLAINJOE.ORG
```

If the server does not support the particular mechanism needed, GSSAPI in this case, authentication will fail. The -Y option can be used to specify an SASL authentication mechanism rather than letting the client and server attempt to negotiate a valid type that is supported by both. As seen earlier, the client can obtain a list of the mechanisms that the server supports by querying the server's rootDSE and viewing the values of the supportedSASLMechanisms attribute.

After becoming accustomed to SASL user IDs, you can incorporate them into the ACLs defined in *slapd.conf*. Following the rule that an SASL ID can be used anywhere a DN is used to represent an authenticated user, SASL IDs can follow the by keyword in an ACL definition. For example, the following definition allows the Kerberos principal *jerry* to edit the mail attribute for all users in the people organizational unit:

```
access to dn=".*,ou=people,dc=plainjoe,dc=org" attrs=mail
     by "uid=jerry,cn=gssapi,cn=auth" write
```

## PART II

Application Integration

## CHAPTER 6

Replacing NIS

One of LDAP's chief advantages is its ability to consolidate multiple directory services into one. This chapter examines the pros and cons of using LDAP as a replacement for Sun's Network Information Service (NIS). NIS is used primarily by Unix clients to centralize management of user information and passwords, hostnames and IP addresses, automount maps (files that control the mounting of remote file systems), and other administrative information. NIS clients for other operating systems, such as Windows NT 4.0, exist, though they aren't particularly common.[*]

While the focus of this chapter is using an LDAP directory as a replacement for NIS domains, many other tools are used to distribute management information on Unix systems; for example, many sites use *rsync(1)* to push administrative files, such as */etc/passwd*, to client machines. While this chapter assumes that you are replacing NIS with an LDAP directory, adapting these techniques I present to other schemes for sharing the data in */etc/passwd*, */etc/hosts*, and other key files should be straightforward:

- Get the information you want to share into the directory.
- Get your clients to use the directory.
- Disable your old information-sharing mechanism.

There are two fundamental strategies for replacing NIS with an LDAP directory. The first solution, illustrated in Figure 6-1, involves setting up an NIS/LDAP gateway: i.e., an NIS server that accepts NIS queries, but answers the queries by retrieving information from an LDAP directory. This strategy doesn't require any client modifications, and therefore works with all NIS clients; it may be the easiest means of transitioning to a new LDAP-based information service. Sun Microsystems Directory Server 4.x supports this approach. Sadly, newer releases (5.x) of Sun's directory services product do not. An alternative solution is the NIS/LDAP gateway provided by a company

---

[*] NIS was superseded by NIS+, which was never widely adopted. Describing how to replace NIS+ is beyond the scope of this book.

named PADL Software (*http://www.padl.com/*). This gateway product is available for servers running Solaris, Linux, FreeBSD, or AIX, and will be discussed later in this chapter.

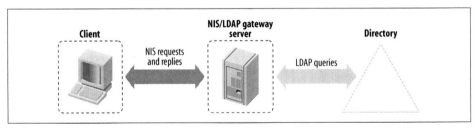

Figure 6-1. NIS/LDAP gateway

The second solution involves making a complete transition to LDAP. If you are willing to disable NIS lookups on all of your clients and install the necessary LDAP libraries and modules, you may prefer this approach. Clients access information directly from an LDAP directory, eliminating the gateway. Many modern operating systems support pluggable information retrieval modules; for example, Unix and Unix-like systems such as Solaris and Linux can use the LDAP Pluggable Authentication Modules (PAM) and Name Server Switch (NSS) modules that have been released by PADL Software under the GNU Lesser General Public License (LGPL).* If you are unfamiliar with PAM and NSS, read the brief overview found in Appendix A.

To implement either solution—an NIS/LDAP gateway server or LDAP-enabled client lookups—we must define the attribute types and object classes needed to move the information served by NIS (or saved in static system files) into an LDAP directory.

More About NIS

Before discussing these strategies for replacing NIS with LDAP, it's worth understanding something about the beast we're trying to replace.† NIS is most commonly used to distribute system password and account maps (i.e., */etc/passwd* and */etc/shadow*) to client machines. It's also used to distribute the information from many other system files, such as */etc/hosts, /etc/services, /etc/group*, and */etc/networks*. It can also distribute a number of files that control the automatic mounting of remote file systems; and with the appropriate wizardry in sed and awk or Perl, it can be coerced into distributing almost any kind of data that can be represented in a text file.

---

* More information on the LGPL license can be found at *http://www.fsf.org/licenses/licenses.html#LGPL*.

† This discussion is necessarily very brief. If you need more information about NIS, see *Managing NFS and NIS*, by Hal Stern, Mike Eisler, and Ricardo Labiaga (O'Reilly).

In the NIS world, the master copy of any shared data resides on a master server, which distributes the data to slave servers. Clients, which are organized into NIS domains (not to be confused with DNS domains), can then access this information from any NIS server, master or slave, that services their domain. The NIS master acts as a directory system agent (DSA) that provides information to clients, which use this information to perform tasks such as authenticating users (i.e., the *passwd* map) and locating other hosts on the network (i.e., the *hosts* map).

The NIS information model is also characterized by a flat namespace. To use the *passwd.byname* map as an example (this map represents the */etc/passwd* file, indexed by username), there can be only one login name of *jerry*. To work around this deficiency, NIS groups client machines into NIS domains, each with its own set of maps (i.e., its own set of virtual administrative files). So, two users with the login name *jerry* can coexist if they can be placed in different domains; for all practical purposes, different NIS domains are different directories (even though they may be served by the same server).

In contrast, LDAP allows you to create a hierarchical namespace to manage these users. Let's assume that we'll use the RDN of a node as its login name. LDAP can then maintain multiple users with the same login name if we make sure that each user belongs to a different parent node (see Figure 6-2).

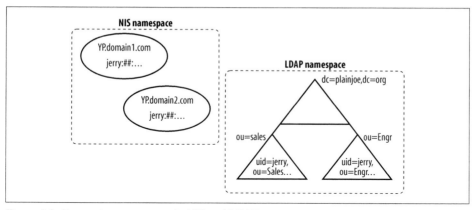

Figure 6-2. Comparing namespaces in NIS and LDAP

One basic rule of system administration is that users should not notice any loss of service when you implement changes. A user does not need to be aware of where their account information is stored. It makes little difference to them, as long as they can access necessary network services. If a change results in a downgrade of service for users (no matter how big of a win for the system administrators), you'll almost certainly be forced to rip it out and go back to the old system; eventually, you'll get tired of answering all the help desk calls. Fortunately, the flexibility of the PAM and NSS interfaces can do a lot to insulate users from a change in information location.

Schemas for Information Services

RFC 2307, "An Approach for Using LDAP as a Network Information Service," which has recently been updated in an Internet-Draft by the LDAPbis working group, defines the attribute types and object classes needed to use an LDAP directory as a replacement for NIS. Despite its experimental status, several vendors such as Sun, Apple, HP, SGI, OpenLDAP, and PADL Software have developed products that support this schema.

RFC 2307 relates directly to information stored in standard NIS maps and how these maps should be viewed by directory-enabled client applications. The list of attribute types and object classes is lengthy; for a complete description of all that is available, refer to the RFC. I will use portions of the RFC 2307 schema in examples later in this chapter. Before trying to implement these examples or experimenting with this schema on your own, consult your directory server's documentation to find out the server's level of support for RFC 2307 and the exact syntax you should use for working with RFC 2307 objects.

The first example shows how to migrate all user accounts and groups into your OpenLDAP server. While there is nothing out of the ordinary about the configuration parameters with which you'll implement this solution, here's a complete listing of the revised *slapd.conf*; note that two new schema files are included, *nis.schema* (the RFC 2307 schema) and *cosine.schema* (which defines items required by *nis. schema*):

```
## slapd.conf for implementing an LDAP-based Network Information Service

## Standard OpenLDAP basic attribute types and object classes
include     /usr/local/etc/openldap/schema/core.schema

## cosine.schema is a prerequesite of nis.schema.
include     /usr/local/etc/openldap/schema/cosine.schema

## rfc2307 attribute types and object classes
include     /usr/local/etc/openldap/schema/nis.schema

## Misc. configure options
pidfile     /var/run/slapd.pid
argsfile    /usr/run/slapd.args
loglevel    256

## SSL configure options
TLSCipherSuite        3DES:RC4:EXPORT40
TLSCertificateFile    /usr/local/etc/openldap/slapd-cert.pem
TLSCertificateKeyFile /usr/local/etc/openldap/slapd-private-key.pem

########################################################
## Define the beginning of example database.
database    bdb
suffix      "dc=plainjoe,dc=org"
```

```
## Define a root DN for superuser privileges.
rootdn          "cn=Manager,dc=plainjoe,dc=org"
rootpw          {SSHA}2aksIaicAvwc+DhCrXUFlhgWsbBJPLxy

## Directory containing the database files
directory       /var/ldap/plainjoe.org
mode            0600

## Create the necessary indexes.
index     objectClass      eq

## These indexes are included to support calls such as getpwuid( ), getpwnam( ), and
## getgrgid( ).
index     cn,uid           eq
index     uidNumber        eq
index     gidNumber        eq
```

Figure 6-3 illustrates the relationships between the posixAccount object class and a standard entry from a Unix password file. There are two attributes, cn and description, that do not directly correspond to a field in the */etc/passwd* file. The RFC 2307 posixAccount object is meant to represent a POSIX account, which doesn't map exactly to the traditional Unix password file.[*] Unix password files have the so-called GECOS field, which has historically been used to store all sorts of information: the user's full name, office number, phone number, and other things that are useful but not used directly by the operating system.[†] The cn attribute ensures that the user's full name (or common name) is present in a posixAccount entry, and the description attribute can be used to store other supplementary information.

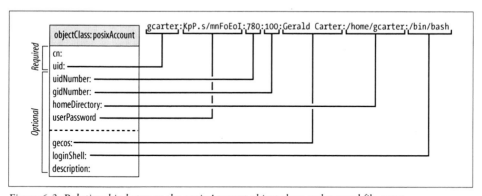

Figure 6-3. Relationship between the posixAccount object class and passwd file entry

---

[*] The Portable Operating System Interface (POSIX) is a specification originally developed by the IEEE to standardize operating system interface programmers. It has since been revised to include topics such as shells, utilities, and system administration.

[†] For some interesting trivia behind GECOS (pronounced /jee' kohs/), refer to *http://www.jargon.net/jargonfile/g/GCOS.html*.

Figure 6-4 illustrates a similar mapping between the posixGroup object class and an entry from the */etc/group* file, which NIS represents using the *group.byname* map.

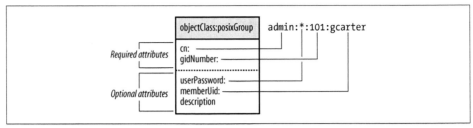

Figure 6-4. Relationship between the posixGroup object class and group file entry

Information Migration

While some organizations may have the resources (such as undergraduate work study students) to re-enter the data held in the NIS maps to the LDAP store, luckily, there are other means available. In addition to the PAM and NSS LDAP reference modules available at PADL Software's web site, you'll also find a set of Perl scripts designed to convert the various */etc* system files (e.g., */etc/passwd* and */etc/hosts*) into LDIF format. Once you've converted the system files to LDIF, you can import them into your LDAP store either online using the *ldapadd(1)* command or by using an offline database creation utility such as the OpenLDAP *slapadd(8c)* tool. These LDAP migration scripts can be found at *http://www.padl.com/OSS/MigrationTools.html*.

After unpacking the migration scripts, you must customize the *migrate_common.ph* script to fit your network settings. Within this Perl script is a variable named $DEFAULT_BASE, which is used to define the base suffix under which the organizational units that will serve as containers for migrated information will be created.

The scripts accept input and output filenames as command-line parameters. If no output filename is present, the scripts write the converted entries to standard output. For example, the following command converts */etc/passwd* into an LDIF file:

```
root# migrate_passwd.pl /etc/passwd /tmp/passwd.ldif
```

Here's what a typical entry from */etc/passwd* looks like after it has been translated:

```
dn: uid=gcarter,ou=people,dc=plainjoe,dc=org
uid: gcarter
cn: Gerald Carter
objectClass: account
objectClass: posixAccount
objectClass: top
objectClass: shadowAccount
userPassword: {crypt}LnMJ/n2rQsR.c
shadowLastChange: 11108
shadowMax: 99999
shadowWarning: 7
```

```
shadowFlag: 134539460
loginShell: /bin/bash
uidNumber: 780
gidNumber: 100
homeDirectory: /home/gcarter
gecos: Gerald Carter
```

All the required fields (cn, uid, uidNumber, gidNumber, and homeDirectory) defined in the RFC schema for a posixAccount are present. There are also a number of shadow fields (shadowLastChange, etc.; see the shadowAccount object in Figure 6-5), which hold values related to password aging. These values are taken automatically from the */etc/shadow* file. If your system doesn't use shadow passwords, the shadowAccount object class values may not be present.

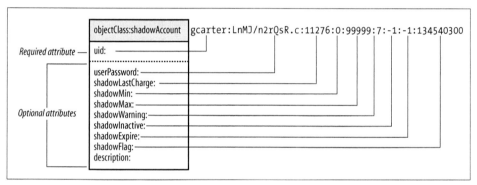

Figure 6-5. Relationship between the shadowAccount object class and /etc/shadow file entry

Different scripts exist to translate each system file into LDIF records. The information in each file is stored in a different organizational unit directly beneath the base suffix (defined in *migrate_common.ph*) in the directory. Each ou listed next is used by convention. The nss_ldap library can be configured to pull information from other locations, as we will see later. Currently, the migration scripts support translating:

- */etc/fstab* (stored in ou=Mounts)
- */etc/hosts* (stored in ou=Hosts)
- */etc/passwd* and */etc/shadow* (stored in ou=People)
- */etc/group* (stored in ou=Group)
- */etc/protocols* (stored in ou=Protocols)
- */etc/rpc* (stored in ou=Rpc)
- */etc/services* (stored in ou=Services)
- */etc/networks* (stored in ou=Networks)
- *netgroups* (stored in ou=Netgroups)

In each case, the PADL migration scripts do not create the top-level organization unit for you. Make sure that these exist prior to attempting to generate LDIF files in the directory. Since we are primarily dealing with users and groups in this chapter, the following entries have already been added to the directory:

```
dn: ou=people,dc=plainjoe,dc=org
objectclass: organizationalUnit
ou: people

dn: ou=group,dc=plainjoe,dc=org
objectclass: organizationalUnit
ou: group
```

The pam_ldap Module

Pluggable Authentication Modules (PAM) are implemented as shared libraries that distance applications from the details of account data storage, mechanisms used to authenticate users, and service authorization processes. PADL Software has developed a pam_ldap module, supported on FreeBSD, HP-UX, Linux, Mac OS 10.2, and Solaris, as part of a reference implementation for RFC 2307. This module allows you to take advantage of LDAP in PAM-aware applications and operating systems. You can download the pam_ldap source code from *http://www.padl.com/OSS/pam_ldap. html*. Most Linux distributions include PADL's pam_ldap and nss_ldap modules with the operating system. You should remove these packages first if you plan to build the latest version from source.

 The pam_ldap and nss_ldap libraries included with Solaris as part of the operating system installation are Sun's own creation and should not be confused with the modules discussed in this chapter.

Once you have obtained and extracted the pam_ldap source code, building the module is a familiar process:

```
$ ./configure
$ make
$ /bin/su -c "make install"
```

PADL's PAM and NSS libraries can make use of the Netscape LDAP SDK and the original University of Michigan LDAP SDK, in addition to the OpenLDAP client libraries. The *configure* script attempts to determine which of these packages is installed on the local system. If you need to inform the *configure* script which LDAP client libraries you have installed and where, use the following configure options:

```
--with-ldap-lib=type   select ldap library [auto|netscape3|
                       netscape4|umich|openldap]
--with-ldap-dir=DIR    base directory of ldap SDK
```

Configuring /etc/ldap.conf

The pam_ldap module (and as we will see shortly, PADL's nss_ldap module) stores its configuration settings in a text file. This file is named *ldap.conf* by default and is normally stored in the */etc* directory. The configuration parameters you can put in this file are summarized in Tables 6-1, 6-2, and 6-3; the list is fairly small and self-explanatory. We will begin customizing this file by exploring how a client locates the LDAP server and authenticates itself.

Table 6-1. ldap.conf parameters shared by pam_ldap and nss_ldap

Parameter	Description
host	The IP address (or hostname) of the LDAP server. The value must be resolvable without LDAP support. If a host is not specified, the nss_ldap library will attempt to locate an LDAP server by querying DNS for an SRV record for _ldap._tcp.<domain>. The current version of the pam_ldap module (v157) will not perform this auto-lookup, but support is planned for a future release. Also refer to the uri parameter.
base	The base DN to use in searches.
ldap_version	The version of LDAP to use when querying the server. Legal values are 2 and 3. Version 3 is used by default if it is supported by the client libraries.
binddn	The DN to use when binding to the LDAP server. This is an optional parameter; it is necessary when access control on directory entries prohibits anonymous searches.
bindpw	The password used when binding to the LDAP server (if the binddn was defined).
port	The port to use when contacting the LDAP server. The default is port 389. Also refer to the uri parameter.
rootbinddn	This parameter allows you to map the effective UID 0 (i.e., the root UID) to a DN that is used to bind to the LDAP server. If enabled, the password for this DN is read from */etc/ldap.secret*. This follows the convention that the root account should be able to access all information on the system.
ssl	This parameter defines the behavior of the PAM and NSS modules for negotiating SSL when binding to the server. By default, SSL is not used. The client can be configured to use LDAPS by setting this parameter to on, or to use the StartTLS Extended command by setting this parameter to start_tls.
scope	The scope to use when searching the LDAP tree. The possible values are sub, one, and base.
uri	This option accepts an LDAP URI defining the host and port of the directory server.

Table 6-2. pam_ldap ldap.conf parameters

Parameter	Description
pam_check_host_attr	A Boolean parameter (defaults to no) that controls checking of the host attribute when authorizing a login.
pam_filter	A string that provides additional filter elements that are ANDed with (uid=%s) when attempting to validate a user. See the pam_login_attribute parameter for related information.
pam_login_attribute	The attribute that should be matched against the user's login name. This parameter lets you use something other than a simple username for authentication—for example, an email address.
pam_lookup_policy	A Boolean parameter (yes or no) that tells pam_ldap whether to contact the root DSE to get the server's password policy. For use with Netscape's directory server 3.x only.
pam_groupdn	Defines the DN of a group whose membership (see the pam_member_attribute parameter) should be used to restrict access to the local host.

Table 6-2. pam_ldap ldap.conf parameters (continued)

Parameter	Description
pam_member_attribute	Defines the group membership attribute.
pam_min_uid pam_max_uid	These two parameters accept an integer representing the minimum and maximun uidNumber values allowed to log in. The default is to place no restrictions on logins.
pam_password	This parameter defines various methods for changing passwords on LDAP servers. It supersedes the older pam_crypt, pam_nds_passwd, and pam_ad_passwd parameters. Possible values include: clear (the default; sends the clear text of the password to the server), crypt (hashes the password locally using the standard crypt( ) function before sending the change to the server), md5 (generates the MD5 hash of the password locally before sending it to the server), nds, racf (provides support for changing passwords stored in a Novell Directory Server), ad (provides support for changing passwords stored in an Active Directory server), and exop (supports the Password Modify extended operation defined in RFC 3062; implemented by OpenLDAP).

Table 6-3. nss_ldap ldap.conf parameters

Parameter	Description
nss_base_shadow nss_base_passwd nss_base_group nss_base_hosts nss_base_services nss_base_networks nss_base_protocols nss_base_rpc nss_base_ethers nss_base_netmasks nss_base_aliases nss_base_netgroup	These parameters allow the naming contexts for various databases in *nsswitch.conf* to be configured as per the recommendations from the RFC 2307 updates. The syntax is: `nss_base_XXX  base?scope?filter` The *filter* is combined with the default filter for the object being requested using a logical AND (&). These parameters are available only when nss_ldap has been configured to use the *--enable-rfc2307bis* option at compile time.
nss_map_attribute nss_map_objectclass	These parameters provide a means of mapping attributes and object classes returned from the directory server to an RFC 2307–equivalent schema item. The syntax is: `nss_map_XX  rfc2307item  mapped_item`

In order for the pam_ldap module to offer any help, it must be able to locate the directory server it will query for information. There are two ways that the module can locate the directory server. The sole method supported by pam_ldap is to explicitly specify the LDAP server using the host or uri parameters in *ldap.conf*. The alternative, utilized only by the nss_ldap library, is to omit the host parameter and create a DNS SRV record that maps the hostname _ldap._tcp.<*domain*> to an IP address. If no host is specified in *ldap.conf*, the nss_ldap library tries to look up a server with this special hostname and uses that server at that address for queries. If you have multiple servers, you can configure round-robin load sharing with either approach.

The following parameters instruct pam_ldap to contact the host *ldap.plainjoe.org* on the default port 389 for all LDAPv3 queries:

```
# Your LDAP server. Must be resolvable without using LDAP.
uri          ldap://ldap.plainjoe.org/
```

```
## Set the version number for LDAP commands. The default is to use Version 3 if
## supported by the client libraries.
ldap_version     3
```

Next, you must define the search parameters for pam_ldap to use when querying the directory. These options correspond to the standard *ldapsearch* command-line options. The following fragment of *ldap.conf* defines the search base, the search scope, and a maximum time limit:

```
## Define the search base
base         dc=plainjoe,dc=org

## Define the scope of the search [sub|base|one]. A subtree search is the default.
scope        sub

## Set a time limit in seconds to wait on a search.
timelimit    30
```

The DN of the user's entry must be located in order to bind to the directory on behalf of the user and thus perform the requested authentication. This search can be done either anonymously or by using a predefined binddn and bindpw. The bindpw string must be stored in *ldap.conf* as clear text, which always makes me nervous. Therefore, my preference is for the first option. Because anonymous searches are implied by the absence of a specified binddn, no additional *ldap.conf* parameters are required.

Finally, add a few parameters to fine-tune the search filter. pam_login_attribute defines which attribute should be matched to the login name entered by the user. pam_filter allows an administrator to further refine the search filter when attempting to locate a user account. In the following configuration file entries, it is specified that the user's login name should be matched against the UID attribute defined in the posixAccount object class. (Note that a UID in this schema is a login name, not a number, as in common Unix usage.)

```
## Define the user login name attribute (defaults to uid).
pam_login_attribute     uid

## The following filter will be used to AND with <pam_login_attribute>=%s.
pam_filter objectclass=posixAccount
```

With these two settings, the pam_ldap library makes the following search to verify that a user account named "carter" is in the directory:

```
(&(objectClass=posixAccount)(uid=gcarter))
```

After verifying the existence of the DN, the PAM module attempts to bind to the directory using the located DN and the password entered by the user. If this bind succeeds, pam_ldap informs the calling application that the user has been successfully authenticated.

The nss_ldap Module

The Name Service Switch (NSS) is similar to PAM except that it only provides a mechanism for information retrieval. PADL Software's nss_ldap module can be obtained from *http://www.padl.com/OSS/nss_ldap.html*. The current implementation can be used on AIX, HP-UX, Linux, and Solaris. Although the pam_ldap module supports FreeBSD and Mac OS 10.2, the nss_ldap library does not. This means that you will not be able to apply the complete solution outlined in this chapter to those platforms.

Compiling PADL's nss_ldap module is almost the same as compiling pam_ldap. The same options are available to the *configure* script (for explicitly defining the LDAP libraries to be used and their locations). The one additional compile-time setting that you will use is *-enable-rfc2307bis*. This change optimizes the search parameters for each *nsswitch.conf* database by using the *nss_base_** parmeters. Otherwise, nss_ldap would query for entries by performing a subtree search beginning at the *base* (from */etc/ldap.conf*). The familiar three-step:

```
$ ./configure  --enable-rfc2307bis
$ make
$ /bin/su -c "make install"
```

installs an appropriately named version of the nss_ldap library in */lib*. For example, the resulting file would be */lib/libnss_ldap.so* on a Linux host and */lib/nss_ldap.so* on a Solaris box. Since the examples in this chapter are based on Linux systems, whenever there is a need to refer to the actual nss_ldap library file, I will use the *libnss_ldap.so* filename.

The nss_ldap module uses the same */etc/ldap.conf* configuration file as PADL's pam_ldap module. The configuration parameters for this module are summarized in Table 6-3. While both pam_ldap and nss_ldap read */etc/ldap.conf* for configuration settings, the parameters prefixed by pam_ do not affect the behavior of nss_ldap.

The */etc/ldap.conf* file must be readable by any process that performs any of the various getXbyY( ) function calls such as getpwnam(jerry) or getgrgid(0). For example, if you have specified a host to which all LDAP queries should be directed, but the user's process is unable to obtain that parameter setting because it cannot read *ldap.conf*, you will begin to notice DNS SRV queries for _ldap._tcp.*domain* as the nss_ldap library attempts to locate an LDAP server. However, if you make the *ldap.conf* file world-readable, think twice about putting a binddn and bindpw in the file.

To configure a service to use the nss_ldap module, add the keyword ldap to the appropriate lines in your */etc/nsswitch.conf* file. PADL's NSS module currently supports the following databases:

    passwd
    group
    hosts

services
networks
protocols
rpc
ethers
netgroups

The following databases are currently unsupported:

netmasks
bootparams
publickey
automount

Mount point lookups using LDAP queries are supported directly by some automount agents, such as Sun's automounter (included with current Solaris releases) and Linux's autofs. This will be covered later in the chapter.

Here's an excerpt from an *nsswitch.conf* file. It specifies that the system should consult the local password, shadow password, and group files before querying the directory server.

```
## Define the order of lookups for users and groups.
passwd:     files ldap
shadow:     files ldap
group:      files ldap
```

Because your directory stores groups in one ou and user accounts in another, you can help reduce the load on your LDAP server by customizing the searches used by nss_ldap. Table 6-3 listed several nss_base_XXX parameters. You will use only the three that correspond to the *nsswitch.conf* ldap entries just listed. Each search needs to be only a one-level search since all relevant entries are stored directly below the corresponding ou (e.g., ou=people and ou=group).

```
## Optimize the nss_ldap searches for these databases.
nss_base_passwd    ou=people,dc=plainjoe,dc=org?one
nss_base_shadow    ou=people,dc=plainjoe,dc=org?one
nss_base_group     ou=group,dc=plainjoe,dc=org?one
```

If all has gone well up to this point (user and group account information has been entered into the LDAP directory, and *libnss_ldap.so* has been installed and configured), the following command should list the accounts in */etc/passwd* first, followed by any posixAccount objects in the directory:

```
$ getent passwd
root:x:0:0:root:/root:/bin/bash
bin:x:1:1:bin:/bin:
<...output deleted...>
gcarter:x:780:100:G. Carter:/home/queso/gcarter:/bin/bash
jerry:x:782:782:Jerry Carter:/home/queso/jerry:/bin/bash
```

The last two lines of output were retrieved from the LDAP server. The "x" in the password field is due to the presence of the shadowAccount object class, as shown in this LDIF listing of the account information for gcarter:

```
dn: uid=gcarter,ou=People,dc=plainjoe,dc=org
uid: gcarter
cn: Gerald (Jerry) Carter
objectClass: account
objectClass: posixAccount
objectClass: top
objectClass: shadowAccount
loginShell: /bin/bash
uidNumber: 780
gidNumber: 100
homeDirectory: /home/queso/gcarter
userPassword: {crypt}GoYLwzMD6cuZE
```

If the shadowAccount object class wasn't present, the nss_ldap module would have filled in the second field of the output from *getent* with the password hash (assuming this attribute was returned from the directory server).

If no posixAccount entries are returned by the *getent* command, then verify that the nss_ldap library was installed correctly, that it has the read and execute permissions set for everyone (*chmod o+rx /lib/libnss_ldap.so**), and that */etc/ldap.conf* is readable by all users (*chmod o+r /etc/ldap.conf*). If all of these appear to be correct, also verify that the information can be retrieved from the directory using *ldapsearch*.

OpenSSH, PAM, and NSS

Once the pam_ldap and nss_ldap shared libraries have been installed and */etc/ldap. conf* has been configured, you can configure individual services to use the new PAM module. We'll start with the SSH daemon, *sshd*. Here's how to set up OpenSSH (*http://www.openssh.com/*) on a Linux system, which uses a separate PAM configuration file per service. (Note that other systems may use a single PAM file for all services; for example, Solaris uses */etc/pam.conf*.) Make sure that PAM is enabled when you compile the *sshd* daemon; otherwise, you will be wasting your time.

The following */etc/pam.d/sshd* configuration file defines the pam_ldap library to be used for authentication (auth) and account management (account). The account management library checks for password aging according to the attribute types defined for the shadowAccount object class and verifies any host-based access rules (covered in the next section). The session module type is ignored by the pam_ldap library. While user password changes are supported by the pam_ldap library, these are not relevent to this example.

```
## /etc/pam.d/sshd
## PAM configuration file for OpenSSH server
auth        required      /lib/security/pam_nologin.so
```

```
auth        sufficient      /lib/security/pam_ldap.so
auth        required        /lib/security/pam_unix.so shadow nullok use_first_pass

account     sufficient      /lib/security/pam_ldap.so
account     required        /lib/security/pam_unix.so

password    required        /lib/security/pam_cracklib.so
password    required        /lib/security/pam_unix.so nullok use_authtok   shadow

session     required        /lib/security/pam_unix.so
session     optional        /lib/security/pam_console.so
```

The use of the sufficient control flag for the auth and account service types indicates that authentication by this module alone is enough to return success to the invoking application. The use_first_pass argument is necessary so that the user is not prompted for an additional password if authentication falls through to the *pam_unix.so* library.

You will have to create a similar configuration file for every other service for which you want to control access.

While configuring *sshd* to use PAM for authentication requires some configuration, nothing needs to be done to make *sshd* use the nss_ldap library. The retrieval of information from the various databases listed in */etc/nsswitch.conf* is handled by the system's standard C library; once you've set up *nsswitch.conf*, you're done. The client application only needs to call the basic get...( ) function, such as getpwnam( ), to obtain the available information.

Authorization Through PAM

Once a user has been authenticated, the account management features of the pam_ldap module provide two means of restricting access to a host, independent of any other PAM modules you may have specified in the configuration file (e.g., the pam_nologin module). Which method you choose depends on whether you wish to bind a host to a group of users or bind a user to a group of hosts.

One Host and a Group of Users

The first authorization method, in which you specify a group of users who are allowed to use a particular host, ties into other information you have already migrated into the directory. The host entry for a machine (generated from */etc/hosts* by the PADL migration scripts) can be extended to include a list of DNs for users (member) that are authorized to log on using pam_ldap. The following LDIF example shows how you can use the extensibleObject class to associate a group of users with a host entry:

```
dn: cn=pogo,ou=hosts,dc=plainjoe,dc=org
objectClass: ipHost
```

```
objectClass: device
objectClass: extensibleObject
ipHostNumber: 192.168.1.75
cn: pogo.plainjoe.org
cn: pogo
member: uid=gcarter,ou=people,dc=plainjoe,dc=org
member: uid=kristi,ou=people,dc=plainjoe,dc=org
member: uid=deryck,ou=people,dc=plainjoe,dc=org
```

In order to configure pam_ldap to honor this group membership, the following two lines must be added to */etc/ldap.conf*:

```
## Define the DN of the entry to contain the groupOfUniqueNames.
pam_groupdn              cn=pogo,ou=hosts,dc=plainjoe,dc=org

## Define the attribute type that should be used in the attempt to match the user's
## DN.
pam_member_attribute     member
```

For OpenSSH, this configuration means that only those users whose DN is listed as one of the values for the member attribute will be allowed *ssh* access to your host.

One User and a Group of Hosts

You can also specify the machines that any given user is allowed to access. To implement this control mechanism, the structural account object class listed in the *cosine.schema* file must be present in the list of object classes for an entry. This is done for you by the PADL migration scripts. Figure 6-6 shows that the account object class requires only one attribute. This attribute, uid, is already required by the posixAccount object class and is therefore guaranteed to be present.

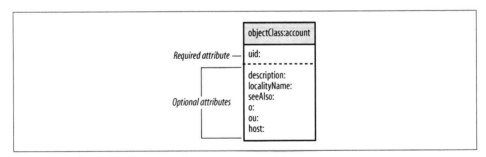

Figure 6-6. Schema for the account object class

While several optional attribute types are available with the addition of this new object class, only the host attribute is of use to pam_ldap. The following LDIF listing shows how the account object class can be used to control access:

```
dn: uid=gcarter,ou=People,dc=plainjoe,dc=org
uid: gcarter
cn: Gerald (Jerry) Carter
objectClass: account
```

```
objectClass: posixAccount
objectClass: shadowAccount
loginShell: /bin/bash
uidNumber: 780
gidNumber: 100
homeDirectory: /home/queso/gcarter
userPassword: {crypt}GoYLwzMD6cuZE
host: queso.plainjoe.org
host: pogo.plainjoe.org
host: tumnus.plainjoe.org
```

This listing shows that the user *gcarter* is allowed to access the hosts *queso*, *pogo*, and *tumnus*. To enable pam_ldap's host-checking functionality, you must enable the pam_check_host_attr parameter in *ldap.conf*:

```
## Enable host attribute lookups.
pam_check_host_attr     yes
```

If the list of hosts does not contain the hostname of the system that the user wants to access, he is denied access. If the host list is empty (i.e., no host attribute is present), the user is denied access by default.

Netgroups

Netgroups have become a daily staple for NIS administrators. They allow machines and/or users to be collected together for various administrative tasks such as grouping machines together for use in the tcp_wrappers files */etc/hosts.allow* and */etc/hosts.deny*. In this next example, you restrict access via *ssh* only to members of the *sysadmin* netgroup:

```
# /etc/hosts.deny
sshd: ALL
...
# /etc/hosts.allow
sshd: @sysadmin
```

Netgroups can be composed solely of individual hosts:

```
sysadmin  (garion.plainjoe.org,-,-)(silk.plainjoe.org,-,-)
```

or other netgroups:

```
all_sysadmin    sysadmin secure_clients
```

or of any combination of the two.

RFC 2307 describes the structural nisNetgroup object class (Figure 6-7), which can be used to represent netgroups as directory entries. The cn attribute holds the name of the netgroup, the nisNetgroupTriple attribute stores the (host, user, NIS-domain) entries, and the memberNisNetgroup attribute stores the names of any nested netgroups.

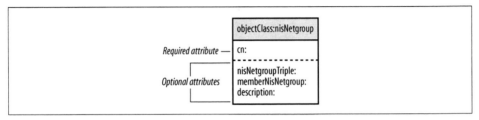

Figure 6-7. nisNetgroup object classes

Before adding any netgroup entries to the directory, you must create the container ou. By convention, I will use the ou=netgroup organizational unit for storing netgroups in this example:

```
dn: ou=netgroup,dc=plainjoe,dc=org
objectclass: organizationalUnit
ou: netgroup
```

After passing through PADL's *migrate_netgroup.pl* tool, the *sysadmin* netgroup will be represented by this LDIF entry:

```
$ ./migrate_netgroup.pl /etc/netgroup
dn: cn=sysadmin,ou=netgroup,dc=plainjoe,dc=org
objectClass: nisNetgroup
objectClass: top
cn: sysadmin
nisNetgroupTriple: (garion.plainjoe.org,-,-)
nisNetgroupTriple: (silk.plainjoe.org,-,-)
```

The *all_sysadmin* netgroup contains the *sysadmin* and the *secure_clients* netgroups, so it will use the memberNisNetgroup attribute:

```
dn: cn=all_sysadmin,ou=netgroup,dc=plainjoe,dc=org
objectClass: nisNetgroup
objectClass: top
cn: all_sysadmin
memberNisNetgroup: sysadmin
memberNisNetgroup: secure_clients
```

After adding these entries to your directory, you must configure the nss_base_netgroup parameter in */etc/ldap.conf* to use the correct search suffix:

```
## /etc/ldap.conf
## <remaining parameters imitted>
## Configure the search parameters for netgroups.
nss_base_netgroup     ou=netgroup,dc=plainjoe,dc=org?one
```

Finally, you must inform the the operating system to pass off netgroup queries to the LDAP directory by updating the *netgroup* entry in */etc/nsswitch.conf*:

```
## /etc/nsswitch.conf
## ...
netgroup:   ldap
```

The *getent* tool can be used to query NSS for specific netgroups by giving the group name as a command-line parameter:

```
$ getent netgroup sysadmin
sysadmin    (garion.plainjoe.org,-,-)(silk.plainjoe.org,-,-)
```

It would also be a good idea to verify that the */etc/hosts.allow* listed in the beginning of the section obeyed the netgroups membership by actually attempting to log on to the machine using *ssh* from a host other than *garion* or *silk*.

There are many services that can use netgroups. The tcp_wrappers security package is only one example. Another frequent use of netgroups is to utilize them to restrict access to exported NFS file systems (refer to the *exports(5)* manpage). Any place where these administrative groups were used in your NIS domain should remain valid for these new nss_ldap-enabled systems.

Security

Up to this point, we haven't discussed security. You've put a lot of sensitive information into your directory, which is now controlling whether users can log into machines on your network. And you could certainly put a lot more information into the directory: telephone numbers, human resources information, etc. Some of this information might be genuinely useful to the public at large; some of it may be highly confidential. But you don't yet know how to keep users from accessing information they shouldn't have access to. In order to have any confidence in a solution, we must examine how certain security issues are addressed by both the PAM and NSS modules.

First, it is important to understand what level of security is desired and exactly what information is being protected. Are you concerned only with protecting passwords? What about usernames as well? From the perspective of system administration, the most important information to protect is related to user and group accounts. Few sysadmins worry about someone being able to snoop a hosts file as it is copied across the network from one machine to another. However, everyone should be concerned about using a clear-text protocol, such as FTP, to transfer */etc/passwd* and */etc/shadow* from one machine to another.

To protect user passwords, we must look at how the PAM module binds to the directory. pam_ldap always uses a simple bind to authenticate a user against an LDAP server. You should avoid sending account credentials across the network in a form that is readable by anyone viewing traffic.

LDAPv3 provides two mechanisms that can be used to protect passwords. One is to use SASL to support more secure methods of authentication such as Kerberos 5 or DIGEST-MD5. However, while this mechanism protects passwords, it doesn't necessarily protect information other than the user's password. It is not supported by pam_ldap at this time. The second solution is to negotiate a secure transport layer that will protect the information used in the LDAP bind request as well as all other information sent to and from the directory server.

Security must be implemented by both the server and the client. It makes no difference if one party is willing to communicate securely but the other is not. Recall the StartTLS-extended command added in RFC 2830. This command allows the client to request a secure transport layer prior to binding to an LDAP server. Both the pam_ldap and nss_ldap modules support using the StartTLS command to negotiate transport layer security. In addition, these modules also support the LDAPS (tcp/636) protocol, which is an older method for accessing an LDAP server securely.

The following *ldap.conf* directive instructs the PADL LDAP modules to issue a Start-TLS command prior to binding to the server:

```
## Use the StartTLS command to negotiate an encrypted transport layer. A value of
## on defines the use of LDAPS when connecting to the directory server.
ssl     start_tls
```

Once you have configured the client, use a tool such as Ethereal or tcpdump to view the network traffic; it's a good idea to verify that things are working as expected.[*] After the initial LDAP Extended Request (i.e., StartTLS), you should see no clear-text traffic between the client and server. It is easy to spot an LDAP simple bind. The following is a bind request using the DN "uid=gcarter,ou=people,dc=plainjoe,dc=org" and the password testing:

```
00 30 f1 11 98 da 00 00 f4 d8 6c 0d 08 00 45 00    .0........l...E..
00 71 b9 a2 40 00 40 06 fd 21 c0 a8 01 4a c0 a8    .q..@.@..!...J..
01 28 a3 2f 01 85 26 8e 13 41 30 62 21 3a 80 18    .(./..&..A0b!:..
19 20 51 ef 00 00 01 01 08 0a 16 aa ab 72 16 ab    . Q..........r..
09 2f 30 3b 02 01 03 60 36 02 01 03 04 28 75 69    ./0;...`6....(ui
64 3d 67 63 61 72 74 65 72 2c 6f 75 3d 70 65 6f    d=gcarter,ou=peo
70 6c 65 2c 64 63 3d 70 6c 61 69 6e 6a 6f 65 2c    ple,dc=plainjoe,
64 63 3d 6f 72 67 80 07 74 65 73 74 69 6e 67       dc=org..testing
```

When the StartTLS command is working correctly, you will be able to notice the initial extended (OID 1.3.6.1.4.1.1466.20037) request and the downloading of the server's certificate, but the remainder of the conversation will appear as gibberish (technically speaking).

Of course, encrypting all of the traffic between the clients and servers does no good if an unauthorized user can obtain information using normal means such as *ldapsearch*. To prevent access to information that could compromise an account (e.g., the userPassword attribute), you must specify access controls that secure account information. The following two access control entries (ACEs) in the database section of

---

[*] More information on Ethereal can be found at *http://www.ethereal.com/*. News regarding tcpdump can be found at *http://www.tcpdump.org/*.

slapd.conf prevent users from viewing passwords belonging to accounts other than their own:

```
## Users can change their own passwords. Other users can attempt to authenticate, but
## can't read the userPassword value.
access to dn=".*,dc=plainjoe,dc=org" attr=userPassword
     by self write
     by * auth

## Default to read access.
access to dn=".*,dc=plainjoe,dc=org"
     by * read
```

It's worth looking at these ACEs in some detail to understand exactly what they say. The first ACE allows a user who has been authenticated by the directory to have write access to his password (self write). Write access implicitly includes read access, and is necessary to allow users to change their passwords. Other users are granted only the ability to authenticate against the given DN (* auth). This is not the same as read access because the client can never obtain the userPassword value. The server compares the password sent by the client in the bind request to the value stored in the directory entry; the password never leaves the server.

The second ACE grants read access to all directory information to all users. Unless you have configured a more privileged account for use by nss_ldap (binddn and bindpw), you must allow anonymous read access to clients using an anonymous bind. However, note that the clients can't obtain the userPassword attribute; the previous ACE blocks access to passwords other than their own.

Remember that access control entries follow the "first match wins" rule. Therefore, the more restrictive ACEs must be defined first. In this example, reversing the order of the ACEs has an ill effect: every read request will match the rule allowing anonymous reads, and the rule restricting access to passwords is never processed.

If you have configured a binddn (uid=nssldap,ou=people,dc=plainjoe,dc=org) for searching the directory, the last ACE can be changed to disallow anonymous reads altogether:

```
## Default to read access.
access to dn=".*,dc=plainjoe,dc=org"
   by dn="uid=nssldap,ou=people,dc=plainjoe,dc=org" read
   by * none
```

Automount Maps

In order to use the *automount* information stored in your directory, you must shift your focus to the automount daemon itself, specifically Linux's kernel-based autofs. As it currently stands, autofs (v3.1.7 and the 4.0 preview releases) supports the undocumented automount and automountMap object classes. However, Red Hat has updated the package in its distribution (autofs-3.1.7-28) to look up mount points based on the nisObject and nisMap classes described in RFC 2307 (and included in *nis.schema*). The LDAPbis workgroup's revisions to RFC 2307 will include new schema items for storing automount information, but for the moment, nisObject and nisMap have the largest support base from Red Hat, Sun, and PADL. Figure 6-8 shows the required and optional attributes for these two new object classes.

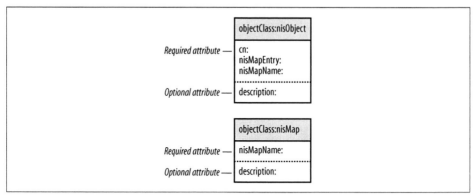

Figure 6-8. nisObject and nisMap object classes

 Red Hat's automount patches can be obtained from either *http://people.redhat.com/nalin/autofs/* or in the latest autofs SRPM at *ftp://ftp.redhat.com/pub/redhat/linux/rawhide/SRPMS/SRPMS/*.

PADL's migration tools include a script (*migrate_automount.pl*) for converting an automount map to LDIF. Here, you will convert a single automount point in */opt* to a directory entry. You can see from the */etc/auto.opt* excerpt that the LDIF entry contains all of the information needed for mounting */opt/src*. This time, PADL's script does create the top-level container (nisMapName=auto.opt) for you:

```
$ grep src /etc/auto.opt
src     -rw,hard,intr   queso.plainjoe.org:/export/u1/src

$ ./migrate_automount.pl /etc/auto.opt /tmp/auto.opt.ldif

$ cat /tmp/auto.opt.ldif
dn: nisMapName=auto.opt,dc=plainjoe,dc=org
objectClass: top
objectClass: nisMap
nisMapName: auto.opt

dn: cn=src,nisMapName=auto.opt,dc=plainjoe,dc=org
objectClass: nisObject
cn: src
nisMapEntry: -rw,hard,intr queso.plainjoe.org:/export/u1/src
nisMapName: auto.opt
```

After adding the new automount entries to the directory using *ldapadd*, the autofs server must be informed of *auto.opt*'s map location, the LDAP server's hostname, and the search base. The following line in */etc/auto.master* instructs the autofs package to look up mounts for */opt* on the host *ldap1* beneath ou=auto.opt,dc=plainjoe,dc=org:

```
## Look up mounts for /opt in the LDAP directory.
   /opt  ldap:ldap1:nisMapName=auto.opt,dc=plainjoe,dc=org  --timeout 300
```

Now you can launch the *automount* daemon; it will obtain all information for mount points in */opt* from the directory server. If you're curious about what's going on, I recommend viewing the *slapd* log file on your server for more information on the autofs LDAP queries.

PADL's NIS/LDAP Gateway

If configuring all your Unix clients to use PAM and installing the various NSS modules is a little more work than your IT shop can bear at the moment, you may prefer the NIS/LDAP gateway solution mentioned at the beginning of this chapter (refer to Figure 6-1 for an illustration). This section examines PADL Software's *ypldapd* daemon as a migration path from NIS- to directory-based information storage. The following excerpt from the *ypldapd(8)* manpage describes *ypldapd*'s position within a network:

> YPLDAP(8)
>
> ypldapd emulates the equivalent process ypserv by providing an RPC call-compatible interface. Rather than consulting 'map' files as ypserv does, however, ypldapd draws its data from LDAP databases.

In theory, *ypldapd* allows an NIS domain to be replaced with a directory-based solution without any client machines being aware of the change. Even non-Unix NIS clients, such as the Windows NT NISgina DLL, will function correctly. As far as NIS clients are concerned, nothing has changed: they still get their data using the NIS protocol from an NIS server. Where the server gets its data from is another matter.

The *ypldapd* package is available in binary form for Solaris, Linux, FreeBSD, and AIX, and can be downloaded with a 30-day evaluation license. PADL's web site provides instructions for obtaining a temporary license via an email request. The user's guide is also available online in either Postscript or MS Word format (*http://www.padl.com/ Products/NISLDAPGateway.html*).

Configuring *ypldapd* is fairly easy. Because it supports the RFC 2307 information service schema, you can use the PADL migration tools described earlier in this chapter to populate the directory with host and user information. PADL includes a copy of its migration tools with the *ypldapd* distribution. However, you may want to download the latest version separately.

PADL provides installation scripts for *ypldapd* that can be executed after unpacking the tar archive in */opt/ypldapd*. Before beginning the installation, you should have or know:

- A license key for *ypldapd*
- The hostname of the LDAP server to query
- The base DN used for searches
- The NIS domain name of the *ypldapd* server

These settings will be stored in */opt/ypldapd/etc/ypldapd.conf*. You can use *ypldapd*'s -c option to specify an alternative configuration file. All other configuration files must be located in */opt/ypldapd/etc/*. Here's an initial *ypldapd.conf*:

```
## NIS domain to serve
ypdomain yp.plainjoe.org

## LDAP server
ldaphost 192.168.1.77

## Search base
basedn dc=plainjoe,dc=org

## Enable caching.
caching on

## Dump caches every half hour.
cache_dump_interval 30

## Use the default naming context mappings.
namingcontexts namingcontexts.conf
```

All of the parameters are fairly self-explanatory. Refer to the *ypldapd(8)* manpage and the *ypldapd* user's manual for complete information on the directives you can use in the configuration file.

Depending on how you have configured access control for the entries in your directory, you may need to assign *ypldapd* a privileged DN to use when it binds to the LDAP server, as it needs to view all user information (i.e., the userPassword attribute value). Otherwise, *ypldapd* uses an anonymous bind, and may therefore be unable to access certain attributes or entries. Here's how to set up a privileged DN:

```
## Define a DN used for binding to the LDAP server.
binddn uid=ypldapproxy,ou=people,dc=plainjoe,dc=org

## Include the clear-text password for the binddn.
bindcred secret
```

This configuration assumes that a user named *ypldapproxy* exists in the directory, and that the following access control rule is defined in *slapd.conf*. Because of

OpenLDAP's "first match wins" algorithm for processing access control rules, this definition should be listed before any others.

```
## Give the ypldapproxy user read access to all information.
access to dn=".*,dc=plainjoe,dc=org"
    by dn="uid=ypldapproxy,ou=people,dc=plainjoe,dc=org" read
```

However, this configuration allows users to view passwords for all accounts using the *ypcat(1)* or *ypmatch(1)* commands. To prevent users from accessing passwords, the hide_password parameter instructs *ypldapd* to implement shadow passwords:

```
## Hide the password field from nonprivileged users.
hide_passwords on
```

Once *ypldapd* is running, you should be able to test the server using the various *yp** commands. For example:

```
# ypwhich
192.168.1.77

# ypmatch gcarter passwd.byname
gcarter:##gcarter:780:100:G Carter:/home/gcarter:/bin/bash
```

CHAPTER 7

Email and LDAP

One of the most important applications of a directory is storing email addresses and other contact information. Although many ad hoc solutions to this problem have been implemented over the years, LDAP provides a natural online publishing service for this type of data. This chapter explores the ins and outs of integrating email clients (MUAs) and mail servers (MTAs) with an LDAP directory. It covers the configuration details of some of the more popular email clients, including Mozilla Mail, Pine, Microsoft Outlook, and Eudora. We'll also discuss the schema required to support these clients and the types of LDAP searches to expect when the application attempts to locate a user in the directory.

On the server side, we'll discuss three popular email servers—Sendmail, Postfix, and Exim—all of which can use a directory. We will cover the level of LDAP support within each MTA, the schema needed to support this integration, and the configuration process for integrating an LDAP directory into a production email environment. This discussion assumes that you are familiar with basic MTA administration and the interaction between SMTP servers.

Representing Users

The server you will build combines the white pages server you created in Chapter 4 and the server for administrative databases you created in Chapter 6 as a replacement for NIS. You already have a head start on integrating user account information because both servers used the ou=people container for storing user account information. With only a few modifications to your directory, the posixAccount and inetOrgPerson object classes can be used to store a single user entry for both authentication and contact information.

Here's an entry for "Kristi Carter," which is similar to those presented in Chapter 4:

```
dn: cn=Kristi W. Carter,ou=people,dc=plainjoe,dc=org
objectClass: inetOrgPerson
cn: Kristi W. Carter
```

```
sn: Carter
mail: kcarter@plainjoe.org
labeledURI: http://www.plainjoe.org/~kristi
roomNumber: 102 Ramsey Hall
telephoneNumber: 222-555-2356
```

In Chapter 6, this same user might have been presented as:

```
dn: uid=kristi,ou=people,dc=plainjoe,dc=org
uid: kristi
cn: Kristi Carter
objectClass: account
objectClass: posixAccount
userPassword: {crypt}LnMJ/n2rQsR.c
loginShell: /bin/bash
uidNumber: 781
gidNumber: 100
homeDirectory: /home/kristi
gecos: Kristi Carter
```

Looking at both examples side by side, some differences can be noted. The first is that the RDN used for each entry is different. It doesn't really matter whether you choose cn=Kristi W. Carter or uid=kristi. Since Unix accounts must already possess a unique login name, the uid attribute is a good choice to prevent name conflicts in ou=people.

The second issue is more serious and shows why the initial directory design should not be rushed. Both the account and inetOrgPerson object classes are structural object classes. Remember that an entry cannot have more than one structural object class and that once an entry is created, its structural class cannot be changed. Some LDAP servers may allow you to reassign an entry's object classes at will, but do not rely on this behavior.

To solve this dilemma, initially create each entry with the inetOrgPerson class and then extend it using the posixAccount auxiliary class. The means that the account entry will have to be filtered from the output of PADL's migration scripts—a simple task using *grep*:

```
$ ./migrate_passwd.pl /etc/passwd | \
  grep -iv "objectclass: account" > passwd.ldif
```

The combined user entry now appears as:

```
dn: uid=kristi,ou=people,dc=plainjoe,dc=org
objectClass: inetOrgPerson
objectClass: posixAccount
cn: Kristi Carter
cn: Kristi W. Carter
sn: Carter
mail: kcarter@plainjoe.org
labeledURI: http://www.plainjoe.org/~kristi
roomNumber: 102 Ramsey Hall
telephoneNumber: 222-555-2356
```

```
uid: kristi
userPassword: {crypt}LnMJ/n2rQsR.c
loginShell: /bin/bash
uidNumber: 781
gidNumber: 100
homeDirectory: /home/kristi
gecos: Kristi Carter
```

One final note before we begin looking at specifics of email integration: the `mail` attribute is optional in the `inetOrgPerson` schema definition. However, it's clearly mandatory when you're trying to support mail clients and servers.

Email Clients and LDAP

When planning a strategy for supporting an application with a directory, you always start by examining the application and determining what schema has the ability to support it. Using a standard schema is vastly preferable to building your own. Of course, with email you don't have the ability to specify what client users will use: at your site, many different clients are probably in use, and you won't make friends by asking users to change. In this section, we'll look at four clients, all of which are in common use: Mozilla Mail, Pine from the University of Washington, Qualcomm's Eudora, and Microsoft's Outlook Express. Fortunately, the `inetOrgPerson` schema supports all of the information items we are concerned with using in this section.

The following parameters are common to all clients:

- The LDAP server is *ldap.plainjoe.org.*
- The base search suffix is `ou=people,dc=plainjoe,dc=org`.

Beyond the basic LDAP search parameters and supporting schema, it is imperative to know what version of LDAP the clients will use. Table 7-1 reveals that 3 out of the 4 mail clients listed use LDAPv2 to bind to the directory server. This means that you must explicitly add support for these connections as OpenLDAP 2.1 rejects LDAPv2 binds in default configurations. Add the following line to the global section of *slapd.conf*:

```
## Allow LDAPv2 binds from clients needed by several mail client packages.
allow     bind_v2
```

then restart the OpenLDAP server to make it recognize the change.

Table 7-1. LDAP versions used by various mail clients

Mail client	LDAPv2 bind	LDAPv3 bind
Mozilla Mail	✓	
Pine 4	✓	
Eudora	✓	
Outlook Express		✓

Mozilla Mail

In 1998, Netscape Communications announced that it would give away the source code to the next generation of Netscape Communicator browser suites. In the Fall of 2002, the 1.0 release of Mozilla finally saw the light of day. Today, this code base is still alive, well, and growing at *http://www.mozilla.org/*. Versions of the browser suite are available for various flavors of Unix, Windows, and Mac OS.

When configuring Mozilla's address book client to access a directory, you must keep two questions in mind:

- Should users be required to authenticate themselves, or should they be able to access directory information anonymously?

- Should the information sent to and retrieved from the LDAP server be sent in clear-text form (i.e., LDAP), or should it be transmitted over SSL (i.e., LDAPS)?

The simplest method of adding a new directory server profile in Mozilla is through the Address Book application shown in Figure 7-1. Select File → New → LDAP Directory to launch the Directory Server Properties dialog shown in Figure 7-2.

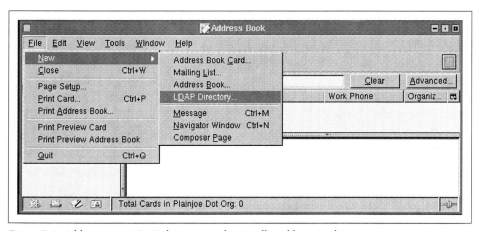

Figure 7-1. Adding a new LDAP directory to the Mozilla Address Book

The Name field lets you provide a descriptive title name for the directory (Plainjoe Dot Org); this name is used in the address book display window, but has no other effect on directory lookups. Put the hostname or IP address of the directory server in the Hostname field (*ldap.plainjoe.org*). Set the Base DN to the base search suffix used when querying the server (ou=people,dc=plainjoe,dc=org). The Port number, which defaults to port tcp/389 for non-SSL directories, should be set to the port on which the LDAP server is listening. By default, Mozilla uses an anonymous bind when searching the server. If a simple bind is preferred, you can define the Bind DN to use

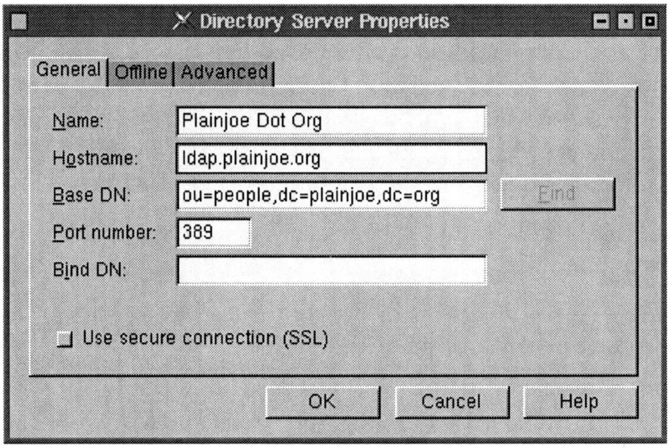

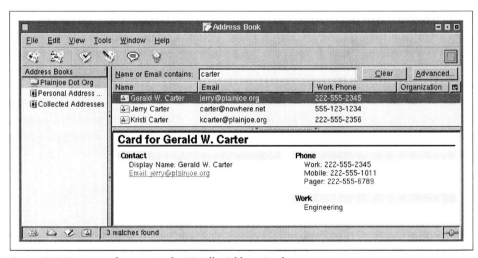

Figure 7-2. Setting directory search parameters

for authentication. Mozilla will prompt you for the corresponding password before it actually performs a search.

Once the directory has been added to the list of address books, you can query the directory by entering a substring to search for, or by using some of the more advanced search dialogs. Figure 7-3 shows the basic substring search test entry box. Any text you enter in this box is used to query the cn, sn, givenName, and mail attributes using a subtree search scope. For example, if you enter the text "carter", the client uses this search filter:

```
(|(mail=*carter*)(cn=*carter*)(givenName=*carter*)(sn=*carter*))
```

Figure 7-3. Basic search screen in the Mozilla Address Book

A simple way to determine the search filters used by any LDAP client is to enable connection logging on your directory server. OpenLDAP uses log level 256 for this purpose. Another possibility is to use a network traffic–monitoring tool such as Ethereal that can decode LDAP requests and replies. More information about Ethereal can be found at *http://www.ethereal.com/*.

The advanced search dialog box (Figure 7-4) allows you to create more elaborate searches. The string entered as the search characteristic is the text for which you're searching; for example, the text "jerry" entered as part of the email address would result in the search filter of (mail=*jerry*).

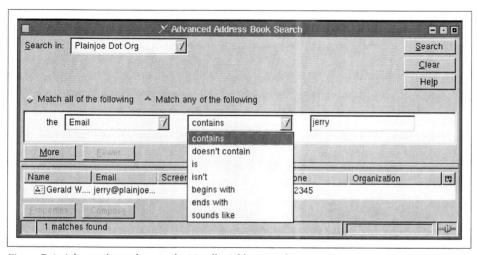

Figure 7-4. Advanced searching in the Mozilla Address Book

If the user selects the "Use secure connection (SSL)" checkbox on the directory properties window displayed in Figure 7-2, Netscape automatically changes the configured port number to tcp/636 (LDAPS). All traffic between the address book client and the directory server will be encrypted. Do not confuse this secure connection with the StartTLS LDAPv3 extension. Mozilla supports LDAPS only for secure communication with the directory server.

For this configuration to work, the LDAP server must be configured to support LDAPS and be listening on the port specified by the Server Port entry field. In addition, the Mozilla client must trust the certificate used by the LDAP server.

The procedure for configuring a directory server to support LDAPS varies from vendor to vendor; refer to your server documentation for details. In the case of OpenLDAP 2, you must generate a certificate and key file for *slapd* (refer to Chapter 3 for details on this) and then instruct the daemon to associate LDAPS with the correct port. The *-h* command-line option tells *slapd* which protocols to support. The command below starts *slapd* with support for LDAP and LDAPS on the default tcp ports 389 (for LDAP) and 636 (for LDAPS):

```
root# /usr/local/libexec/slapd -h "ldap:/// ldaps:///"
```

Unless the LDAP server's certificate can be verified by a certificate authority (CA), Mozilla will ask you whether it should trust the server before continuing the connection. If you decide that this will be too much trouble (or confusing) for your users, avoid self-signed certificates (or set up your own CA).

Pine 4

Pine is a popular, console-based email client developed by the University of Washington. The source distribution of the mail client is available at *http://www. washington.edu/pine/*; precompiled versions are available for most modern Unix and Unix-like systems. Support for retrieving addresses from an LDAP directory was introduced in Pine 4.00. A Windows version of Pine, known as PC-Pine, offers similar features to the Unix version, including LDAP support. PC-Pine is available from the University of Washington at *http://www.washington.edu/pine/pc-pine/*.

If you are using a precompiled version of Pine, you must ensure that LDAP support was enabled when the package was built. LDAP-enabled versions of Pine should allow you to configure a new directory from the Setup menu, as shown in Figure 7-5.

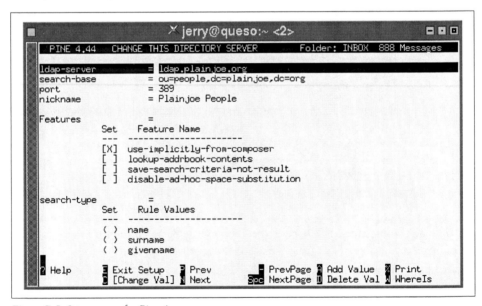

Figure 7-5. Setup menu for Pine 4

Pine's directory configuration screen supports the common LDAP search parameters, including:

ldap-server
> The IP address or hostname of the directory server (*ldap.plainjoe.org*)

search-base
> The base search suffix (ou=people,dc=plainjoe,dc=org)

port
> The tcp port on which the server is listening (389)

nickname
> A descriptive display name (Plainjoe People)

Pine allows users to construct searches using up to four search attributes. By default, it uses the name (cn), surname (sn), given name (givenName), and email (mail) attributes. The default search filters only append the wildcard onto the end of the user's search string. For example, by default, Pine converts an email search for the string "kristi" into the search filter:

```
(|(cn=kristi*)(mail=kristi*)(sn=kristi*)(givenName=kristi*))
```

However, Pine offers a fair amount of flexibility for more adventurous users; you can change the kind of substring match (e.g., exact match, match at the beginning, match at the end, match anywhere), change the attributes Pine uses in the search, or specify a custom search filter. All of these settings can be accessed from Pine's directory configuration screen.

One shortcoming of Pine's LDAP implementation is the lack of support for LDAPS (and the fact that it uses LDAPv2). Although Pine supports SSL, it supports SSL only for POP or IMAP access to mailboxes. Pine cannot use SSL to access an LDAP directory.

Eudora

Qualcomm's Eudora has become a popular mail client on both Windows and Mac OS platforms. Configuring access to an LDAP directory in Eudora is similar to configuring LDAP for Mozilla. To start, go to the Modify Database window shown in Figure 7-6 by selecting the LDAP protocol from the directory window (Tools → Directory Services) and clicking the New Database button.

The Network tab allows you to specify connection information for the directory server. If you configure Eudora to use a login name and password to search the directory, the username must be in the form of a DN. The Search Options view shows that Eudora, by default, performs a substring match on the cn attribute; you can customize the search using standard search filter syntax. The Attributes dialog shown in Figure 7-6 provides a way to select which attributes are shown in response to a directory query. Eudora displays all the attributes for each entry that the search returns.

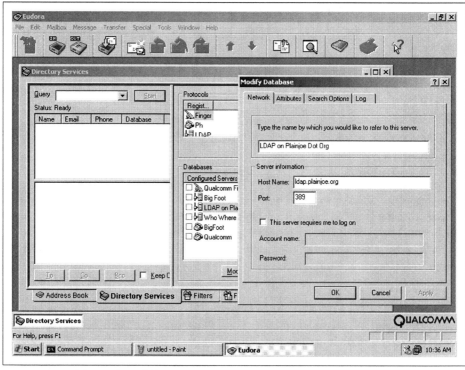

Figure 7-6. Modify Database dialog views used by Eudora 5.1 for Windows

You can define more descriptive names for attribute types using the Attributes window; for example, you can display the cn attribute type as "Real Name."

Eudora 5.1 does not support LDAPS when searching directories.

Microsoft Outlook Express

Microsoft Outlook in its various incarnations has become one of the most important mail clients on Windows networks. This section examines the version of Outlook Express that is included with Microsoft's Internet Explorer.

To configure Outlook Express to use a directory, start with the Directory Services configuration dialog, shown in Figure 7-7. To get to this dialog, select Tools → Accounts. The General tab contains settings for the directory server host information, such as the server's hostname and display name. The Advanced tab provides a means to define the port on which the server is listening and the base search suffix.

To search for someone in a directory, Outlook users go to the Find People dialog shown in Figure 7-8. Outlook Express uses a combination of the cn, sn, mail, and givenName attributes to generate the search filter. A search for the user "carter" is

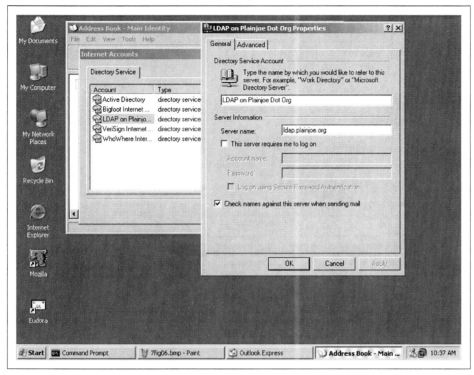

Figure 7-7. The Directory Services configuration window from Outlook Express 5.5

translated into a search filter very similar to the one used by both Mozilla Mail and Pine:

```
(|(mail=carter*)(cn=carter*)(sn=carter*)(givenname=carter*))
```

Searches can be customized using the Advanced tab of the Find People dialog in Figure 7-8.

Like both Mozilla and Eudora, Outlook Express can perform authenticated binds when searching a directory. If you check "This server requires me to logon," Outlook asks for a user ID and password, which it uses when binding to the server. Unlike Eudora, which expected a DN only for the username, Outlook Express supports two different styles of usernames. When using a simple bind, Outlook expects the login name to be the DN used in the bind request. However, if the "Logon using Secure Password Authentication" box is checked, Outlook negotiates with the directory server to use the NTLMv1 challenge/response authentication model (or possibly the GSSAPI SASL mechanism).

Refer to your directory server's documentation to determine whether it supports NTLM authentication. OpenLDAP does not currently support this feature.

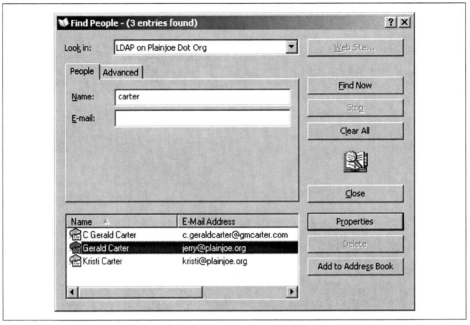

Figure 7-8. Using the Find People dialog to search an LDAP directory

Outlook Express is a little more friendly than Mozilla when it comes to using LDAPS to connect to a directory server. On Windows 98, simply indicating that the directory server should be accessed using SSL on port 636 is enough. It is not necessary to tell Internet Explorer or Outlook to trust the self-signed certificate used by an OpenLDAP server. I'll let you decide whether this is a good thing; Mozilla was less trusting, requiring you to tell it to trust the LDAP server's certificate.

Mail Transfer Agents (MTAs)

The remainder of this chapter discusses LDAP support within several popular MTAs. You can skim this material if you want an overview of various mail servers, or you can focus on the details regarding your specific MTA and skip the others. In either case, I assume that you have some familiarity with the Simple Mail Transport Protocol (SMTP) and mail servers in general.

Before we begin, Table 7-2 provides a summary of the LDAP versions used by the mail servers presented in this section. The same rule for enabling LDAPv2 binds described in the beginning of this chapter still holds true for two out of the three mail servers listed.

Table 7-2. LDAP versions used by various mail servers

Mail transfer agent	LDAPv2 bind	LDAPv3 bind
Sendmail	✓	
Postfix		✓
Exim	✓	

Sendmail

Sendmail is the default MTA on most current versions of Unix. A number of alternatives have appeared in the past few years (such as Postfix, Qmail, and Exim), but if you work with Unix or Linux systems, chances are you'll deal with Sendmail. Sendmail introduced support for retrieving information from an LDAP directory in Version 8.9. However, this support didn't really stabilize until later versions (this discussion focuses on Version 8.12). It by no means attempts to give comprehensive coverage of Sendmail. For information on the details of configuring and running a Sendmail server, refer to *Sendmail,* by Bryan Costales and Eric Allman (O'Reilly).

Sendmail's LDAP integration falls into four categories: support for retrieving mail aliases from a directory, support for accessing generic Sendmail maps using LDAP queries, expansion of Sendmail classes at startup using information obtained from a directory, and support for retrieving specific mail-routing information from an LDAP directory. We will return to the specifics of these features in later sections.

In order to support any of these functions, Sendmail must be compiled with the *LDAPMAP* option enabled. Here's how to modify *site.config.m4* to compile LDAP against the client libraries installed by OpenLDAP 2:

```
dnl .../devtools/Site/site.config.m4
dnl Enable LDAP features in Sendmail during compilation
dnl
APPENDDEF (`confMAPDEF´, `-DLDAPMAP´)dnl
APPENDDEF(`confLIBS´, `-lldap -llber´)dnl
dnl
dnl The following two entries are needed so
dnl that make can find the the ldap header files
dnl and libraries
APPENDDEF(`confINCDIRS´, `-I/opt/ldap/include´)dnl
APPENDDEF(`confLIBDIRS´, `-L/opt/ldap/lib´)dnl
```

Refer to the *sendmail/README* file for any relevant details about your server's operating system, particularly if you're using LDAP libraries other than OpenLDAP. The previous example was used to build Sendmail 8.12.6 linked against OpenLDAP client libraries on a Linux system. The resulting *sendmail* binary should be checked to ensure that the *LDAPMAP* option was properly enabled. Here we have a Linux host named *garion* that includes several compile-time options that were enabled by default. The only one to be concerned with is the *LDAPMAP* flag that you specified in *site.config.m4*:

```
$ cd sendmail-8.12.6/obj.Linux.2.4.19.i686/sendmail
$ echo | ./sendmail -bt -d0
Version 8.12.6
 Compiled with: DNSMAP LDAPMAP LOG MATCHGECOS MIME7TO8
                MIME8TO7 NAMED_BIND NETINET NETUnix NEWDB
                PIPELINING SCANF USERDB USE_LDAP_INIT XDEBUG


============ SYSTEM IDENTITY (after readcf) ============
      (short domain name) $w = garion
  (canonical domain name) $j = garion.plainjoe.org
         (subdomain name) $m = plainjoe.org
             (node name) $k = garion
```

Sendmail 8.12 includes what developers have described as an experimental schema file for OpenLDAP 2. The attributes and object classes are not defined in any Internet-Draft or RFC and may change in future releases. Because we are mainly concerned with exploring the specifics of sendmail, this is of little risk to us. However, if other applications made use of it, changes to the directory schema would require tight control so no dependencies are broken. Figure 7-9 displays the six object classes defined Sendmail's schema file. All of the attributes are defined as strings (either as a Directory String or an IA5String).

 There is a syntax error in the *sendmail.schema* file included with Sendmail 8.12.6. The `sendmailMTAAliasGrouping` attribute uses an invalid combination with String matching rules. This can be fixed by changing the SYNTAX for this attribute to use the Directory String OID (1.3.6.1.4.1.1466.115.121.1.15).

To install the Sendmail objects and attributes, simply copy *sendmail.schema* to the *schema/* directory:

```
root# cp cf/sendmail.schema /usr/local/etc/openldap/schema
```

and then include it in the global section of *slapd.conf*:

```
## Add support for Sendmail 8.12 objects and atrributes.
include  /usr/local/etc/openldap/schema/sendmail.schema
```

As usual, *slapd* will need to be restarted to recognize the new items.

Maps

To access information quickly, Sendmail uses a number of maps in which it retrieves dates by searching for a unique key value. These maps can take various forms; some of the more common ones are the Berkeley DBM or YP/NIS maps. Within the *sendmail.cf* file, an LDAP map is designated by the ldap keyword. If you're hacking

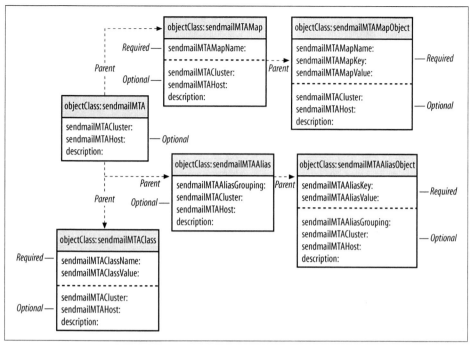

Figure 7-9. Object classes defined in sendmail.schema

the Sendmail configuration directly, you can use LDAP for any of the maps, but that's beyond the scope of this book. We will work only with Sendmail's m4 configuration generator.

Sendmail provides support for several frequently used maps as FEATURE( )s. Any of these features that accept an optional argument to refine the search can also accept the keyword LDAP to specify that the lookup should be performed using directory calls. The most basic definition of an access_db table using LDAP would look like:

```
FEATURE(`access_db´, `LDAP´)
```

The default *sendmail.cf* entry generated for this m4 macro is:

```
Kaccess ldap -k (&(objectClass=sendmailMTAMapObject)
               (sendmailMTAMapName=access)
               (|(sendmailMTACluster=${sendmailMTACluster})
                 (sendmailMTAHost=$j))
               (sendmailMTAKey=%0))
           -1 -v sendmailMTAMapValue
```

The *-k* option defines the search, and the *-v* parameter specifies the name of the attribute's value to return. *-1* indicates that the search must return only one value or else it will be considered a failure. Table 7-3 contains a complete list of LDAP-specific options. It is best to refer to the Sendmail documentation (*doc/op/op.ps*) for a complete list of all lookup parameters.

Table 7-3. Configuration options for use with LDAP maps

Switch	Description
-1	The search must return a single value or else it is considered to be a failed lookup.
-b suffix	The DN to use as the base search suffix.
-d binddn	Defines a DN to use when binding to the directory.
-h hostname	The LDAP server hostname.
-k filter	Defines the search filter.
-l time -Z size	Define the time and size limits for a given search. The time limit is given in seconds.
-M method	The method of authentication to use when binding to the LDAP server: LDAP_AUTH_NONE, LDAP_AUTH_SIMPLE, or LDAP_AUTH_KRBV4.
-n	Retrieves attribute names only, not values. This is the same as the attrsOnly Boolean flag used during ldap_search( ).
-P pwfile	The file containing the credentials for -d binddn.
-p port	The port to use when connecting to the LDAP server.
-R	Does not automatically chase referrals.
-r deref	Controls how Sendmail should dereference aliases when searching: never, always, search, or find.
-s	The search scope (base, one, or sub).
-V sep	Retrieves both the attribute name and value separated by the *sep* character.
-v	Defines the attribute type that contains the value of the search result.

It is possible to define your own defaults for LDAP searches using the confLDAP_DEFAULT_SPEC variable in your m4 source file. This is a common place to set the hostname of the LDAP server and the base suffix used in searches. We will see an example of this later when we discuss aliases.

Table 7-4 lists all of the the Sendmail m4 features that support LDAP queries.

Table 7-4. Sendmail features that can be defined to use LDAP searches

Feature	sendmailMTAMapName	Description
access_db	access	List of hosts or networks that should be allowed to relay mail
authinfo	authinfo	Provides a separate map for storing client authentication information
bitdomain	bitdomain	A table for mapping bitnet hosts to Internet addresses
domaintable	domain	Makes use of a table that maps domain names to new domain names
genericstable	generics	Utilizes a table that contains rules for rewriting sender addresses in outgoing mail
mailertable	mailer	Includes support for a mailer table that contains rules for routing mail to specific domains
uucpdomain	uucpdomain	A table for mapping UUCP hosts to Internet addresses
virtusertable	virtuser	Includes support for a domain-specific version of aliasing

Aliases

Before implementing mail alias lookups via LDAP, let's begin with a simple *sendmail.mc* configuration file for a central mail hub for the plainjoe.org domain. Figure 7-10 illustrates how this host fits into the plainjoe.org network. Clients on the network spool messages to the mail hub, which ensures that all outgoing messages have a send in the form of *user@plainjoe.org*:

```
divert(-1)
########################################################
 Sendmail m4 file for plainjoe.org mail hub on local
 network.
########################################################
divert(0)
OSTYPE(`linux')dnl
FEATURE(`use_cw_file')dnl
dnl
dnl Masquerading settings
dnl
EXPOSED_USER(`root')dnl
MASQUERADE_AS(`plainjoe.org')dnl
MASQUERADE_DOMAIN(`plainjoe.org')dnl
FEATURE(`masquerade_envelope')dnl
FEATURE(`masquerade_entire_domain')dnl
dnl
FEATURE(`relay_entire_domain')dnl
FEATURE(`local_procmail')dnl
define(`PROCMAIL_MAILER_PATH', `/usr/bin/procmail')dnl
define(`STATUS_FILE', `/var/log/mail.stats')dnl
dnl
dnl Mailer settings
dnl
MAILER(`smtp')dnl
MAILER(`procmail')dnl
```

The *ALIAS_FILE* m4 option (*AliasFile* in *sendmail.cf*) allows an administrator to define the location of the aliases file (even within an LDAP directory). A very basic */etc/mail/aliases* might appear as:

```
postmaster:          root, mailadmin@plainjoe.org
nobody:              /dev/null
```

Here, the postmaster alias maps to the *root* account and the address *mailadmin@plainjoe.org*. Any mail addressed to *nobody@plainjoe.org* is sent to the bit bucket (*/dev/null*).

To use Sendmail's default LDAP search parameters for aliases, simply add:

```
define(`ALIAS_FILE', `ldap:')dnl
```

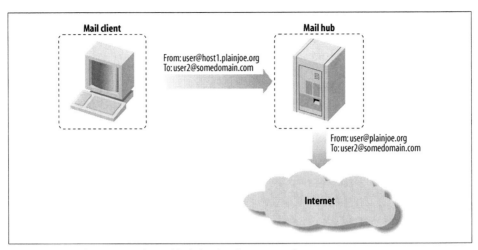

Figure 7-10. Utilizing a simple mail hub for the plainjoe.org domain

to the source m4 configuration file. This will generate a search similar to the one shown for the access_db lookup. However, this default search does not restrict the returned results to a single value (i.e., there is no *-1* option specified).

```
ldap -k (&(objectClass=sendmailMTAAliasObject)
        (sendmailMTAAliasGrouping=aliases)
        (|(sendmailMTACluster=${sendmailMTACluster})
          (sendmailMTAHost=$j))
        (sendmailMTAKey=%0))
     -v sendmailMTAAliasValue
```

You could integrate the mail aliases into the existing ou=people organizational unit within your directory. There is one main problem with this, however: all of the object classes defined in *sendmail.schema* are defined as structural. The user accounts with ou=people cannot have a second structural class. You should therefore create a new ou to store aliases for Sendmail. Other applications may arise in the future that also require a portion of the directory for storing data. In preparation, the naming scheme ou=*servicename*,ou=services,dc=plainjoe,dc=org has been chosen to organize subtrees. Figure 7-11 shows your new directory namespace.

The LDIF needed to create these three new ous should be very familiar by now:

```
dn: ou=services,dc=plainjoe,dc=org
objectClass: organizationalUnit
ou: services

dn: ou=sendmail,ou=services,dc=plainjoe,dc=org
ou: sendmail
objectClass: organizationalUnit

dn: ou=aliases,ou=sendmail,ou=services,dc=plainjoe,dc=org
objectClass: organizationalUnit
ou: aliases
```

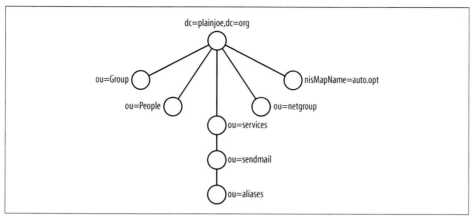

Figure 7-11. New ou=aliases for use by Sendmail

Next, you will create the directory entries corresponding to the */etc/mail/aliases* entries for postmaster and nobody:

```
dn: sendmailMTAKey=postmaster,ou=aliases,ou=sendmail,
 ou=services,dc=plainjoe,dc=org
objectClass: sendmailMTAAliasObject
sendmailMTAAliasValue: root
sendmailMTAAliasValue: mailadmin@plainjoe.org
sendmailMTAKey: postmaster

dn: sendmailMTAKey=postmaster,ou=aliases,ou=sendmail,
 ou=services,dc=plainjoe,dc=org
objectClass: sendmailMTAAliasObject
sendmailMTAAliasValue: /dev/null
sendmailMTAKey: nobody
```

The final step is to configure the actual lookup in *sendmail.mc*. Because you expect to use additional LDAP searches in Sendmail, it is best to define any global defaults using confLDAP_DEFAULT_SPEC. Specify that all LDAP requests should be sent to the host *ldap.plainjoe.org*:

```
define(confLDAP_DEFAULT_SPEC, `-h ldap.plainjoe.org´)dnl
```

The ALIAS_FILE definition will contain the base suffix, search filter, and requested attribute values. By default, Sendmail uses a subtree scope, which is fine for the alias searches:

```
define(`ALIAS_FILE´, `ldap:-k
(&(objectClass=sendmailMTAAliasObject)(sendmailMTAKey=%0)) -v sendmailMTAAliasValue
-b "ou=aliases,ou=sendmail,ou=services,dc=plainjoe,dc=org"´)dnl
```

After generating and installing the new *sendmail.cf* file:

```
$ cd sendmail-8.12.6/cf/cf
$ sh Build sendmail.cf
$ /bin/su -c "cp sendmail.cf /etc/mail/sendmail.cf"
```

you can test aliases using Sendmail's verify mode (*sendmail -bv*):

```
$ sendmail -bv postmaster@plainjoe.org
root... deliverable: mailer local, user root
mailadmin@plainjoe.org... deliverable: mailer local, user mailadmin
```

Before continuing on to Sendmail's ldap_routing feature, you may be wondering what advantage was achieved by storing Sendmail's aliases in LDAP. After all, you did create a new subtree within the directory, and it certainly does seem that some information, such as usernames, will end up being duplicated from the organizational unit. How did you reduce the duplication of data?

By shifting your focus from account management to service management, you can see that your directory provides a means of sharing basic Sendmail configuration data among multiple servers. This means that you no longer have to manage duplicate */etc/mail/aliases* files on each of your Sendmail hosts. Remember that the default Sendmail LDAP queries include:

```
(|(sendmailMTACluster=${sendmailMTACluster})(sendmailMTAHost=$j))
```

as part of the search filter. A Sendmail installation can be defined as a member of a cluster using the confLDAP_CLUSTER variable:

```
define(`confLDAP_CLUSTER´, `MailCluster´)
```

This provides a means of associating directory entries with individual hosts ($j) or groups of servers (${sendmailMTACluster}).

Mail routing using LDAP

Sendmail's LDAP mail-routing functionality can be described as an LDAP virtusertable. This is a domain-specific form of aliasing that supports the handling of virtual domains. It provides rules for rewriting recipient addresses or rerouting a message to the appropriate host. The following virtual user table entry would route messages that are addressed to *joe@foo.com* to the host *somehost.foo.com*:

```
joe@foo.com     somehost.foo.com
```

Under its default configuration, Sendmail's ldap_routing uses the inetLocalMailRecipient auxiliary object class defined in the expired Internet-Draft *draft-lachman-laser-ldap-mail-routing-xx.txt*. A version of this draft is included with the OpenLDAP source distribution. There are no required attributes in this object class, as you can see in Figure 7-12.

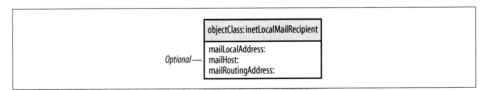

Figure 7-12. inetLocalMailRecipient object class used by Sendmail's FEATURE('ldap_routing')

The three optional attributes in `inetLocalMailRecipient` are:

`mailLocalAddress`
> The RFC 822–compliant mail address of the message recipient

`mailHost`
> The DNS name specifying the host to which the message should be relayed

`mailRoutingAddress`
> The RFC 822–compliant mail address to which the original recipient address should be rewritten

OpenLDAP includes a definition for the `inetLocalMailRecipient` object and associated attributes in *misc.schema*. You must include this file in *slapd.conf* and restart OpenLDAP before you can support Sendmail's `ldap_routing` feature:

```
## Support the inetLocalMailRecipient object.
include   /usr/local/etc/openldap/schema/misc.schema
```

To enable LDAP mail routing, add the following feature definition to *sendmail.mc*:

```
FEATURE(`ldap_routing')
```

We must also inform Sendmail which mail domains should be routed. Without control over which email domains Sendmail should attempt to look up in the directory, each incoming message triggers a lookup, resulting in severely degraded performance on high-traffic sites.

To define a single routable domain, Sendmail provides the `LDAPROUTE_DOMAIN` m4 macro. The configuration for your server requires you to add this line to your *sendmail.mc* source file:

```
LDAPROUTE_DOMAIN(`plainjoe.org')
```

> A list of LDAP-routable domains can be read from a file defined by the `LDAPROUTE_DOMAIN_FILE` macro. Sendmail 8.12 introduced support for retrieving such class values from a directory using the syntax `LDAPROUTE_DOMAIN_FILE(`@LDAP')`. More information on file class macros can be found in the documentation included with Sendmail.

As mentioned previously, `ldap_routing` uses the `inetLocalMailRecipient` object class. It is possible to use an alternative schema by defining the `ldap_routing` feature as:

```
FEATURE(`ldap_routing',mailHost,mailRoutingAddress,bounce,detail)
```

The *mailHost* and *mailRoutingAddress* entries are just LDAP map configuration lines; they default to:

```
ldap -1 -T TMPF -v mailHost
  -k (&(objectClass=inetLocalMailRecipient)
     (mailLocalAddress=%0))
```

They also default to:

```
ldap -1 -T TMPF -v mailRoutingAddress
  -k (&(objectClass=inetLocalMailRecipient)
     (mailLocalAddress=%0))
```

The search filters and the resulting attributes can be redefined to better suit your directory, if required. Both the *bounce* and *detail* parameters specify actions to take if a lookup does not return any routing information. The default behavior is to accept addresses not located by the LDAP search. Sendmail's *cf/README* file has more details on changing this if you are interested.

The default searches used by ldap_routing do not define an LDAP server, nor do they include a search suffix. The confLDAP_DEFAULT_SPEC option can be used to specify defaults for all of Sendmail's LDAP queries (maps, aliases, classes, and mail routing):

```
define(`confLDAP_DEFAULT_SPEC´, `-h ldap.plainjoe.org -b
  ou=people,dc=plainjoe,dc=org´)dnl
```

This is fully compatible with the configuration used to retrieve mail aliases from the directory. The ALIAS_FILE option used its own base suffix (*-b*) which overrode any matching default set by confLDAP_DEFAULT_SPEC.

With three optional attributes in the inetLocalMailRecipient object class, Sendmail must consider six unique routing cases. Note that if the mailLocalAddress attribute is absent, Sendmail will ignore the entry altogether. The possible results are described in Table 7-5.

Table 7-5. Possible results from an ldap_routing search

mailHost value	mailRoutingAddress value	Result
A local host	Exists	The recipient is rewritten to mailRoutingAddress and delivered to the local host.
A local host	Does not exist	The mail is delivered to the original address on the local host.
A remote host	Exists	The mail is relayed to the mailRoutingAddress at the mailHost.
A remote host	Does not exist	The mail is relayed to the original address at mailHost.
Does not exist	Exists	The recipient is rewritten to mailRoutingAddress and delivered to the local host.
Does not exist	Does not exist	The mail is delivered locally to the original address or possibly bounced as a unknown user.

The following LDIF listings help explain the entries in Table 7-5. Here, you extend the original user entries in the ou=people subtree. You could have created a new organizational unit beneath ou=sendmail. However, adding the mail-routing information to a user's entry means that when a user's account is deleted, the mail-routing information is removed as well.

In the first listing, the `mailLocalAddress` and `mailHost` attributes cause mail addressed to *kcarter@plainjoe.org* to be relayed to the host designated by *mail.engr.plainjoe.org*'s DNS MX record for local delivery:

```
dn: uid=kristi,ou=people,dc=plainjoe,dc=org
objectclass: inetOrgPerson
objectclass: posixAccount
objectclass: inetLocalMailRecipient
cn: Kristi Carter
sn: Carter
mail: kcarter@plainjoe.org
mailLocalAddress: kcarter@plainjoe.org
mailHost: mail.engr.plainjoe.org
<...remaining attributes not shown...>
```

The following example adds the `mailRoutingAddress` attribute. With this attribute, all mail addressed to *kcarter@plainjoe.org* is relayed to the host named by the MX record for *mail.engr.plainjoe.org*, but only after the recipient address has been rewritten to *kristi@engr.plainjoe.org*:

```
dn: uid=kristi,ou=people,dc=plainjoe,dc=org
objectclass: inetOrgPerson
objectclass: posixAccount
objectclass: inetLocalMailRecipient
cn: Kristi Carter
sn: Carter
mail: kcarter@plainjoe.org
mailLocalAddress: kcarter@plainjoe.org
mailHost: mail.engr.plainjoe.org
mailRoutingAddress: kristi@engr.plainjoe.org
<...remaining attributes not shown...>
```

These rewrites can be verified using Sendmail's rule set–testing mode:

```
$ /usr/sbin/sendmail -bt
> /parse kcarter@plainjoe.org
  <...intervening ruleset output deleted...>
mailer relay, host mail.engr.plainjoe.org,
    user kristi@engr.plainjoe.org
```

This output shows that mail received for *kcarter@plainjoe.org* will be forwarded to the host *mail.engr.plainjoe.org* after rewriting the recipient address to *kristi@engr. plainjoe.org*.

The `mailLocalAddress` attribute can also be used to specify that all mail for a domain should be relayed to another host. The following LDIF entry relays all mail addressed to the *@plainjoe.org* domain to the host denoted by *hq.plainjoe.org*'s MX record:

```
dn: o=plainjoe.org,ou=people,dc=plainjoe,dc=org
objectclass: organization
objectclass: inetLocalMailRecipient
o: plainjoe.org
description: plainjoe.org mail domain
mailLocalAddress: @plainjoe.org
mailHost: hq.plainjoe.org
```

It should be noted that Sendmail gives exact matches for the mailLocalAddress precedence over entries returned by matching the @*domain* syntax.

Postfix

Our next stop during this tour of MTAs is to examine Wietse Venema's Postfix
mailer. This MTA is a popular replacement for Sendmail because it has:

- Feature and interface compatibility with Sendmail
- A simpler configuration
- A history of fewer security holes

This section focuses on Postfix's ability to integrate with an LDAP directory. I
assume that the terminology and configuration files are familiar to Postfix administrators. If this is your first exposure to Venema's MTA, the Postfix web site (*http://
www.postfix.org/*) offers several good documents on the software's design philosophy and architecture. It may also be helpful to refer to *Postfix*, by Richard Blum
(Sams Publishing) for case studies of working installations.

After the gory details of configuring LDAP queries in Sendmail, Postfix's configuration files are a welcome relief. In comparison to Sendmail, Postfix's configuration is
much more intuitive.

We will begin by ensuring that the proper features are enabled when you compile Postfix. The source distribution for Postfix can be downloaded from *http://www.postfix.org/*.
Assuming that the OpenLDAP 2 client libraries have been installed in the directory */usr/
local/lib/*, the following commands clear all remaining intermediate files from a previous build (just to be safe), and then create the necessary Makefiles to enable LDAP client support:

```
$ cd postfix-1.1.2/
$ make tidy
$ make makefiles CCARGS="-I/usr/local/include -DHAS_LDAP" \
> AUXLIBS="-L/usr/local/lib -lldap -llber"
$ make
$ /bin/su -c "make install"
```

Refer to the *LDAP_README* file included with the Postfix distribution for details
about building the software on your server platform.

Postfix 1.1.2 will not compile when using the OpenLDAP 2.1 client
libraries. You must use the most recent OpenLDAP 2.0 libraries in this
case (or libraries from some other vendor described in the *README_
FILES/LDAP_README* document). Note that this does not affect
communications with an OpenLDAP 2.1 server.

Once you have built and installed Postfix, verify that LDAP support has been
included. To do so, use the *postconf* utility installed with the Postfix server. The *-m*

switch informs *postconf* to display the list of supported storage mediums for tables. The output should look something like this:

```
$ /usr/sbin/postconf -m
static
nis
regexp
environ
ldap
btree
unix
hash
```

The exact list will vary, depending on how you've built Postfix. Your immediate concern is to verify that *ldap* is listed as a supported storage medium. However, it's important to understand what's going on. Postfix maintains six tables, any of which may be stored on any of the media reported by *postconf -m*. Table 7-6 introduces each of the tables and shows which core program acts as the table's main client.

Table 7-6. Postfix tables and associated core programs

Table	Description	Core program
Access	Provides information about which messages to accept or reject based on sender, host, network , etc.	*smtpd*
Aliases	Provides information on redirecting mail received for local users.	*local*
Canonical	Provides information on local and nonlocal addresses.	*cleanup*
Relocated	Provides information on "user has moved to a new location" bounce messages.	*qmgr*
Transport	Provides information on delivery methods and relay hosts for the domain.	*trivial-rewrite*
Virtual	Provides information used in redirecting local and nonlocal users or domains.	*cleanup*

The remainder of this section shows how to configure a Postfix server to retrieve local aliases via LDAP queries. The following configuration file, *main.cf*, is the starting point for our discussion:

```
## /etc/postfix/main.cf
## Postfix configuration file for the plainjoe.org SMTP server.
##    Written by <jerry@plainjoe.org>

## Host/domain information
myhostname = garion.plainjoe.org
mydomain = plainjoe.org
myorigin = plainjoe.org

## Who is local?
mydestination = localhost $myhostname

## Who do we accept mail relaying from?
mynetworks = 192.168.1.0/24 127.0.0.0/8

## Program locations
command_directory = /usr/sbin
```

```
daemon_directory = /usr/libexec/postfix
queue_directory = /var/spool/postfix
mail_owner = postfix

## Sendmail-compatible mail spool directory
mail_spool_directory = /var/spool/mail
```

As before, an alias entry maps a local username to an email address; this address can be either another local user or a user on a remote system. In your LDAP schema, a local user is represented by the uid attribute of the posixAccount object class. The aliased entry is represented by the mail attribute of the inetOrgPerson object class. Note that you do not use the sendmailMTA and related schema objects presented in the previous section, but rely on the original object classes and attributes used by the mail clients presented in the first half of this chapter.

This schema does not address the case of mapping one local user to another for email delivery. Nor does it allow the use of external files to list the addresses that should be used as expansions for aliases; this feature is useful for supporting a local mailing list. This limitation is a result of the attributes chosen and not of Postfix's LDAP implementation.

Here's a typical LDIF entry for a user account that has an email alias. Mail for this account (a guest account) is forwarded to *jerry@plainjoe.org*:

```
## User account including a mail alias
dn: uid=guest1,ou=People,dc=plainjoe,dc=org
uid: guest1
cn: Guest Account
objectClass: posixAccount
objectClass: inetOrgPerson
userPassword: {CRYPT}Fd8nE1RtCh5G6
loginShell: /bin/bash
uidNumber: 783
gidNumber: 1000
homeDirectory: /home/guest1
gecos: Guest Account
sn: Account
mail: jerry@plainjoe.org
```

To inform the Postfix daemons that they should read the alias map from an LDAP directory, add the following entry to the server's *main.cf*:

```
alias_maps = ldap:ldapalias
```

The ldap keyword denotes the type of lookup table; the ldapalias string is the name of the table. This name is used as a prefix for parameter names; it identifies which settings are associated with this table.

After specifying that Postfix should look up alias information from the directory, you have to define several parameters that tell Postfix how to search the directory. These should be familiar by now. The most common settings include the LDAP server name (server_host), the search base (search_base), the search scope (scope), the search filter (query_filter), and the resulting attribute value to return (result_attribute). Each of these parameters is prefaced by the LDAP table name (ldapalias_). Add these definitions to *main.cf*:

```
## Parameters for LDAP alias map
ldapalias_server_host = localhost
ldapalias_search_base = ou=people,dc=plainjoe,dc=org
ldapalias_scope = sub
ldapalias_query_filter = (uid=%s)
ldapalias_result_attribute = mail
```

You can test the alias table lookup using the *postmap(1)* utility to verify that mail to the user *guest1* will be forwarded to the mail account at *jerry@plainjoe.org*:

```
$ postmap -q guest1 ldap:ldapalias
jerry@plainjoe.org
```

After starting the Postfix daemons (*/usr/sbin/postfix start*), you can test your configuration further by sending a test message to *guest1@garion*. This *slapd* log entry (which comes from a logging level of 256) proves that Postfix did query the server using the filter "(uid=guest1)":

```
Aug 15 10:53:37 ldap slapd[6728]: conn=24 op=1 SRCH
base="ou=people,dc=plainjoe,dc=org" scope=2 filter="(uid=guest1)"
```

The following excerpt from the header of the delivered message shows that the message was delivered to *guest1@garion.plainjoe.org*. However, the message was then forwarded to *jerry@plainjoe.org*, as specified by the value of the mail attribute for the *guest1* account:

```
Return-Path: <root@plainjoe.org>
Delivered-To: jerry@plainjoe.org
Received: from XXX.XXX.XXX.XXX ([ XXX.XXX.XXX.XXX ] helo=garion.plainjoe.org)
        by gamma.jumpserver.net with esmtp (Exim 3.36 #1)
        id 18M1Sc-0003tj-00
        for jerry@plainjoe.org; Wed, 11 Dec 2002 01:39:14 -0600
Received: by garion.plainjoe.org (Postfix)
        id 15CA23FB62; Tue, 10 Dec 2002 11:40:23 -0600 (CST)
Delivered-To: guest1@garion.plainjoe.org
Received: by garion.plainjoe.org (Postfix, from userid 0)
        id F042E3FB69; Tue, 10 Dec 2002 12:40:22 -0500 (EST)
To: guest1@garion.plainjoe.org
Subject: testing Postfix/LDAP lookups
Message-Id: <20021210174022.F042E3FB69@garion.plainjoe.org>
Date: Tue, 10 Dec 2002 12:40:22 -0500 (EST)
From: root@plainjoe.org (root)
```

There are many possibilities beyond the simple example presented here. Your *query_filter* used only a single attribute, but nothing prevents the use of more complex filters that match on multiple attributes. Furthermore, many additional LDAP parameters allow you to fine-tune the way Postfix interacts with the directory. Table 7-7 gives a complete listing of all LDAP-related Postfix parameters as well as the default setting for each one.

Table 7-7. Postfix LDAP parameters

Parameter	Default	Description
bind	yes	Defines whether an LDAP bind request should be issued prior to performing the query. This value must be yes or no.
bind_dn	" "	The DN used when binding to the LDAP directory.
bind_pw	" "	The clear-text password used when binding to the directory using the bind_dn value.
cache	no	Determines whether to enable client-side caching of LDAP search results, as described in the *ldap_enable_cache(3)* manpage.
cache_expiry	30 seconds	Defines the cache expiration timeout when cache=yes.
cache_size	32 KB	Specifies the size of the LDAP cache when cache=yes.
dereference	0	Controls whether Postfix should dereference aliases when searching the directory. Possible values are 0 (never), 1 (when searching), 2 (when locating the base object for the search), and 3 (always).
domain	none	A list (possibly a table lookup) of domain names that restricts when a query is made. This means that a local "user" (with the @...) will not be queried, nor will any email address that does not match one of the domains listed. For example: ltable_domain = plainjoe. org, hash:/etc/postfix/ moredomains
query_filter	(mailacceptinggeneralid=%s)	The RFC 2254–style LDAP search filter.
result_attribute	maildrop	The attribute value that should be read as a result of the query_filter.
scope	sub	The scope of the directory search; must be one of sub, base, or one.
search_base	none	The DN that acts as the base search suffix for the query.
server_host	localhost	The hostname of the LDAP server to which queries should be submitted. The value is of the form *hostname*[: *port*][,*hostname*[:*port*], ...].

Table 7-7. Postfix LDAP parameters (continued)

Parameter	Default	Description
server_port	389	The port on which the server_host is listening (unless overridden by the *hostname:port* syntax).
special_result_attribute	none	Allows administrators to define an attribute that returns DNs from an LDAP search. If this value is present in the entry returned by a successful search, another query is issued using the returned DN as the search_base.
timeout	10 seconds	The maximum amount of time, in seconds, that can elapse before the search is abandoned.

Exim

The Exim MTA is another Sendmail alternative. It was first developed in 1995 by Dr. Philip Hazel while at Cambridge University. For the full details on configuring Exim, Philip Hazel's book, *Exim: The Mail Transfer Agent* (O'Reilly), provides an excellent tutorial on the various configuration details.* If you are not familiar with Exim, it is a good idea to visit *http://www.exim.org/* to obtain an overview of Exim's mail architecture. We will be looking at Exim 4.10.

Like Sendmail and Postfix, Exim supports various types of file and database lookups, such as mySQL, Berkeley DBM, and LDAP. In its default form, the Exim Makefile supports only linear searches in files (*lsearch*) and database lookups (*dbm*). To enable LDAP lookups, a handful of Makefile variables must be set. These variables are presented in Table 7-8.

Table 7-8. Exim LDAP-related Makefile variables

Variable	Description
LOOKUP_LDAP	This variable must be set to yes to include LDAP lookup support in the *exim* binary.

LOOKUP_INCLUDE LOOKUP_LIBS	These variables provide a means of supplementing the existing CFLAGS and LDFLAGS variables when building Exim. To support LDAP lookups, they must specify the locations of include files and LDAP libraries. For example:
	
	`LOOKUP_INCLUDE=-I/opt/ldap/include`
	`    LOOKUP_LIBS=-L/opt/ldap/lib -llldap -llber`

LDAP_LIB_TYPE	This variable defines which LDAP client libraries will be used. Possible values are UMICHIGAN, OPENLDAP1, OPENLDAP2, NETSCAPE, and SOLARIS.

---

* At the time of this writing, Hazel's book covers Exim 3. The current release discussed in this chapter is Exim 4. There have been some substantial changes between the two versions.

Build the mail server with the following LDAP settings in Exim's *Local/Makefile*:

```
## Included in Exim's Local/Makefile to enable LDAP lookup support
LOOKUP_LDAP=yes
LOOKUP_INCLUDE=-I /usr/local/include
LOOKUP_LIBS=-L/usr/local/lib -lldap -llber
LDAP_LIB_TYPE=OPENLDAP2
```

It is a good idea to verify that the OpenLDAP libraries have been linked to the *exim* binary using some type of tool, such as *ldd(1)*, to view linking dependencies:

```
$ ldd /usr/exim/bin/exim
    libresolv.so.2 => /lib/libresolv.so.2 (0x40026000)
    libnsl.so.1 => /lib/libnsl.so.1 (0x40037000)
    libcrypt.so.1 => /lib/libcrypt.so.1 (0x4004b000)
    libdb-4.0.so => /lib/libdb-4.0.so (0x40078000)
    libldap.so.2 => /usr/local/lib/libldap.so.2 (0x4010f000)
    liblber.so.2 => /usr/local/lib/liblber.so.2 (0x40146000)
    libc.so.6 => /lib/libc.so.6 (0x40153000)
    libdl.so.2 => /lib/libdl.so.2 (0x4027b000)
    libsasl2.so.2 => /usr/lib/libsasl2.so.2 (0x4027e000)
    libssl.so.2 => /lib/libssl.so.2 (0x40290000)
    libcrypto.so.2 => /lib/libcrypto.so.2 (0x402bd000)
    /lib/ld-linux.so.2 => /lib/ld-linux.so.2 (0x40000000)
```

Once the Exim binaries have been built and installed (we'll assume that the default location of */usr/exim/* is the installation directory), the next step is decide what data should be retrieved from the directory. Our discussion of Postfix defined a useful schema for retrieving mail aliases for local users; let's see how this same schema applies to Exim. The schema makes use of the uid attribute type (posixAccount) as the key and the mail attribute type (inetOrgPerson) as the resulting value. For completeness's sake, here's the LDIF entry for a user account with a mail alias; it's the same entry you used for the Postfix server. All mail that would be delivered to the local user named *guest1* should be forwarded to the address *jerry@plainjoe.org*.

```
## User account including a mail alias
dn: uid=guest1,ou=People,dc=plainjoe,dc=org
uid: guest1
cn: Guest Account
objectClass: posixAccount
objectClass: inetOrgPerson
userPassword: {CRYPT}Fd8nE1RtCh5G6
loginShell: /bin/bash
uidNumber: 783
gidNumber: 1000
homeDirectory: /home/guest1
gecos: Guest Account
sn: Account
mail: jerry@plainjoe.org
```

Exim searches are defined using the data keyword. The general syntax for a table lookup is:

```
data = ${lookup db_type {db_search_parameters}}
```

LDAP queries can use a *db_type* of:

ldap

> Indicates that the search will return a single value and that Exim should interpret multiple values as a failure

ldapdn

> Specifies that the search will match one entry in the directory and that the returned value is the DN of that entry

ldapm

> Defines searches that may return multiple values

To inform Exim that local alias data should be retrieved from an LDAP directory, you must configure an appropriate *redirect* router. To do so, you create an ldap_ aliases entry in */usr/exim/configure*:

```
## Alias Director, which retrieves data from an LDAP director. The name
## "ldap_aliases" has been arbitrarily chosen.
ldap_aliases:
  driver = redirect
  data = ${lookup ldap \
    { ldap://ldap.plainjoe.org/\
      ou=people,dc=plainjoe,dc=org\
      ?mail?sub?(uid=${local_part})} }
```

The driver keyword is used to define the type of router being implemented. In contrast to both Sendmail and Postfix, Exim uses an LDAP URL to define the LDAP host, port, search base, retrieved attribute values, scope, and filter. The line continuation character (\) has been used to make the line more readable. The variable ${local_part} is the username extracted from the local recipient's mail address (for example, the ${local_part} of *jdoe@garion.plainjoe.org* would be *jdoe*). So you can read the query specification as: "Using the LDAP server at *ldap.plainjoe.org* (on the default port of tcp/389), perform a substring search of the uid attribute, searching for the local part of the email address, and returning the value of the mail attribute. Perform the search with a search base of ou=people,dc=plainjoe,dc=org."

 It is possible to define multiple servers for LDAP queries with the ldap_default_servers parameter in Exim's *configure* file. This option accepts a colon-separated list of servers and ports that are tried one by one until a server is successfully contacted. This setting would utilize two directory servers, *ldap1* and *ldap2,* for fault tolerance purposes:

```
ldap_default_servers = ldap1::389:ldap2::389
```

Using Exim's address-testing mode, you can verify that mail sent to *guest1@garion* will indeed be forwarded to *jerry@plainjoe.org*:

```
root# exim -v -bt guest1@garion
jerry@plainjoe.org
    <-- guest1@garion.plainjoe.org
  deliver to jerry@plainjoe.org
```

```
router = dnslookup, transport = remote_smtp
host plainjoe.org [xxx.xxx.xxx.xxx]
```

The log file for *slapd* (loglevel 256) shows that the lookup for (uid=guest1) was performed as expected:

```
Aug 16 17:05:09 ldap slapd[3574]: conn=36 op=1 SRCH
base="ou=people,dc=plainjoe,dc=org" scope=2 filter="(uid=guest1)"
```

The LDAP URL format does not allow any space for defining credentials to be used when binding to the server. The default behavior is to perform an anonymous bind and not request any limits on search results. Exim can request a simple bind using credentials specified by the *user* and *pass* options. Table 7-9 lists several parameters that can be included in the LDAP query as *option=value* to specify authentication information as well as search limits.

Table 7-9. Additional Exim LDAP query parameters

Parameter	Description
user	The DN used when binding to the directory server
pass	The clear-text password used when binding to the directory server with a non-empty user
size	The upper limit on the number of entries returned from the lookup
time	The upper limit, in seconds, on the time to wait for a response to a lookup

To use these additional parameters when performing an LDAP lookup, they must preceed the URL in the *data* string. For example, to bind to the LDAP server as the user cn=Mail Admin,dc=plainjoe,dc=org using the password secret, you would define the following query:

```
data = ${lookup ldap \
    { user="cn=Mail Admin,dc=plainjoe,dc=org"\
      pass=secret \
      ldaps://ldap.plainjoe.org/\
      ou=people,dc=plainjoe,dc=org\
      ?mail?sub?(uid=${local_part})}  }
```

Because Exim uses LDAPv2 binds, it cannot take advantage of SASL authentication or the StartTLS LDAv3 extension. However, it can understand URLs that use *ldaps://*. This is important when sending a DN and password to the directory server in clear text.

It should also be mentioned that because the pass value is stored in clear text, it is preferable to preface the data line with the hide keyword (i.e., hide data = …) directive so that the line cannot be displayed by ordinary users using the *exim -bP* command.

## CHAPTER 8

Standard Unix Services and LDAP

In Chapter 6, we examined the possibilities of integrating an LDAP directory into basic authentication services by using the PAM and NSS modules. In Chapter 7, we integrated LDAP into the network mail infrastructure in both clients and servers. This chapter takes LDAP integration a step further by exploring how other standard Unix services can make use of our directory. The applications we will explore are Apache, FTP (ProFTPD), Samba, RADIUS (FreeRadius), DNS (BIND 9), and printing (LPRng and LPD). It is impossible to cover all the services a network may provide, but by showing a few concise, real-world solutions to common problems, I hope to give you tools and ideas that you can apply to any network applications you encounter in the future.

The applications discussed in this chapter will communicate directly with the LDAP directory. Servers that do not possess native LDAP support can use the PAM and NSS solutions presented in Chapter 6.

The Directory Namespace

Although we will eventually need to modify it, we will start by using the namespace developed in Chapters 6 and 7. Our directory root is dc=plainjoe,dc=org, and user-related information is stored beneath the people organizational unit directly below the root, as shown in Figure 8-1. The group organizational unit contains any posixGroup entries as well as any administrative group (groupOfNames) objects used in access control rules for the directory.* We will need to add additional organizational units, which we will do later in this chapter.

---

* Examples of using administrative groups in ACLs and the groupofNames object can be found in Appendix E.

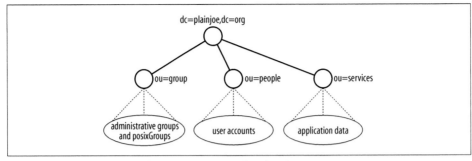

Figure 8-1. Initial namespace for the directory used in this chapter

An FTP/HTTP Combination

The first set of services that we will explore is the combination of the ProFTPD server (*http://www.proftpd.org/*) and Apache (*http://www.apache.org/*). In this scenario, we would like to build a new web server and allow users to publish web content using an FTP client. All user and group accounts already exist in the LDAP directory, but just to make things interesting, assume that your theoretical web server platform cannot make use of either PAM or NSS to access any of this information.

The solution we would like to deploy is illustrated in Figure 8-2. Users should be able to put files into ~*<username>*/public_html on the web server using FTP. ProFTPD must authenticate user connections using information stored in the LDAP directory. These files should then be accessible via a web browser at *http://www.plainjoe.org/*~*<username>*. Because the server is not using an nss_ldap library, Apache must obtain the home directory path for users directly from the *LDAP* server.

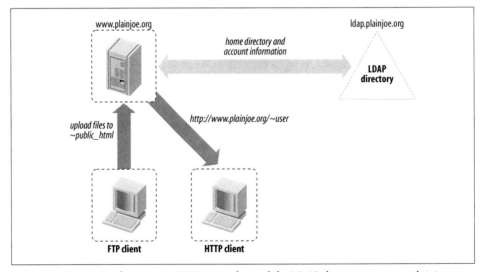

Figure 8-2. Interaction between ProFTPD, Apache, and the LDAP directory on www.plainjoe.org

Two add-ins, both developed by John Morrissey (*http://www.horde.net/~jwm*), will help you implement your new web server. We will begin by looking at ProFTPD's LDAP features.

ProFTPD

Morrissey's LDAP authentication module (mod_ldap) is included with current releases of the ProFTPD server.* Our focus will be on the ProFTPD Release v1.2.7. Building mod_ldap is controlled by an option to the configure script (*--with-modules=mod_ldap*). After extracting the source code, the following commands build the binaries and tools to include support for mod_ldap:

```
$ ./configure --with-modules=mod_ldap
$ make
$ /bin/su -c "make install"
```

You can specify multiple modules as arguments to the *--with-modules* option by separating each module name in the list with a colon (e.g., *--with-modules=mod_ldap:mod_linuxprivs*). For more information on the various modules supported by the ProFTPD package, refer to the documentation included with the software or the online versions at *http://www.proftpd.org/docs/*.

ProFTPD's *-l* command-line option can be used to verify that the mod_ldap module was included in the final binary. The actual list of modules may vary depending on the OS used during compilation, but at a minimum, you must see mod_ldap listed:

```
$ proftpd -l
Compiled-in modules:
  mod_core.c
  mod_auth.c
  mod_xfer.c
  mod_site.c
  mod_ls.c
  mod_unixpw.c
  mod_log.c
  mod_ldap.c
```

The *sample-configurations/* subdirectory included in the source distribution contains settings for several common scenarios. We'll use the following *proftpd.conf* file as starting point. The parameters are fairly self-explanatory, but you can review the configuration documentation included in the *docs/* directory of the *proftpd* source distribution if you need more information.

```
## ####################################################
## ProFTPD configuration file
```

---

* ProFTPD's mod_ldap module should not be confused with any of Apache's modules of the same name (*http://modules.apache.org/*).

```
## (/usr/local/etc/proftpd.conf)
## Global directives
## ################################################
ServerType              standalone
DefaultServer           on
Port                    21
Umask                   022
User                    nobody
Group                   nobody

## <- LDAP parameters will go here. ->

# Normally, files should be overwritable.
<Directory /*>
  AllowOverwrite                on
</Directory>
```

Your first step is to restrict a user to her individual *~/public_html* subdirectory when connecting. We will assume that this directory already exists. The DefaultRoot option defines the path that will be passed to the chroot( ) call by the *proftpd* server.

```
## Limit users to their web directory.
DefaultRoot     ~/public_html
```

The next step is to instruct the *proftpd* daemon to use the mod_ldap module for authentication. The LDAPDoAuth keyword accepts up to three arguments. The first either turns the module on or off. The second argument is the base suffix to use when searching the directory. The final argument allows an administrator to define a customized search filter. In the absence of an explicit filter string, the default of (&(uid=%u)(objectclass=posixAccount)) is used.

```
## Limit users to their web directory. Use the default search filter.
LDAPDoAuth      on "ou=people,dc=plainjoe,dc=org"
```

Of course, you also must define the hostname of the directory server:

```
## Define the LDAP server to contact.
LDAPServer      ldap.plainjoe.org
```

By default, the ProFTPD daemon uses an anonymous bind when searching an LDAP directory. However, if you include the LDAPDNInfo directive in the configuration file, the daemon uses a DN and password to bind to the *LDAP* server. We'll stick with anonymous binds since Chapter 6 allowed nss_ldap clients to enumerate account information this way.

The mod_ldap module supports two means of authenticating user connections once their directory entries are located. The LDAPAuthBinds directive controls which method is used. If it is set to off, mod_ldap searches the *LDAP* server anonymously (or uses a simple bind as the LDAPDNInfo entry) to retrieve all of the user information including the userPassword attribute. The module then hashes the password entered by the user (if necessary) using the local system's crypt( ) function and compares it to the value obtained from the directory search. This means that the userPassword must be stored in either {CLEAR} or {CRYPT} formats.

The preferred and default method (LDAPAuthBinds on) authenticates the connecting user by binding to the directory server. In this case, ProFTPD locates the DN of the connecting user by searching the directory (either anonymously or as the LDAPDNInfo). However, the userPassword attribute is never requested from the *LDAP* server under this configuration. The module then binds to the directory again, using the user's DN and the password that the user entered. If this bind succeeds, ProFTPD considers the user to be authenticated.

To configure ProFTPD for the preferred authentication method, add the following line to *proftpd.conf*:

```
## Require that an incoming user can successfully bind to the LDAPServer.
LDAPAuthBinds      on
```

The final hurdle to overcome is to inform *proftpd* how to resolve UIDs and GIDs when listing files without using the standard getpwuid( ) and getgrgid( ) calls. The LDAPDoUIDLookups and LDAPDoGIDLookups directives instruct *proftpd* to query the directory server using the specified base suffix. Each directive accepts an optional parameter if you find it necessary to override the respective default search filters of (&(uidNumber=*UNIX uid*)(objectclasses=posixAccount)) and (&(gidNumber=*UNIX gid*) (objectclasses=posixGroup)). These filters work well with your directory, so there is no need to change them.

```
## Look up UIDs and GIDs in the directory.
LDAPDoGIDLookups   on "ou=group,dc=plainjoe,dc=org"
LDAPDoUIDLookups   on "ou=people,dc=plainjoe,dc=org"
```

Assuming that you have a valid user named *kristi* in the directory, you can verify that mod_ldap and *proftpd* are working by connecting to the server (*www.plainjoe.org*) and uploading a file:

```
$ ncftp -u kristi -p testpass www.plainjoe.org
NcFTP 3.1.3 (Mar 27, 2002) by Mike Gleason (ncftp@ncftp.com).
Connecting to 192.168.1.100...
ProFTPD 1.2.7 Server (ProFTPD Default Installation) [www.plainjoe.org]
Logging in...
User kristi logged in.
Logged in to localhost.
ncftp / > put index.html
index.html:                        1.38 kB   69.43 kB/s
ncftp / > ls -l
-rw-r--r--  1 kristi   ftpusers    464 Dec 18  2002 index.html
```

Table 8-1 lists the entire set of directives for mod_ldap.

Table 8-1. Parameters for the ProFTPD mod_ldap 2.7 module

Directive	Default	Description
LDAPAuthBinds	on	Should the connecting user be authenticated by binding to the directory server using the located DN and the user's password (on), or should the module hash the password locally and compare it with the userPassword attribute obtained from the directory (off)?
LDAPDefaultAuthScheme	crypt	Specifies the hashing scheme for passwords that are not prefixed by a type string ({ }). Possible values are crypt and clear.
LDAPDefaultGID	None	Specifies the default Unix GID to be assigned to the user if the gidNumber attribute is unavailable.
LDAPDefaultUID	None	Specifies the default Unix UID to be assigned to the user if the uidNumber attribute is unavailable.
LDAPDNInfo	"" ""	Defines the DN and password to use when binding to the directory server for searches.
LDAPDoAuth	off	Should mod_ldap be enabled for authentication?
LDAPDoGIDLookups	off	Should mod_ldap attempt to resolve GID numbers to names by querying the directory for matching posixGroup entries?
LDAPDoUIDLookups	off	Should mod_ldap attempt to resolve UID numbers to names by querying the directory for matching posixAccount entries?
LDAPForceDefaultGID	off	Forces the GID of all connected users to the LDAPDefaultGID, even if a gidNumber attribute can be obtained.
LDAPForceDefaultUID	off	Forces the UID of all connected users to the LDAPDefaultUID, even if a uidNumber attribute can be obtained.
LDAPHomedirOnDemand	off	Instructs mod_ldap to create the user's home directory (from the homeDirectory attribute) if it does not already exist. The directive also accepts a second parameter that sets the mode of the new directory.
LDAPHomedirOnDemandSuffix	""	Specifies additional subdirectories to be created in the event that LDAPHomedirOnDemand has been enabled. Multiple directories can be included in a whitespace-delimited list.
LDAPNegativeCache	off	Instructs mod_ldap to cache negative responses to UID/GID resolution attempts.
LDAPQueryTimeout	LDAP client library default	Specifies the maximum amount of time, in seconds, to wait for a search to complete.
LDAPSearchScope	subtree	Defines the LDAP search scope as onelevel or subtree.

Table 8-1. Parameters for the ProFTPD mod_ldap 2.7 module (continued)

Directive	Default	Description
LDAPServer	localhost	Specifies the hostname of the directory server. An alternative to port 389 can be defined using the syntax *server:port*. Multiple servers can be specified; separate server hostnames by spaces.
LDAPUseTLS	off	This parameter is available only if mod_ldap.c has been modified to define USE_LDAPV3_TLS. If enabled, mod_ldap will use the StartTLS extension when contacting the *LDAP* server. If the directory does not support TLS, mod_ldap will downgrade to an unencrypted channel and simply report failure to the *proftpd* server.

Apache

Now that users can upload files to your web server, Apache must be configured to resolve URLs such as *http://www.plainjoe.org/~kristi*. Traditionally, Apache administrators have used a subdirectory named *public_html* in home directories to provide a simple mechanism for users to publish personal web pages. This associates the tilde (~) with a home directory by asking the operating system to provide the details about the user from the local system password file, NIS map, or LDAP directory via NSS modules.

Because we have chosen not to implement any nss_ldap functionality on the server, we will have to use another means of instructing Apache how to determine a user's home directory location. Morrissey's mod_ldap_userdir module allows us to do just that.

This module obtains the path to a user's home directory by searching an LDAP directory for a posixAccount entry with a matching uid value. Our LDAP directory already supports the schema required for mod_ldap_userdir, so the new work to be done is localized to the web server. As usual, we focus only on the aspects of Apache needed to integrate the server with an LDAP directory. Full coverage of Apache configuration is well beyond the scope of a single chapter, as is the case with all of the server packages discussed in this chapter. For more information on Apache and its *httpd. conf*, refer to *Apache: The Definitive Guide*, by Ben and Peter Laurie (O'Reilly).

The first step is to download the latest version of the module from *http://www.horde.net/ ~jwm/software/mod_ldap_userdir/*. Building mod_ldap_userdir requires adding only a single option (*--with-activate*) to the configure script. However, unless the Apache eXtenSion tool is located in a directory in your $PATH, it will also be necessary to set the absolute path to the *apxs* binary. These are the steps I used to build the module for an Apache 1.3.23 installation, although an Apache 2.0 installation is no different:

```
$ ./configure --with-activate --with-apxs=/usr/sbin/apxs
$ make
```

```
$ /bin/su -c "make install"
/usr/sbin/apxs -i -a mod_ldap_userdir.so
[activating module 'ldap_userdir' in /etc/httpd/conf/httpd.conf]
cp mod_ldap_userdir.so /usr/lib/apache/mod_ldap_userdir.so
chmod 755 /usr/lib/apache/mod_ldap_userdir.so
cp /etc/httpd/conf/httpd.conf /etc/httpd/conf/httpd.conf.bak
cp /etc/httpd/conf/httpd.conf.new /etc/httpd/conf/httpd.conf
rm /etc/httpd/conf/httpd.conf.new
```

The build process will fail if *configure* cannot locate the necessary LDAP libraries and header files. The two options, *--with-sdk-headers=<path>* and *--with-sdk-libs=<path>*, can be used to specify the path to the LDAP SDK header files and libraries. The final *make install* command should copy the compiled library to the directory containing the other installed Apache modules (normally */usr/lib/apache/*) and activate the module in *httpd.conf*. Here is the LoadModule line created in Apache's configuration from the installation (the comments are my own):

```
## Activate the LDAP userdir module (this may also require an AddModule
## mod_ldap_userdir.c directive later in the file depending on the server's
## configuration).
LoadModule ldap_userdir_module /usr/lib/apache/mod_ldap_userdir.so
```

The module itself has seven directives, which are presented in Table 8-2. Your web server uses four of these directives:

```
<IfModule mod_ldap_userdir.c>
    LDAPUserDirServer        ldap.plainjoe.org
    LDAPUserDirSearchScope   subtree
    LDAPUserDirBaseDN        ou=people,dc=plainjoe,dc=org
    LDAPUserDir              public_html
</IfModule>
```

Table 8-2. Directives for mod_ldap_userdir

Directive	Default	Description
LDAPUserDir	public_html	The expected name of the subdirectory.
LDAPUserDirServer	None	The hostname of the LDAP directory server.
LDAPUserDirDNInfo	None	The DN and password to be used to bind to the directory. The password should be given in clear text.
LDAPUserDirBaseDN	""	The base search suffix to use when searching the directory.
LDAPUserDirFilter	(&(uid=%v)(objectclass=posixAccount))	The RFC 2254–compliant LDAP search filter to use when querying the directory.

Table 8-2. Directives for mod_ldap_userdir (continued)

Directive	Default	Description
LDAPUserDirSearchScope	subtree	The scope of the LDAP search; can be a onelevel or subtree.
LDAPUserDirUseTLS	off	Whether to use the StartTLS extended operation (on) or an unencrypted connection (off) when searching the directory.

The values for each directive in your configuration are fairly self-explanatory. LDAPUserDirServer, LDAPUserDirSearchScope, and LDAPUserDirBaseDN set the standard LDAP search parameters: the server's hostname (*ldap.plainjoe.org*), the search scope (subtree), and the base suffix (ou=people,dc=plainjoe,dc=org). The search filter is not set explicitly because the default filter string, (&(uid=%v)(objectclass=posixAccount)), works nicely with your directory; it matches the current username against the uid attributes of all posixAccount objects.

By default, Apache binds to the directory anonymously. However, you could specify a DN and password to be used when binding to the *LDAP* server by defining the LDAPUserDirDNInfo parameter. There is no need to avoid anonymous searches in this case because the uid and homeDirectory attributes have already been made available anonymously to support other services such as ProFTPD.

Once all of these pieces are in place, you can verify that the module is working correctly by viewing the *index.html* file uploaded to *~kristi/public_html* in the previous section. If there are any errors, the two places to look for clues are Apache's *error_log* and OpenLDAP's syslog messages.

User Authentication with Samba

This book has concentrated on Unix services, with only a few exceptions; email applications often cross platform boundaries, as do requirements for file and printer sharing. The Samba project (*http://www.samba.org/*) has become a staple for administrators seeking to integrate Unix file and print servers with Windows clients. Samba is a suite of programs that implement the server portion of the SMB (Server Message Block) protocol, later renamed CIFS (Common Internet File System).

Samba includes several client programs and administrative tools in addition to its server components. Adequate coverage of Samba is well beyond the scope of this book. For more information about Samba, see *Sams Teach Yourself Samba in 24 Hours*, Second Edition, by Gerald Carter (Sams Publishing), or *Using Samba*, Second Edition, by Jay Ts, Robert Eckstein, and David Collier-Brown (O'Reilly).

To support the challenge/response authentication methods used by Microsoft clients, Samba requires a list of hashed passwords separate from the normal Unix account information stored in */etc/passwd* (or in the posixAccount object class). This collection of LanManager and Windows NT password hashes is normally stored in a file named *smbpasswd(5)*; the format of each entry is:

```
username:uid:LM_HASH:NT_HASH:account flags:timestamp
```

Samba's *smbpasswd* file has several disadvantages for sites with many users:

- Lookups are performed sequentially. When servicing a domain logon request from a Windows NT/2000/XP client, there are a minimum of two lookups. These lookups can be a performance bottleneck.

- Attempts at using a single *smbpasswd* file for multiple standalone servers requires the administrator to use external tools, such as a combination of *rsync(1)* and *ssh(1)* or *scp(1)*, to replicate the file. This solution also requires that the set of Unix users and groups be synchronized between the servers, perhaps using the methods outlined in Chapter 6.

- The format of the *smbpasswd* file limits the number of attributes that can be maintained for each user. When Samba is acting as a Windows Primary Domain Controller, there are many additional fields, such as the location of a user's roving profile, that should be maintained on an individual basis.

Configuring Samba

All of these deficiencies can be addressed by moving the information from a local, flat file into sambaAccount objects in an LDAP directory. The LDAP support in Samba 2.2.7a must be enabled at compile time using the *--with-ldapsam* configure script option.* This support requires the OpenLDAP 2 client libraries to be present when compiling Samba. Here's a typical Samba build:

```
root# ./configure --with-ldapsam
<...output deleted...>
checking whether to use LDAP SAM database... yes
root# make
root# make install
```

After installing the LDAP-enabled version of the Samba, the next step is to create a working configuration file (*smb.conf*) for the *smbd(8)* and *nmbd(8)* binaries. The following *smb.conf* creates a single file share named [files]:

```
## smb.conf file for LDAP-enabled Samba server
[global]
  netbios name      = TASHTEGO
  workgroup         = PEQUOD
```

---

* The LDAP support in Samba 2.2 has no relationship to the LDAP support in a Windows 2000 domain or in Windows 2000 Active Directory servers.

```
security          = user
encrypt passwords = yes

## LDAPsam-related passwords
ldap admin dn = "cn=smbadmin,ou=people,dc=plainjoe,dc=org"
ldap server   = ldap.plainjoe.org
ldap ssl      = start_tls
ldap port     = 389
ldap suffix   = "ou=people,dc=plainjoe,dc=org"
## The following is the default LDAP filter used if one is not explicitly defined.
ldap filter   = "(&(uid=%U)(objectclass=sambaAccount))"

## Define the file service to be shared.
[files]
path      = /export/files
read only = no
```

If you've been following along, the LDAP-related parameters should be familiar. Table 8-3 provides descriptions of the various parameters as well as the default value assigned to each option.

Table 8-3. Samba's LDAPsam smb.conf parameters

Parameter	Default	Description
ldap admin dn	""	The DN used by *smbd* when connecting to the *LDAP* server. This DN should be able to read all attribute values for sambaAccount entries, including lmPassword and ntPassword.
ldap filter	(&(uid=%u)(objectclass=sambaAccount))	The RFC 2254–compliant search filter to use when locating a user's Samba account information.
ldap port	636	The tcp port to use when contacting the *LDAP* server.
ldap server	localhost	The FQDN of the directory server.
ldap ssl	on	The parameter that specifies how *smbd* connects to the *LDAP* server. The possible values are off (do not use encryption when communicating with the directory), on (use LDAPS when contacting the directory server), and start_tls (use the StartTLS command to establish an encrypted transport layer).
ldap suffix	""	The base search suffix to use when querying the directory.

Samba must obtain the Windows password hashes from the directory in order to authenticate a user using encrypted passwords. Due to their security-sensitive nature, the hashes should never be retrievable by an anonymous user. To bind to the host specified by the ldap server parameter, Samba requires a valid ldap admin dn value and a password. The clear-text password is not stored in Samba's configuration file (*smb.conf* is often world-readable, so storing the password in this file would be pointless). Rather, the password is stored in the *secrets.tdb* file located in */usr/local/samba/private/* by default. The password is still stored in clear text, but the permissions assigned to this file should restrict read and write access to the superuser account.

Samba's *smbpasswd(8)* utility is normally used to perform duties such as manipulating user entries in the *smbpasswd(5)* file, joining the Samba server to a Windows domain, and changing passwords for remote Windows users. Use it to store the ldap admin dn password by executing:

```
root# /usr/local/samba/bin/smbpasswd -w secret
Setting stored password for "cn=smbadmin,ou=people,dc=plainjoe,dc=org" in secrets.tdb
```

Because *secrets.tdb* can be read or written only by root, you must execute this command as root. If the *smbpasswd* command does not support the -w option, either LDAPsam support was not properly enabled when compiling Samba, or a non-LDAP–enabled version of the tool exists in your $PATH.

Currently, the Samba server uses a simple bind when contacting the directory server to retrieve user information. Given the access rights required by the ldap admin dn account and the clear text–equivalent nature of the LanManager and NT password hashes, it is strongly advised that the ldap ssl parameter be left enabled or set to use the StartTLS operation.

Configuring OpenLDAP

To store sambaAccount entries in the directory, your *LDAP* server must support the appropriate schema. Samba developers provide a definition of the sambaAccount schema for use with OpenLDAP 2 servers in the file *examples/LDAP/samba.schema* (included in the Samba source distribution). Copy *samba.schema* to an appropriate location, such as */usr/local/etc/openldap/schema/*, and include it in the server's configuration by adding the appropriate include statements to the *slapd.conf* file. Two dependencies are noted at the beginning of the *samba.schema* file: *cosine.schema* (for the uid attribute) and *inetorgperson.schema* (for the displayName attribute). After you've finished editing the schema portion of *slapd.conf*, it should look like this:

```
## /usr/local/etc/openldap/slapd.conf

## core.schema is required for all servers.
include  /usr/local/etc/openldap/schema/core.schema

## Included from Chapter 6
include  /usr/local/etc/openldap/schema/cosine.schema
include  /usr/local/etc/openldap/schema/nis.schema

## Included from Chapter 4
include  /usr/local/etc/openldap/schema/inetorgperson.schema
```

```
## Dependencies for samba.schema: cosine.schema and inetorgperson.schema needed to
## support --with-ldapsam in Samba
include  /usr/local/etc/openldap/schema/samba.schema
```

Figure 8-3 shows attributes used by the sambaAccount object class. The *Samba-LDAP-HOWTO* file (also distributed with the Samba source distribution) defines each attribute and its expected values. All of the attributes are stored as ASCII string values (IA5String).

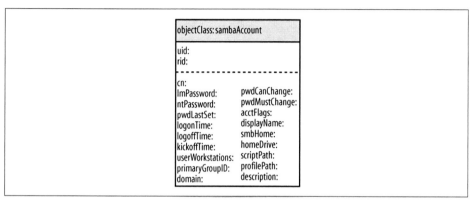

Figure 8-3. sambaAccount object class

In addition to the schema changes, you must add a new access control rule to prevent normal users (authenticated or not) from retrieving LanMan/NT password hashes (the lmPassword and ntPassword attributes) from the directory. Since OpenLDAP never uses these attributes for authenticating a bind request, there is no reason for a user to access these attributes. The other attributes of the sambaAccount object class do not contain any sensitive information, so it doesn't matter who reads them. The first and last *slapd.conf* ACLs are repeats from Chapter 6. The second access rule denies all users except *smbadmin* access to the lmPassword and ntPassword attributes. This ACL could be modified to allow users to change their own password hashes without any adverse security affects. The third allows the cn=smbadmin user to write to all entries in the ou=people subtree. You could tighten down this ACL by restricting the *smbadmin*'s access to the attributes of the a sambaAccount object only, but the simpler version is presented here:

```
## Previous ACL from Chapter 6
access to attrs=userPassword
    by self write
    by * auth

## Don't let users snoop Windows passwords.
access to attrs=lmPassword,ntPassword
    by dn="cn=smbadmin,ou=people,dc=plainjoe,dc=org" write
    by * none

## Allow the Samba admin user to add new entries and modify existing ones.
access to dn.subtree="ou=people,dc=plainjoe,dc=org"
```

```
    by dn="cn=smbadmin,ou=people,dc=plainjoe,dc=org" write
    by * read

## Previous ACL from Chapter 6
access to dn.subtree="ou=group,dc=plainjoe,dc=org"
    by * read
```

I have already added Samba's ldap admin dn to *smb.conf*, but have yet to explain what its directory entry looks like. Samba will bind to the directory as the user, so it must possess a userPassword attribute value. However, it is not necessary that this entry have a numeric UID or other POSIX attribute. The person structural object class in OpenLDAP's *core.schema* file includes just the attributes you need: a name and a password. Figure 8-4 displays the required and optional attributes held by a person in the directory.

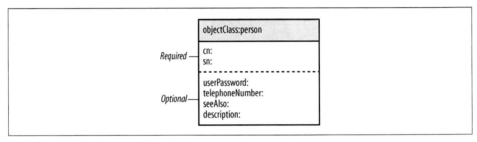

Figure 8-4. person object class

A simple LDIF representation of the cn=smbadmin entry would be:

```
dn: cn=smbadmin,ou=people,dc=plainjoe,dc=org
objectclass: person
cn: smbadmin
sn: smbadmin
userPassword: {SSHA}xDG3/Cfj7ATgJ9yPOexS2lGD+infJqCj
```

In this case, the userPassword attribute holds the SSHA hash of the passphrase string "secret."

You have now finished all the configuration details, and are ready to add a real sambaAccount entry. When you've done this, you can start testing.

Adding and Using a sambaAccount

Just as entries in the *smbpasswd(5)* file supplement entries in the local system *passwd* file, the sambaAccount entries in the directory supplement the basic Unix account information. *smbd* always queries the server's operating system for attributes such as the Unix home directory and user ID. By using both the posixAccount and the sambaAccount auxiliary object classes, you can store all of this information in your directory.

The only requirement Samba places on sambaAccount or *smbpasswd* entries is that the operating system must provide a valid set of Unix attributes for the user (e.g., a Unix UID and primary GID). The example presented here uses the directory structure presented earlier in this chapter and therefore assumes that a posixAccount entry already exists for all valid Unix users.

To add the sambaAccount information required for validating Windows users, we turn to the *smbpasswd(8)* utility. The *-a* option specifies the username of the account to be added, and the *-s* option specifies the initial password. For example, to add a user named *kristi*, execute the following command as root:

```
root# smbpasswd -a kristi -s testpass
LDAP search "(&(uid=kristi)(objectclass=sambaAccount))"
      returned 0 entries.
Added user kristi.
```

The message about the LDAP query returning 0 entries is normal. *smbpasswd(8)* initially looks for a preexisting account with the specified username. Since you are adding a new account, this search returns 0 entries. The resulting entry in the directory (with sambaAccount attributes highlighted), including the preexisting posixAccount attributes, appears as:

```
dn: uid=kristi,ou=people,dc=plainjoe,dc=org
objectClass: inetOrgPerson
objectClass: posixAccount
objectClass: sambaAccount
cn: Kristi Carter
cn: Kristi W. Carter
sn: Carter
mail: kcarter@plainjoe.org
labeledURI: http://www.plainjoe.org/~kristi
roomNumber: 102 Ramsey Hall
telephoneNumber: 222-555-2356
userPassword: {SSHA}7eXyEM+Q+1BVUGFz/MOWYUCONdovP3uM
loginShell: /bin/bash
uidNumber: 781
gidNumber: 100
homeDirectory: /home/kristi
gecos: Kristi Carter
uid: kristi
pwdLastSet: 1040186720
logonTime: 0
logoffTime: 2147483647
kickoffTime: 2147483647
pwdCanChange: 0
pwdMustChange: 2147483647
rid: 2570
primaryGroupID: 1201
lmPassword: 3AE6CCCE2A2A253F93E28745B8BF4BA6
ntPassword: 35CCBA9168B1D5CA6093B4B7D56C619B
acctFlags: [UX        ]
```

We can confirm that Samba can authenticate the new user by using *smbclient*:

```
$ smbclient //tashtego/files -Ukristi%testpass
Domain=[PEQUOD] OS=[Unix] Server=[Samba 2.2.7a]
smb: \>
```

FreeRadius

The FreeRadius server project (*http://www.freeradius.org/*) is the implementation of the Remote Authentication Dial-In User Service (RADIUS) protocol used by many corporations and Internet service providers to authenticate users connecting from remote locations. Complete coverage of FreeRadius or RADIUS servers goes beyond the scope this chapter. RFC 2865 explains the details of the protocol. For a more practical look at RADIUS, you should refer to the FreeRadius web site as well as *RADIUS*, by Jonathon Hassel (O'Reilly).

The FreeRadius server daemon, *radiusd*, can use an LDAP directory in two different ways. First, it can use LDAP as a data store for RADIUS attribute values. RADIUS attributes are defined by the RADIUS protocol and should not be confused with LDAP attributes.* The only similarity between the two types of attributes is that both have names and are used to store values. The FreeRadius administrator defines the mapping between RADIUS attributes and the LDAP attributes used to represent them. We'll look at the configuration details after we have compiled a working RADIUS server. The second option is to use the directory as an authentication service by binding to the *LDAP* server on behalf of a user. In this way, *radiusd* can determine whether to accept or reject incoming connection requests.

In the 0.8 release, the rlm_ldap module used by *radiusd* to access a directory is included in a default installation. No additional flags are required to enable LDAP support at compile time. Running the basic `configure && make && /bin/su -c "make install"` is enough to achieve a working *radiusd* in most environments.

Without getting too bogged down in the specifics of the FreeRadius configuration file, *radiusd.conf*, it is worth explaining the general layout. Configuration options can be described as either existing within the scope of a section bounded by { }s or global. Global parameters define information such as the location of directories necessary to the general operation of *radiusd* or the number of threads that the main server should spawn. Scoped parameters can be subdivided into module settings and component implementations.

FreeRadius modules are shared libraries defined by the project's RLM interface. The modules block in *radiusd.conf* contains parameters specific to each library. The RLM

---

* A list of RADIUS attributes linked with the corresponding RFCs can be found at *http://www.freeradius.org/rfc/attributes.html*.

interface describes several different components that a module can implement. The two components of interest to us are authorize and authenticate.

The authorization component is used by *radiusd* to look up information about a user account. The authorize section can contain several different module names. Each module is queried in order for an entry matching the login name of the user in question until a record is located or all modules have reported failure. Part of the authorization component's responsibility is to describe the authentication method used to validate this account. The authenticate section defines possible authentication mechanisms. The method actually used for a specific request is determined by the information returned by the authorize section.

Here is the working configuration file for a basic server to authenticate connections against the list of local accounts:

```
## radiusd.conf: FreeRADIUS server configuration file

##
## Global parameters: directory/logfile locations, etc.
##
prefix = /opt/radius
exec_prefix = ${prefix}
sysconfdir = ${prefix}/etc
localstatedir = ${prefix}/var
sbindir = ${exec_prefix}/sbin
logdir = ${localstatedir}/log/radius
raddbdir = ${sysconfdir}/raddb
radacctdir = ${logdir}/radacct
confdir = ${raddbdir}
run_dir = ${localstatedir}/run/radiusd
log_file = ${logdir}/radius.log
libdir = ${exec_prefix}/lib
pidfile = ${run_dir}/radiusd.pid

# CLIENTS CONFIGURATION
$INCLUDE  ${confdir}/clients.conf

##
## MODULE CONFIGURATION
##
modules {

    ## Unix /etc/passwd-style authentication
    unix {
        passwd = /etc/passwd
        shadow = /etc/shadow
        group = /etc/group
        radwtmp = ${logdir}/radwtmp
    }

    ## Local files. The user's file contains a single entry to default all
    ## authentication to the local system.
```

```
##      DEFAULT Auth-Type := System
files {
    usersfile = ${confdir}/users
    acctusersfile = ${confdir}/acct_users
    compat = no
}
}

##
## Authorization: obtain information about the user
##
authorize {
    files
}

##
## Authentication: validate the user request
##
authenticate {
    unix
}
```

To test your server, you must make sure that the following entry is defined in *radiusd*'s *clients.conf* file to allow connections over the loopback interface:

```
## Allow connection requests from localhost.
client 127.0.0.1 {
    secret = testing123
    shortname = localhost
    nastype = other
}
```

You can test your configuration by starting *radiusd* in debug mode. This will produce a large amount of log information printed to standard output.

```
root# radiusd -X -A
<...preceding output omitted...>
Ready to process requests.
```

Using *radtest(1)*, you can verify that the local user *guest1* with password *test1* can be successfully authenticated:

```
$ radtest guest1 test1 localhost 0 testing123
Sending Access-Request of id 50 to 127.0.0.1:1812
    User-Name = "guest1"
    User-Password = "\263\033\037\2760@3\022X\327\334\343\025\265\347}"
    NAS-IP-Address = garion
    NAS-Port = 0
rad_recv: Access-Accept packet from host 127.0.0.1:1812, id=50, length=20
```

Now that you have a working RADIUS configuration, it is time to move on and integrate the new server with your directory.

FreeRadius and OpenLDAP

If you want the RADIUS server to utilize the directory for authentication only, no schema modifications to your existing *LDAP* server are necessary. You can simply use the posixAccount entry for a user, as you did with the ProFTPD server.

The first step is to define the parameters for the rlm_ldap module instance. All of the parameters shown here should be intuitive. The module will perform an anonymous bind to our *LDAP* server and search for a posixAccount entry whose uid attribute matches the username of the connecting user. Once this entry is found, the library will attempt to bind to the directory as the user to verify the user's credentials. All of the communication takes place after the StartTLS command has been executed to ensure privacy.

```
ldap {
    server = "ldap.plainjoe.org"
    port = "389"
    basedn = "ou=people,dc=plainjoe,dc=org"
    filter = "(&(objectclass=posixAccount)(uid=%{Stripped-User-Name:-%{User-Name}}))"
    start_tls = yes
}
```

There are many more parameters that can be defined for the rlm_ldap module. A complete list is given, along with descriptions, in Table 8-4.

Table 8-4. rlm_ldap module parameters

Parameter	Default	Description
access_attr	None	The attribute located below the basedn that must exist in the user's entry. The user is denied access if the attribute is not returned by the initial search.
access_attr_used_for_allow	yes	Controls how the access_attr directive is used. When disabled, the presence of the access_attr in an entry will deny the user access.
basedn	None	Searches base DN.
compare_check_items	no	Specifies whether the module should compare the check items in the RADIUS request with the check items in the directory.
default_profile	None	DN of the entry containing the default RADIUS profile.
dictionary_mapping	{confdir}/ldap.attrmap	Location of the file containing the RADIUS/LDAP attribute mappings.
filter	(uid=%u)	An RFC 2254 search filter.
groupname_attribute	cn	Attribute used when searching for a RADIUS groupname.

Table 8-4. rlm_ldap module parameters (continued)

Parameter	Default	Description
groupmembership_attribute	None	The attribute containing the DN of the group of which the user is a member.
groupmembership_filter	(|(&(objectClass=GroupOfNames)(member=%{LdapUserDn}))(&(objectClass=GroupOfUniqueNames)(uniquemember=%{Ldap-UserDn})))	The RFC 2254 search filter used to query a group for membership.
identify password	None	DN and password to use when performing a nonanonymous bind to the directory server for searches.
ldap_cache_timeout	0	Number of seconds until the LDAP client library cache expires. A setting of 0 disables the cache.
ldap_cache_size	0	The cache size to pass to the LDAP client libraries. A size of 0 specifies an unlimited size.
ldap_connections_number	5	The total number of LDAP connections to maintain for the RADIUS server.
ldap_debug	0	OpenLDAP debug flags (see *slapd.conf*'s loglevel parameter).
net_timeout	10	The number of seconds to wait for a response from the *LDAP* server in the event of a network failure.
password_header	None	Header (such as {CRYPT}) to strip from the beginning of a password before performing a compare operation against checkItems in the request.
password_attribute	None	The name of the attribute containing the password for a user.
port	389	TCP port to use when contacting the directory server.
profile_attribute	None	The attribute containing the DN of the user's radiusprofile object.
server	localhost	Hostname of the *LDAP* server.
start_tls	no	If enabled, the module will send a StartTLS command prior to any other LDAP operations.
timelimit	20	Number of seconds the *LDAP* server has to perform the search (server-side time limit).

Table 8-4. rlm_ldap module parameters (continued)

Parameter	Default	Description
timeout	20	Number of seconds to wait for a response to the LDAP query.
tls_mode	no	If enabled, the module will contact the directory using LDAPS.

The next step required to put this new module instance into play is adding a definition to the authenticate section that can be used as a value for the Auth-Type attribute in the *users* file:

```
authenticate {
    authtype LDAP {
        ldap
    }
}
```

Now you can change the authentication default in *raddb/users* to LDAP:

```
## raddb/users file defined by the files authorize component
##
## Authenticate all users by binding to the LDAP directory.
DEFAULT Auth-Type := LDAP
```

After restarting *radiusd* (again in debug mode), test the new configuration using a preexisting LDAP user entry (uid=kristi and userPassword=testpass):

```
$ ./radtest kristi testpass localhost 0 testing123
Sending Access-Request of id 147 to 127.0.0.1:1812
    User-Name = "kristi"
    User-Password = "1q\325\026\020\315p\214X\310\227\376\014]F\332"
    NAS-IP-Address = garion
    NAS-Port = 0
rad_recv: Access-Accept packet from host 127.0.0.1:1812, id=147, length=20
```

From the client's point of view, nothing appears to be different. The server, however, yields much more information. You should be able to locate a line where the module binds to the directory on behalf of the user.

```
auth: type "LDAP"
modcall: entering group authtype
<...remaining output omitted...>
rlm_ldap: bind as uid=kristi,ou=people,dc=plainjoe,dc=org/test to
ldap.plainjoe.org:389
rlm_ldap: waiting for bind result ...
rlm_ldap: user kristi authenticated successfully
  modcall[authenticate]: module "ldap" returns ok
```

This is definitely the least intrusive way to integrate FreeRadius with an existing directory and will work with any LDAPv3 server. The next step is to use your directory as a data store for the information currently stored in FreeRadius's *users* file. This, however, will require that you learn about some new schema items.

The FreeRadius project provides an LDAP schema file for use with OpenLDAP 2.x servers. The *RADIUS-LDAPv3.schema* file can be found in the *doc/* directory of the FreeRadius source code distribution. The schema defines many new attributes used to store RADIUS attribute values and a single structural object class named radiusprofile, shown in Figure 8-5, which is used to represent RADIUS users. To keep our focus on LDAP and not RADIUS, we will only concern ourselves with how radiusAuthType maps the Auth-Type RADIUS attribute. Descriptions of the other attributes can be found in the RADIUS RFC.

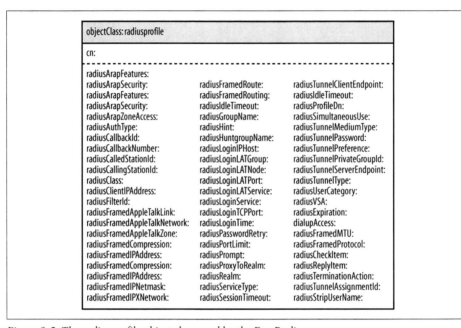

Figure 8-5. The radiusprofile object class used by the FreeRadius server

First, copy the new schema file to */usr/local/etc/openldap/schema/*:

```
root# cp RADIUS-LDAPv3.schema /usr/local/etc/openldap/schema/
```

Next, you must include a reference to this file in *slapd.conf*. Because a radiusprofile object includes the lmPassword and ntPassword attributes from the *samba.schema* file, it must be placed after the latter file has been parsed:

```
## /usr/local/etc/openldap/slapd.conf

## core.schema is required for all servers.
include  /usr/local/etc/openldap/schema/core.schema
```

```
## Included from Chapter 6
include  /usr/local/etc/openldap/schema/cosine.schema
include  /usr/local/etc/openldap/schema/nis.schema

## Included from Chapter 7
include  /usr/local/etc/openldap/schema/inetorgperson.schema

## Dependencies for samba.schema: cosine.schema and inetorgperson.schema needed to
## support --with-ldapsam in Samba
include  /usr/local/etc/openldap/schema/samba.schema

## Support for FreeRadius depends on samba.schema for LM/NT password attributes.
include /usr/local/etc/openldap/schema/RADIUS-LDAPv3.schema
```

The mapping between LDAP attributes and RADIUS attributes is stored in a text file named *ldap.attrmap* by default. Conventionally, this file is stored in the *raddb/* directory, but both the name and location are configurable via the rlm_ldap module's dictionary_mapping parameter. Because we will be using the default schema file, the corresponding attribute dictionary is sufficient. If you decide to use a custom schema, you may have to modify the dictionary as well.

Your next hurdle is decide where to store the radiusprofile entries in the directory. Your first choice might be to store them with the other user account information below the people ou. The problem is that you cannot add the radiusprofile object to your existing users' accounts. You can either change the radiusprofile definition to an auxiliary object or choose to store objects of this type somewhere else. Following the trend of using provided schemas whenever possible, we will create a new organizational unit to hold FreeRadius users and establish a link between the posixAccount and the radiusprofile objects.

First, create a new ou=radius entry below the services ou (created in Chapter 7 for Sendmail):

```
dn: ou=radius,ou=services,dc=plainjoe,dc=org
objectclass: organizationalUnit
ou: radius
```

Next, create a profile for the user *kristi*. The difficulty with this is choosing the RDN for the entry. You have already chosen the uid attribute as the unique naming convention for entries below ou=people. However, the radiusprofile object includes only the cn attribute. The informational RFC 2377 defines an auxiliary uidObject class for situations such as this one. This allows you to include the uid attribute as the RDN for new entries regardless of the structural object class and still maintain your internal naming conventions. You could just use an extensibleObject, but the uidObject is a cleaner approach. Here is the resulting RADIUS user entry:

```
dn: uid=kristi,ou=radius,ou=services,dc=plainjoe,dc=org
objectclass: radiusprofile
objectclass: uidObject
uid: kristi
```

```
cn: Kristi Carter
radiusAuthType: LDAP
```

Finally, link the posixAccount entry for *kristi* to her RADIUS information by storing the DN of the radiusprofile object in uid=kristi,ou=people,dc=plainjoe,dc=org. This time we will use the extensibleObject to add the extra attribute. To make the new attributes easier to see, most of the existing optional attributes have been omitted from this LDIF excerpt. Added attributes are shown in bold.

```
## Existing optional attributes have been omitted from the display.
dn: uid=kristi,ou=people,dc=plainjoe,dc=org
objectClass: inetOrgPerson
objectClass: posixAccount
objectClass: sambaAccount
objectclass: extensibleObject
cn: Kristi Carter
cn: Kristi W. Carter
sn: Carter
loginShell: /bin/bash
uidNumber: 781
gidNumber: 100
homeDirectory: /home/kristi
uid: kristi
rid: 2570
radiusprofileDN: uid=kristi,ou=radius,ou=services,dc=plainjoe,dc=org
```

The two module configuration changes to be made are changing the locations of the dictionary file for LDAP/RADIUS attributes (dictionary_mapping) and specifying the LDAP attribute containing the DN of the user's RADIUS information (profile_attribute):

```
ldap {
    server = "ldap.plainjoe.org"
    port = "389"
    basedn = "ou=people,dc=plainjoe,dc=org"
    filter = "(&(objectclass=posixAccount)(uid=%{Stripped-User-Name:-%{User-Name}}))"
    start_tls = yes

    profile_attribute = "radiusProfileDn"
    dictionary_mapping = ${raddbdir}/ldap.attrmap
}
```

You can now remove the local copy of the *users* file from the RADIUS server and add the ldap module to the authorize block in *radiusd.conf*. The files module is still listed because it also contains directives affecting local accounting policies.

```
##
## Authorization: obtain information about the user
##
authorize {
    files
    ldap
}
```

This example brings up two important points:

- Relationships between entries in a directory can be represented by storing the DNs as reference links.

- Using auxiliary objects such as the uidObject to maintain a standard naming convention can help reduce the management costs associated with locating related entries.

I'll leave it up to you to use the *radtest* tool to verify that the server is working correctly.

Resolving Hosts

Now let's turn our attention to data describing hosts on a network. One of the most fundamental services provided in any TCP/IP network is the resolution of machine names to network addresses. The most widespread mechanism for looking up IP addresses is the Domain Name System (DNS). Again, coverage of DNS is beyond the scope of this book; for more information, see *DNS and BIND*, Fourth Edition, by Cricket Liu and Paul Albitz (O'Reilly).

Chapter 1 already made it clear that LDAP is not a replacement for a specialized directory service such as DNS. However, you can use LDAP effectively as a backend storage system for DNS zone files. Stig Venaas has written such a patch for Bind 9 using its new *simplified database interface* (SDB). The latest release of the patch for BIND 9.1 (or later) and the necessary schema file for OpenLDAP 2 can be obtained from *http://www.venaas.no/ldap/bind-sdb/*. For performance reasons, I recommend that you obtain the latest patch, rather than using the one included in the *contrib/* subdirectory of the latest BIND 9 release.

Venaas has included a brief list of the steps necessary for integrating LDAP-sdb support in Bind 9. Here are the instructions contained in the *INSTALL* file of the ldap-sdb archive:

1. Copy the *ldap.c* source file to the *bin/named/* subdirectory of the BIND 9 source tree.

2. Copy the *ldap.h* header file to the *bin/named/include/* subdirectory of the BIND 9 source tree.

3. Edit *bin/named/Makefile.in* and add the following lines:

   ```
   DDRIVER_OBJS = ldapdb.@O@
   DDRVIVER_SRCS = ldapdb.c
   DDRIVER_LIBS = -lldap -llber
   ```

   The Makefile variables may already exist; if this is the case, simply append the references to the LDAP files to the existing definitions. You may also need to add the path to the LDAP include files and libraries to the *DDRIVER_INCLUDES* and *DDRIVER_LIBS* respectively.

4. Edit *bin/named/main.c* and add the line #include <ldapdb.h> below #include "xxdb.h"; add the line ldapdb_init( ); below xxdb_init( ); and finally, add ldapdb_clear( ); below xxdb_clear( );.

After making these changes, you're ready to build the LDAP-enabled *named* binary by executing ./configure && make && /bin/su -c "make install". It is a good idea to ensure that the new server is working with an existing set of zone files before continuing. Here is a zone file for the *plainjoe.org* domain; it contains four hosts, *localhost*, *dns1*, *ldap*, and *ahab*:

```
plainjoe.org. IN SOA dns1.plainjoe.org. root.dns.plainjoe.org. (
                    3           ; Serial
                    10800       ; Refresh after 3 hours
                    3600        ; Retry after 1 hour
                    604800      ; expire after 1 week
                    86400 )     ; minimum TTL of 1 day
; Name Servers
plainjoe.org.               IN    NS    dns1.plainjoe.org.

; Addresses for local printers
localhost.plainjoe.org.     IN    A     127.0.0.1
dns1.plainjoe.org.          IN    A     192.168.1.10
ldap.plainjoe.org.          IN    A     192.168.1.70
ahab.plainjoe.org.          IN    A     192.168.1.80
```

Figure 8-6 shows the schema for the structural dNSZone object class. This schema allows you to store DNS records in the directory. All of the attributes used to represent the various DNS records (MX, A, PTR, etc.) are optional, which means that a dNSZone entry can represent any type of DNS record.

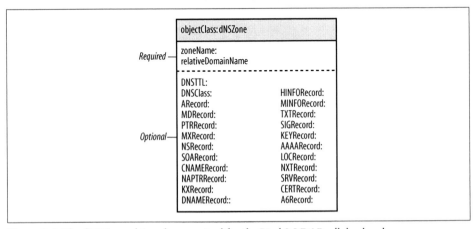

Figure 8-6. The dNSZone object class required for the Bind 9 LDAP-sdb backend

I have chosen to place all *plainjoe.org* hosts in the hosts organizational unit. The following LDIF entry represents the A record for the host *ahab.plainjoe.org*:

```
dn: relativeDomainName=ahab,ou=hosts,dc=plainjoe,dc=org
aRecord: 192.168.1.80
objectClass: dNSZone
relativeDomainName: ahab
dNSTTL: 86400
zoneName: plainjoe.org
```

After placing your DNS zone data into the LDAP directory, you need to tell the *named* server how to locate the zone information. The database keyword specifies the SDB type holding the zone information; in this case, you're using an LDAP database. Any remaining arguments after the database type are passed directly to the SDB backend module. Here, you use an LDAP URI to define the directory server's hostname and the base search suffix. The final number (172800) specifies the default time-to-live (TTL) for entries that do not possess a dNSTTL attribute value.

```
zone "plainjoe.org" in {
    type master;
    database "ldap ldap://192.168.1.70/ou=hosts,dc=plainjoe,dc=org 172800";
};
```

You can now use the *dig* utility to test the new LDAP-served DNS zone. Figure 8-7 describes what will happen when the *dig* or *nslookup* tools are executed.

```
$ dig ahab.plainjoe.org +short
; <<>> DiG 9.1.0 <<>> ahab.plainjoe.org +short
;; global options: printcmd
192.168.1.80
```

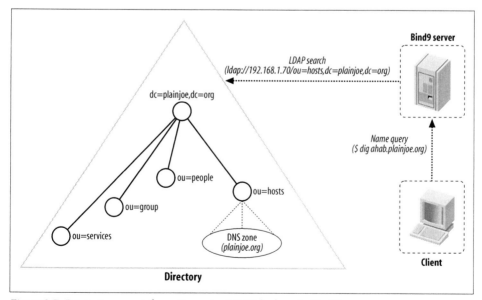

Figure 8-7. Retrieving zone information using LDAP lookups in Bind 9

The *zone2ldap* tool included with the Bind distribution provides a quick way to transfer existing zone files into an LDAP directory. Newer versions of this utility can also be downloaded from Venaas's web site. I decided against using it because it creates an entry for each component of the FQDN for each host. For example, the host *ahab.plainjoe.org* results in three entries: one for dc=org, one for dc=plainjoe,dc=org, and one for relativeDomainName=ahab,dc=plainjoe,dc=org. For more information, refer to the *zone2ldap* manpage.

Central Printer Management

Now that you've moved your DNS zone data into an LDAP directory, you have the leisure to ask, "What's the big deal?" DNS already has highly effective mechanisms for distributing and replicating zone data; it's not like user account data, which needs to be kept consistent on every machine. So have you accomplished anything, aside from being able to point to a directory server that's serving the zone data to your DNS servers? Clearly, you need to be able to justify the effort you've spent, and to do so, you need to find another application that can make use of the same data.

Network printers are devices that are associated with entries in DNS and possess additional attributes used to support a non-DNS application (i.e., printing). Our next step is to design a directory-based solution for managing printer configuration information that simplifies the process of adding, deploying, and retiring printers. A printer should be accessible to its clients as soon as it has been added to the directory. The namespace shown in Figure 8-8 was designed with this philosophy in mind. All printer configuration information is stored below the ou=printers organizational unit. The immediate three children, config, global, and location, are used to group printers and maintain configuration parameters.

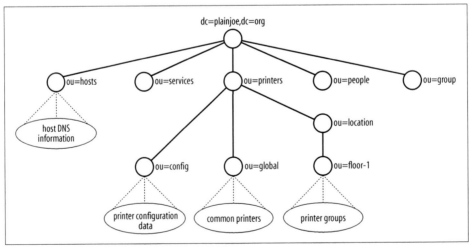

Figure 8-8. LDAP namespace for directory-based storage of printer configuration data

The `config` organizational unit sits at the root of the actual configuration tree. Each printer has an entry containing information such as the printer's name and maximum print job size. For network printers, the entry also contains DNS information, such as IP address and hostname. The `ou=config,ou=printers,dc=plainjoe,dc=org` entry acts as the base suffix for the *lp.plainjoe.org* DNS zone used by your BIND 9 server. This means that if an administrator removes a printer's entry from the `config` organizational unit, it is immediately removed by DNS as well. Devices that are physically connected to a host acting as the spooler are not considered network printers for the purposes of this discussion.

Printers listed beneath the `ou=global` entry should be available to all clients on the network. The entries here contain only a printer's name; the actual configuration data can be accessed by querying for the attributes of `cn=`*printername*`,ou=config,` `ou=printers,dc=plainjoe,dc=org`. The `ou=location` tree has a similar function to the global tree. The `location` organizational unit is a holder for another group of organizational units, one of which is shown in Figure 8-8. Each organizational unit at this level represents a group of printers. Each client on the network can list one or more group names; the clients are then allowed to access the printers in the groups that they have listed.

The major difficulty in dealing with printers is deciding on an acceptable schema for representing printer capabilities and data. Currently, there is no standardized printer schema. The closest we have to a standard is the Internet-Draft *draft-fleming-ldap-printer-schema-XX.txt*. We only need to implement a subset of the schema in this document (see Figure 8-9).* The *printer.schema* file also includes a modified version of the schema presented in *Network Printing*, by Todd Radermacher and Matt Gast (O'Reilly). These additional object classes and attributes support the information needed to generate printcap entries for use with the Berkeley print spooler (LPD) or Patrick Powell's LPRng (*http://www.lprng.com/*).

 The *printer.schema* file should be viewed as an example only. While it can be used in a production directory, my hope is that a final standardized schema will soon be available and supported by printing vendors.

Begin populating the `printers` organizational unit with a simple network printer named hp2100. The `printer-uri` attribute was developed by the IETF's Printer Working Group to represent different printing systems such as *ipp://*, *lpr://*, etc. All of the printers in your directory will use a printer URI of the form *lpr://<printer-name>*. This printer also exists as a host in DNS under the name *hp2100.lp.plainjoe.org*.

---

* The *printer.schema* file is available online at the web site for this book (*http://www.oreilly.com/catalog/ldapsa*).

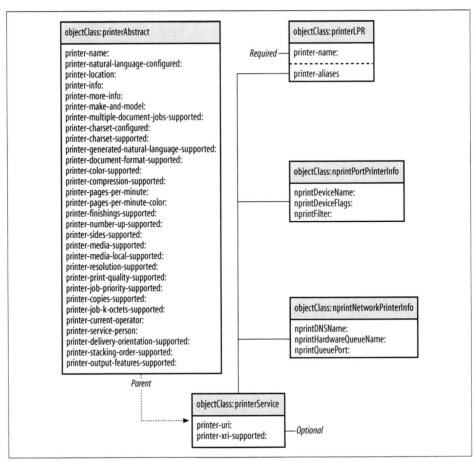

Figure 8-9. The abstract printerAbstract class, structural printerService class, and auxiliary classes printerLPR, nprintPortPrinterInfo, and nprintNetworkPrinterInfo included in the printer.schema file

Immediately, however, we have a problem: the dNSZone and the printerService objects are both structural classes. Luckily, the default Bind 9 LDAP lookups do not use the objectclass value in searches. Therefore, you can use the extensibleObject class in the place of dNSZone. The other solution would be to define a new auxiliary object class that contained all of the attributes contained in a dNSZone object. I choose to use an extensibleObject to prevent the introduction of new schema items into our discussion.

Now that the object class conflict has been resolved, we can return to our discussion of printer attributes. The printer's domain name is stored in the relativeDomainName and zoneName attributes. The printer-name and nprintHardwareQueueName represent the remote machine (rm) and remote printer (rp) printcap variables.

```
dn: printer-uri=lpr://hp2100,ou=config,ou=printers,dc=plainjoe,dc=org
aRecord: 192.168.1.220
printer-name: hp2100
nprintHardwareQueueName: raw
printer-uri: lpr://hp2100
relativeDomainName: hp2100
objectClass: printerService
objectClass: nprintNetworkPrinterInfo
objectClass: extensibleObject
printer-job-k-octets-supported: 10000
zoneName: lp.plainjoe.org
```

You get extra points if you noticed that the nprintDNSName attribute is missing. This attribute doesn't appear because the fully qualified hostname can be determined from the relativeDomainName and zoneName attributes. Because the nprintDNSName serves the same purpose, it can be left out. The script for generating a printcap entry attempts to retrieve the nprintDNSName attribute first; in its absence, the script generates the remote printer's name by concatenating the relativeDomainName and zoneName attribute values.

Your system must be able to represent nonnetworked printers in the same namespace as networked printers. Nonnetworked printers don't have the attributes associated with a dNSZone (replaced by an extensibleObject) that are required to support DNS lookups. Of course, since such an entry describes a nonnetworked device, this detail is of no concern. Here's the LDIF representation of a nonnetworked printer:

```
dn: printer-uri=lpr://bjc240,ou=config,ou=printers,dc=plainjoe,dc=org
printer-name: bjc240
printer-uri: lpr://bjc240
objectClass: printerService
objectClass: printerLPR
objectClass: nprintPortPrinterInfo
nprintDeviceName: /dev/lp0
printer-aliases: canon
```

Directory entries that exist below the ou=global and ou=location roots contain only a printer's name. The next two directory entries state that the printer *hp2100* is available for all network hosts (because it is in the global organizational unit), and the printer *bitsink* is available only to clients within the floor-1 group (because it is in the floor-1 group, which is within the location subtree):

```
dn: printer-name=hp2100,ou=global,ou=printers,dc=plainjoe,dc=org
printer-name: hp2100
objectClass: printerService

dn: printer-name=bitsink,ou=floor-1,ou=location,ou=printers,dc=plainjoe,dc=org
printer-name: bitsink
objectClass: printerService
```

The nprintHostPrinter AUXILIARY object class (see Figure 8-10) allows you to extend an existing entry for a network host to define membership in a printing group, and lets you list any host-specific printers that should be available to users. The entry for workstation *queso.plainjoe.org* associates it with the floor-1 printing group (i.e., ou=floor-1,ou=location,ou=printers,dc=plainjoe,dc=org) and includes a reference to the specific printer named draft-printer:

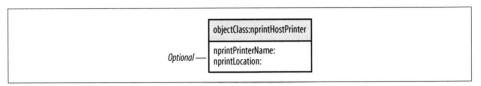

Figure 8-10. nprintHostPrinter object class

```
dn: relativeDomainName=queso,ou=hosts,dc=plainjoe,dc=org
aRecord: 192.168.1.74
nprintLocation: floor-1
objectClass: dNSZone
objectClass: nprintHostPrinter
relativeDomainName: queso
dNSTTL: 86400
nprintPrinterName: draft-printer
zoneName: plainjoe.org
```

Finally, you must be able to retrieve information from the directory and format it in a way that is usable by the local printing system. The *generate_printcap.pl* Perl script supports the *printer.schema* used in this section and generates *printcap* files from the directory that are compatible with the BSD printing system. This script supports the common LDAP searching options, such as the directory server's name and base suffix. The script also accepts the hostname of the client to receive the *printcap* file. Table 8-5 presents the complete set of parameters supported by *generate_printcap.pl*.

Table 8-5. Options to generate_printcap.pl

Parameter	Default	Description
--base	none	The base suffix used when searching the directory
--debug	off	Enables extra debugging output
--help		Summarizes command usage and parameters
--host	$HOSTNAME	The host for which you want to generate the *printcap* file
--printcap	printcap.$HOSTNAME	The name of the generated *printcap* file
--server	localhost	The hostname of the *LDAP* server to query

The following command generates a *printcap* file for *queso.plainjoe.org*, given the directory entries represented by Figure 8-11:

```
$ generate_printcap.pl --host=queso \
  --base="dc=plainjoe,dc=org" \
  --server=ldap.plainjoe.org
```

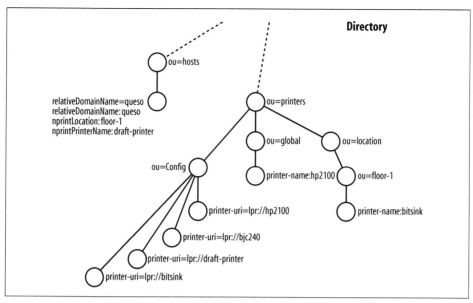

Figure 8-11. Printing information and entries for the host queso.plainjoe.org

```
Searching ou=global,ou=printers,dc=plainjoe,dc=org...
Using entry for "relativeDomainName=queso,ou=hosts,dc=plainjoe,dc=org"
Searching ou=floor-1,ou=location,ou=printers,dc=plainjoe,dc=org...
Finished generating printcap (printcap.queso)
```

generate_printcap.pl uses an anonymous bind when connecting to the *LDAP* server. This means that the OpenLDAP server must be configured with the following access control rule, which allows read-only access to information about printers:

```
access to dn.children="ou=printers,dc=plainjoe,dc=org"
        by * read
```

The resulting *printcap* file is:

```
#
# Printcap file generated automatically on Sun Jan 20 19:33:37 2002 for host queso
#
#######################################################################
# printer-uri=lpr://hp2100,ou=config, ou=printers, dc=plainjoe,dc=org
# objectclass: nprintNetworkPrinterInfo
hp2100:\
     :sh:\
     :mx#10000:\
     :lf=/var/spool/lpd/hp2100/lpd-err:\
     :sd=/var/spool/lpd/hp2100:\
     :lp=/dev/null:\
     :rm=hp2100.lp.plainjoe.org:\
     :rp=raw:
#######################################################################
```

```
##################################################################
# printer-uri=lpr://bitsink,ou=config, ou=printers, dc=plainjoe,dc=org
# objectclass: nprintNetworkPrinterInfo
bitsink:\
     :sh:\
     :mx#0:\
     :lf=/var/spool/lpd/bitsink/lpd-err:\
     :sd=/var/spool/lpd/bitsink:\
     :lp=/dev/null:\
     :rm=bitsink.lp.plainjoe.org:\
     :rp=bitsink:
##################################################################


##################################################################
# printer-uri=lpr://draft-printer,ou=config,ou=printers,dc=plainjoe,dc=org
# objectclass: nprintPortPrinterInfo
draft-printer:\
     :sh:\
     :mx#0:\
     :lf=/var/spool/lpd/draft-printer/lpd-err:\
     :sd=/var/spool/lpd/draft-printer:\
     :lp=/dev/lp0:\
     :sd=/var/spool/lpd/draft-printer:\
     :if=/opt/printers/filters/hpif.sh:
##################################################################
```

The details of writing Perl scripts such as *generate_printcap.pl* to manage information in an LDAP directory using the Net::LDAP module will be presented in Chapter 10.

Whenever you're trying to integrate network services into LDAP, remember to focus on reduction of data. Storing information in a directory has no benefit by itself; it is only worthwhile if it decreases the cost of managing the data (i.e., makes life easier for you and the people you work with). If data is used only by a single application on a single host, the information could be kept in a local database file just as easily. However, if the information is needed by several services on multiple hosts, as with user accounts or printer settings, storing the information in an LDAP directory reduces the cost of updating data by ensuring that each change needs to be made only once.

## CHAPTER 9

LDAP Interoperability

What is a chapter on interoperability doing in a book on LDAP? After all, I've presented LDAP throughout this book as a standard protocol, and standards are supposed to minimize, if not eliminate, interoperability problems. One of the major selling points of LDAP is its potential for consolidating vendor-specific or application-specific directories. We've seen many examples of this: using LDAP as a replacement for NIS, as a backend data store for DNS, and as a replacement for many ad hoc databases used in email management.

Still, while LDAP minimizes interoperability problems, "minimize" is definitely the key word. The core features of LDAP are standardized, but things such as schemas are not. There are many common object classes and attributes that can be extended by a vendor. Not only can schemas be extended, the protocol can be extended as well by creating additional operations using extensions and controls, and not all vendors support the same ones.

For each service that can be consolidated into an LDAP directory, there must be a corresponding client-side application that can access the old information in the new directory. That's not always an easy order to fill; we've already seen some clever workarounds to help older applications access an LDAP directory, such as using the pam_ldap library presented in Chapter 6 to enable non-LDAP–aware applications to authenticate users in the directory. Furthermore, sooner or later you will encounter an LDAP-enabled application that requires the directory service to implement a specific schema or extended operation.

The goal of this chapter is to discuss several technologies that you can use to solve problems of this sort. Every directory integration project is unique. I will show how to solve a number of common directory integration problems—and although the problems I discuss are typical enough, they're only a small fraction of the problems you're likely to face. The most effective way to prepare yourself to solve the problems posed by your environment is to examine the tools, concepts, and architectures that can be combined into a solution to meet the needs of your users.

Interoperability or Integration?

The terms interoperability and integration each have a different place within our coverage of LDAP. For our purposes, directory integration means enabling client applications to access data in an LDAP directory, a topic that has been covered extensively in previous chapters. Interoperability should address communication between LDAP servers themselves. The distinction between integration and interoperability begins to blur when one LDAP server becomes the client of another LDAP server.

Whenever you start thinking about interoperability or integration, your first step should be to ask what level of interoperability or integration your application requires. There are a number of solutions that provide interoperability or integration in various forms. Knowing what your application requires will make it much easier to decide which solution is appropriate. Table 9-1 lists some common approaches to interoperability and integration issues.

Table 9-1. Common directory interoperability solutions

Problem	Possible solution	Example
"What can I do if my application doesn't speak LDAP?"	Gateways that translate one directory access protocol into another	The NIS/LDAP gateway presented in Chapter 6
"How can users in a non-Unix administrative domain access services on Unix hosts?"	Cross-platform authentication services	Authenticating non-Microsoft clients against an active directory
"How can I join information contained in different directories?"	Distributed, multivendor directories glued together by referrals and references	Connecting directories from different vendors into a single DIT
"How can I unify access to the databases and directories held by multiple departments in my organization?"	Metadirectories that provide an integrated view of several disjointed directories and databases	Using an LDAP proxy server to translate entries from a second directory into the format needed by client applications
"How can I implement replication or synchronization between directories from different vendors?"	Push/pull agents that synchronize information from one directory to another	Customizing scripts or in-house tools that suck data from one server and uploading it to another directory after translating it into a format understood by the second server

This chapter examines ways to implement each approach. No single approach is a solution in and of itself; they're tools that you can use to assemble a solution that works in your environment. My intent, therefore, is to spur your imagination and introduce you to the different types of glue that are available for coordinating directory services.

Directory Gateways

Gateways are not a new concept; we've seen gateways between different email formats, different network filesystems, and so on for years. When building a gateway for directory services, one directory protocol is used as the frontend (the "face" presented to application clients). Another protocol is used between the gateway and the backend storage mechanism. The irony of using a directory gateway to unify access to an LDAP server is that LDAP itself was originally designed as a gateway protocol for X.500.

PADL's *ypldapd* daemon, presented in Chapter 6, is an example of a gateway between NIS and LDAP. Packages such as *ypldapd* tend to do one thing and do it well. In many respects, such a gateway can simply be viewed as another LDAP client. The gateway consumes LDAP information and makes that information available to its clients through another protocol.

Another example of an NIS/LDAP gateway is the NIS service distributed with Microsoft's "Windows Services for Unix (SFU)." This Active Directory add-on provides tools for importing data from a NIS domain into Active Directory. Once NIS data has been incorporated into Active Directory, SFU can provide services for NIS clients from the Active Directory domain. For more information on the SFU product, see *http://www.microsoft.com/windows/sfu/*.

The main advantage of using a gateway is that you usually don't have to modify any clients. This alone can save a great deal in the cost of administration. The disadvantage of using a gateway is that translating requests and replies from one protocol to the other requires additional overhead. Furthermore, clients can't take full advantage of the LDAP directory service; they're limited to the services offered by the gateway. In many environments, these disadvantages are relatively minor.

Cross-Platform Authentication Services

Cross-platform authentication is a term heard most often in IT departments that want to authenticate logons to Unix services using Microsoft's Active Directory,* or authenticate logons to Windows clients using a Unix-based LDAP server. In this scenario, we're not interested in interoperability between directory services, but between a specific directory service and nonnative clients (for example, Active Directory and Unix clients).

---

* Active Directory can be described as a network operating system (NOS) directory service that uses LDAPv3 as its primary access protocol and is, along with Kerberos 5, the major piece of Microsoft's larger domain infrastructure model. So while it is possible to use Active Directory as a vanilla LDAP directory service, I have never encountered a network that used Active Directory without a specific need for integration with other Microsoft technologies. More information about Active Directory can be found at *http://www.microsoft.com/ad* and in *Windows 2000 Active Directory Services* (O'Reilly).

Cross-platform authentication is the Holy Grail for many administrators, not just those dealing with Microsoft operating systems. Novell's eDirectory (formally called NDS) is available on a variety of platforms, including Windows, Linux, and Solaris. Novell provides tools such as a PAM module for NDS to integrate host authentication services with their directory. However, while Microsoft does provide some tools and sample source code for integrating Unix clients into an Active Directory domain (*http://msdn.microsoft.com/library/en-us/dnactdir/html/kerberossamp.asp*), there is currently no way to implement an Active Directory domain using non-Microsoft servers and technologies.

In all fairness, Microsoft's small offering of packages for Unix servers does not prevent Unix clients from using the user and group account information stored in an Active Directory domain. There are at least three methods for using Active Directory to authenticate Unix requests:

- The NIS/Active Directory gateway included in Microsoft's "Services for UNIX" package allows Unix clients to access information stored in Active Directory. We discussed this product briefly in the previous section.

- PADL's PAM and NSS LDAP libraries can act as a proxy server between the Unix services and Active Directory. The modules map attributes and object classes stored in Active Directory to something more suitable for consumption by Unix applications.

- Active Directory domains use Kerberos 5 for authenticating users. Interoperability between the implementations of Kerberos on Windows and other platforms is better than you might expect, but perhaps not as good as you would hope.

The remainder of this section examines the PAM/NSS solution in depth. At the end of this section, we'll discuss how to use Kerberos to enhance interoperability between OpenLDAP and Active Directory. The examples use a single Active Directory domain with the name *ad.plainjoe.org* using the default options provided by the *dcpromo* installation process. The domain name implies that the domain naming context is dc=ad,dc=plainjoe,dc=org.

Chapter 6 covered how to install and configure the PADL libraries with an OpenLDAP server supporting the RFC 2307 (NIS) schema. Using these modules to access information held by an Active Directory server is almost the same. The pam_ldap library requires no additional compilation options for Active Directory support. The changes are solely to the module's configuration file.

The following excerpt from */etc/ldap.conf* provides the module with the information it needs to contact the Active Directory server. For those unfamiliar with the Active Directory namespace, by default all users and groups are stored in the cn=Users container directly below the top-level entry in the domain. Therefore, if the default container is used, a one-level search beginning at cn=Users,dc=ad,dc=plainjoe,dc=org should be sufficient to locate any user or group in an Active Directory domain:

```
## /etc/ldap.conf for PADL pam_ldap and nss_ldap libraries
##
## Define the hostname of the Windows Domain Controller to contact.
host            windc.ad.plainjoe.org

## Active Directory does support LDAPv2, but make v3 the default.
ldap_version    3

## Users and groups are stored one level below this entry in the directory.
base            cn=users,dc=ad,dc=plainjoe,dc=org
scope           one
```

With a default installation, the PAM library searches the directory using the filter (&(objectclass=posixAccount)(uid=%s)), in which %s is expanded to the login name entered by the user. By default, Active Directory does not support the posixAccount object class or the uid attribute. To work around this, you need to develop a different search filter that can successfully locate users in an Active Directory domain.

User accounts in Active Directory are represented by the user object class; the login name is stored with the sAMAccountName attribute. Therefore, an appropriate filter for this application is (&(objectclass=user)(sAMAccountName=%s)), and you can apply this filter by setting the pam_filter and pam_login_attribute parameters as follows:

```
pam_filter           (objectclass=user)
pam_login_attribute  sAMAccountName
```

Finally, you must tell pam_ldap how to change the user's password in Active Directory. The pam_ldap library provides support for changing passwords in a variety of directory servers, including the SunOne server, the password modify extended operation (RFC 3062), Novell's NDS, and Microsoft's Active Directory. The pam_password parameter decides which mechanism is selected. By specifying the ad password change mechanism, you allow users to update their Windows password using a PAM-aware application such as Linux's */usr/bin/passwd*:

```
pam_password         ad
```

Be aware that this setting does not affect how the actual authentication is done; Chapter 6 describes the authentication process. To summarize, the PAM library performs these steps:

1. It requests an entry matching the search filter from the directory server.

2. It attempts to bind to the directory server using the DN of the returned entry and the clear text of the password.

 SASL support in pam_ldap, both for searching and for user authentication, is planned for a future release.

Step 1 is a problem because by default Active Directory does not allow LDAP clients to make anonymous searches for user or group account information. There are several ways around this problem. One solution is to specify values for the binddn and bindpw parameters in /etc/ldap.conf. Because this file must be readable by all users on the system, the account credentials stored in the configuration file will be exposed to anyone who can log onto the host. You will have to be the judge of how this security concern will impact your network. A second solution is to allow anonymous searches of specific attributes within Active Directory. This has the same effect on pam_ldap as defining an account to use when searching the Active Directory domain, but now anyone can search for usernames using basic LDAP requests. I'll cover both methods for the sake of completeness, even though allowing anonymous access to Active Directory is often avoided by administrators.

To relax the access control lists on users and groups within Active Directory, launch the Active Directory Users and Computers administration tool. To view the properties of the Users container, right-click on the Users icon and select Properties... from the menu that appears (see Figure 9-1).

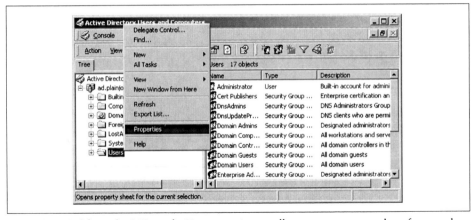

Figure 9-1. Modifying the ACL on the Users container to allow anonymous searches of user and group names

Next, move to the security tab of the resulting dialog box and select the Advanced button. You need to add three entries to the access control list, as shown in Figure 9-2:

- The Everyone group requires the List Contents permission on the User container itself.

- The Everyone group requires the ability to read certain properties of User objects. This permission should apply to the User container and all of its children.

- The Everyone group requires the ability to read certain properties of Group objects. This permission should apply to the User container and all of its children.

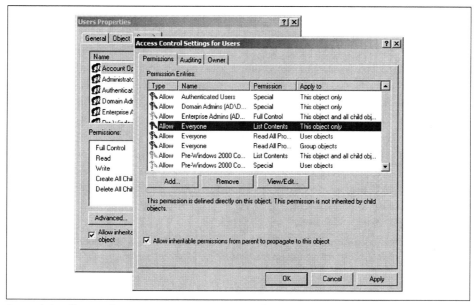

Figure 9-2. Allowing the Everyone group access to read user attributes

To simplify this exercise, the Everyone group has been given the permission to read all properties for a user. This list can be shortened to the attributes that compose an entry in the *passwd(5)* file (the actual password is not needed). Again, you will have to judge whether this fits within the boundaries of your network security policies. Note that Read All Properties does not include the permission to read a user's password anonymously.

Enabling anonymous access frequently leaves a bad taste in the mouths of Active Directory admins. Because of this, you should choose to use an account named *padl* for searching the directory. This user account was created using normal means with the default set of security policies. Now, you must add the directives in *ldap.conf* for binding to the Active Directory server:

```
## Bind as the user padl in the ad.plainjoe.org domain
binddn    cn=padl,cn=Users,dc=ad,dc=plainjoe,dc=org
bindpw    padl-secret
```

Now that pam_ldap can locate the DN for an account using a search based on the sAMAccountName attribute, it is time to move on to the second problem: the PAM library currently sends the user (and binddn) credentials in clear text. The obvious solution to this problem is to use SSL to secure the information in transit.

Active Directory on a Windows 2000 server does not implement the StartTLS extended operation for negotiating a secure transport layer,* but it does support the

---

* The Windows 2003 Server release due in April 2003 reportedly supports the StartTLS extension.

LDAPS protocol on port 636. There are two preconditions for implementing this solution:

- The Windows Active Directory server must support 128-bit encryption. If you're using Windows 2000, you can obtain 128-bit encryption by installing the high-encryption version of the latest service pack. See *http://www.microsoft.com/ windows2000/downloads/servicepacks/* for details on obtaining and installing Windows 2000 updates.

- The Active Directory server must have been issued a digital certificate. Our network will use the Certificate Authority (CA) included with the Windows 2000 Advanced Server OS. For more details on installing the Windows 2000 Certificate Authority, refer to the Windows 2000 Resource Kit online at *http:// www.microsoft.com/windows2000/techinfo/reskit/en-us/default.asp*.

 After installing the Windows Certificate Authority, reboot the server before attempting to connect using the LDAPS protocol.

After the directory server has been configured to support LDAPS, add the following lines to */etc/ldap.conf*:

```
## Instruct pam_ldap and nss_ldap to use LDAPS when connecting to the directory.
ssl       on
port      636
```

By default, pam_ldap does not verify the LDAP server's certificate (see the tls_ checkpeer parameter from Chapter 6). For our purposes, that's acceptable.

 The OpenLDAP 2.1 client tools will fail if the server's certificate cannot be verified. This can result in some strange problems if you are using *ldapsearch* to issue queries to Active Directory. To work around this problem, place the following line in the OpenLDAP client library configuration file (*/usr/local/etc/openldap/ldap.conf*):

```
TLS_REQCERT never
```

At this point, the Unix client can potentially validate connection requests for a PAM-enabled service using Active Directory. However, as we saw in Chapter 6, PAM and NSS solutions are often implemented together. Next you must configure the nss_ldap module to retrieve Unix account information from Active Directory, in combination with using pam_ldap for authentication. The problem you need to deal with this time is that Active Directory does not normally maintain any attributes related to Unix accounts.

The exception to this rule is the NIS server included in Microsoft's SFU. To support NIS clients, the SFU installation process modifies the Active Directory schema to include attributes and object classes for storing information such as Unix user and group identifiers (numeric UIDs and GIDs), Unix-style home directory paths, and

Unix login shells. So you can extend the Active Directory schema by installing the SFU package, and using the schema it provides—even if you don't intend to use Microsoft's NIS server itself.

Another approach is to extend the Active Directory schema yourself. After all, it's really just another LDAPv3 server. The AD4Unix plugin developed by CSS Solutions (*http://www.css-solutions.ca/ad4unix/*) allows you to manage Unix-related attributes using the standard "Active Directory Users and Computers" Microsoft Management Console (MMC) interface. The MKSADExtPlugin extension is freely distributed in binary form as a Windows Installer (MSI) package. The installation process gives you the opportunity to import the SFU schema without installing SFU itself.

 Modifying the schema of an Active Directory forest should not be taken lightly. Once you've extended the schema, you cannot remove any of the new classes or attributes. Make sure to back up the directory server before proceeding.

Active Directory designates one domain controller as the schema master; all schema changes must take place on this server. In order for the MKSADExtPlugin installer to import the schema changes, two conditions must be met:

- The user attempting the schema update must be a member of the Schema Admins group.
- The domain controller serving as the Schema Master must be configured to allow schema changes.

By default, a Windows 2000 Active Directory installation does not allow the schema to be modified; this limitation has been removed in Windows 2003. To change this setting, you must register and open the "Active Directory Schema" MMC snap-in. To register the snap-in with the operating system, execute the following command on the domain controller:

```
C:\WINNT\System32\> regsvr32.exe schmmgmt.dll
```

The Active Directory Schema snap-in should now appear in the list of available modules for the MMC. After opening the MMC application and adding the schema management tool, as shown in Figure 9-3, you can access the Change Schema Master dialog window by selecting the Operations Master... option from the right-click context menu on the Active Directory Schema icon. Check the box that determines whether the schema may be modified.

Now that the directory server is configured to access the imported schema, the MKSADExtPlugin installation process can begin. You may see messages about components being successfully registered. These are normal and can be safely ignored.

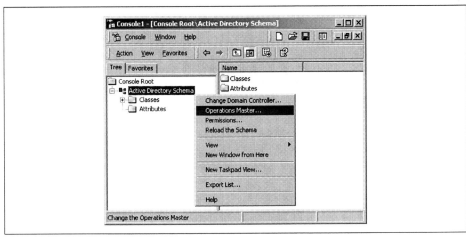

Figure 9-3. Using the "Active Directory Schema" MMC snap-in

When the Windows Installer has completed, you will see the configuration tool for MKSADExtPlugin's general settings under the Start menu. This application, shown in Figure 9-4, allows you to specify a range of numeric UIDs and GIDs that are automatically allocated to Active Directory users and groups as necessary. These IDs are allocated by the snap-in but can be set manually. The "Allowed NIS" field defines the syncNisDomain attribute for a user. This attribute is provided for the SFU NIS server and is not needed by either *pam_ldap* or *nss_ldap*. However, unless a user is placed in one of the listed NIS domains, the remaining Unix attributes will not be available, as shown in the user properties dialog in Figure 9-5.

Back on the Unix side, the NSS library can handle the AD/SFU schema only if it is compiled with the *--enable-schema-mapping* option. The *--enable-rfc2307bis* option is frequently used in combination with schema mapping to define individual suffixes for the various NSS databases such as *passwd* and *netgroup*. The installation steps now become:

```
$ ./configure --enable-schema-mapping --enable-rfc2307bis
$ make
$ /bin/su -c "make install"
```

The */etc/nsswitch.conf* file should include the settings used in the earlier discussion of nss_ldap (see Chapter 6):

```
## Portion of /etc/nsswitch.conf needed to support LDAP lookups in AD
passwd: files ldap
shadow: files ldap
group:  files ldap
```

Since pam_ldap and nss_ldap share a common configuration file, setting up the latter doesn't require much effort. The nss_ldap library must be instructed to map necessary attribute and object class names on the AD server to a member of the RFC

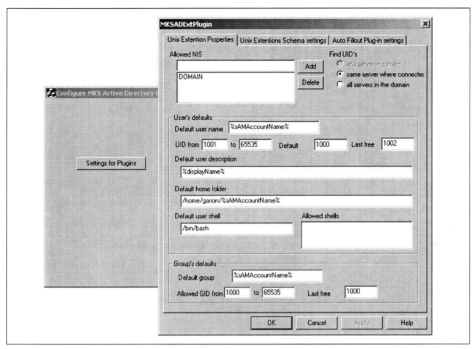

Figure 9-4. The AD4Unix configuration application

2307 schema commonly used to represent Unix service information. To do this, use the nss_map_attribute and nss_map_objectclass parameters:

```
## Excerpt from /etc/ldap.conf
## <...other parameters not shown...>
## Map AD attributes and objectclasses to ones expected by nss_ldap.
nss_map_objectclass    posixAccount      User
nss_map_objectclass    shadowAccount     User
nss_map_attribute      uid               sAMAccountName
nss_map_attribute      uniqueMember      Member
nss_map_attribute      homeDirectory     msSFUHomeDirectory
nss_map_objectclass    posixGroup        Group
nss_map_attribute      gecos             name
```

Certain attributes, such as the uidNumber and gidNumber, are not mentioned in the configuration file. If a mapping is not defined for an attribute or an object class, nss_ldap assumes that the attribute has the same name in the directory. If you browse the directory using the Active Directory Schema snap-in, you can verify that these two attributes are included in the SFU schema.

It is time to test the configuration. Start by configuring a user named *kristi* in Active Directory. Next, verify that this user has been assigned to an NIS domain and that the appropriate Unix attributes have been stored in the directory (refer to Figure 9-5 for an example). The client on which the PADL libraries have been installed should

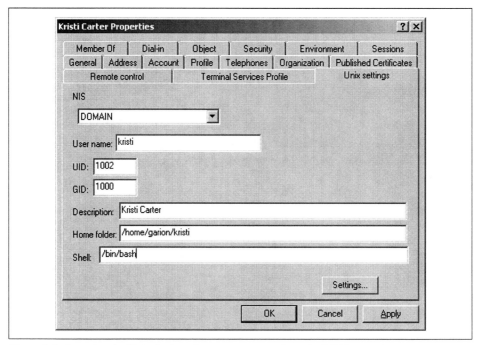

Figure 9-5. Accessing the Unix Settings for a user account from the MMC snap-in

be able to map the Active Directory user *kristi* to a valid Linux user using the *getent* tool:

```
$ getent passwd kristi
kristi:x:1002:1000:Kristi Carter:/home/garion/kristi:/bin/bash
```

To test the PAM portion of this setup on a Linux host, define the following *auth* section for the OpenSSH service in */etc/pam.d/sshd*. The modules are stacked so that if a user can be validated by Active Directory, the authentication test returns succes:

```
## Portion of /etc/pam.d/sshd
##
## If a user can be authenticated using LDAP, that is enough.
auth   required    /lib/security/pam_env.so
auth   sufficient  /lib/security/pam_ldap.so
auth   sufficient  /lib/security/pam_unix.so use_first_pass likeauth
auth   required    /lib/security/pam_deny.so
```

The Active Directory user *kristi* should be able to log onto the Linux host (*garion*) using the Active Directory password associated with her account:

```
$ ssh kristi@garion
kristi@garion's password:
Last login: Sat Oct  5 20:29:14 2002 from ahab.plainjoe.org

[kristi@garion kristi]$ id
uid=1002(kristi) gid=1000(Domain Users) groups=1000(Domain Users)
```

If anything fails at this point, here are some items to check:

- Ensure that both the users and group containers can be searched using the account specified by the `binddn` in */etc/ldap.conf*, or that the containers allow for anonymous searches

- If the LDAPS protocol is suspect, verify that everything works as expected with `ssl no` in */etc/ldap.conf*. If this works, verify that the Active Directory server has a valid certificate. When all else fails, use a network-monitoring tool such as Ethereal, or run OpenLDAP's *ldapsearch* with a debug value of -1 to isolate the point of failure in the SSL negotiation.

- Verify that the `gidNumber` on the Unix Settings tab of the account properties can be resolved to a real group in Active Directory.

- Follow the PAM and NSS troubleshooting tips provided in Chapter 6.

A Short Discussion About Kerberos

No discussion of Active Directory authentication or interoperability would be complete without at least some mention of Microsoft's Kerberos 5 implementation, and how well it plays with other Kerberos distributions, such as the one from MIT. Microsoft has provided a white paper at *http://www.microsoft.com/windows2000/techinfo/planning/security/kerbsteps.asp* on the varying levels of trust that can be achieved between Active Directory and MIT Kerberos realms. If Kerberos is new to you, the following web sites provide general information on its protocol and how it works:

- The MIT Kerberos Project, *http://web.mit.edu/kerberos/www/*

- Windows 2000 Kerberos Authentication, *http://www.microsoft.com/TechNet/prodtechnol/windows2000serv/deploy/kerberos.asp*

Why is Kerberos mentioned in a chapter on directory interoperability? Because one of the first, and sometime the most difficult, hurdles in directory interoperability is being able to access information without having to remember which username and password goes with which service. While this isn't an interoperability problem in the strict sense, practically speaking, your directory isn't worth much if it makes things harder for you and your users. When Active Directory is part of the equation, there are two scenarios for using Kerberos authentication:

- Have the non-Microsoft clients use a Windows Kerberos authentication service (AS) for authentication.

- Establish a trust relationship between the Active Directory domain and a non-Microsoft Kerberos realm.

To implement the first solution, you can use PAM modules that support Kerberos tickets, or you can have the Unix service function as a service principal in the Active Directory domain. The second solution is feasible only if an existing Kerberos realm is in place.

I won't describe how to implement either of these solutions in detail because many of Microsoft's applications have not been kerberized. For example, it would be convenient to search an OpenLDAP server from Microsoft Outlook running on a member of an Active Directory domain without having to define an OpenLDAP-specific login name/password combination. However, there's no configuration that allows current versions of Outlook to use the GSSAPI SASL mechanism to authenticate when connecting to an OpenLDAP server.* Perhaps things will be easier in the future. For now, Kerberos may or may not help in your directory interoperability needs. You will have to test and decide for yourself.

Distributed, Multivendor Directories

Standard protocols go a long way to promote interoperability. While the schema for representing an LDAP referral can vary from vendor to vendor, the method of returning referral information to clients is defined as part of the core LDAPv3 protocol. This means that LDAP servers from various vendors can be linked into a single, logical, distributed directory.

But why go through all the trouble of building a multivendor directory? Why not settle on a single LDAP vendor, who has no doubt made it easy to build distributed directories by developing schemas to represent referrals and solving other problems that aren't addressed by the standards? And, as I've said elsewhere, we shouldn't use technologies just because they're there; if LDAP doesn't make life easier for us as administrators, and for the users of our systems, there's little point going through the effort of setting up an LDAP directory at all, let alone a distributed, multivendor directory.

However, sooner or later a single-vendor directory will force you to make decisions that you're uncomfortable with. Let's assume that you're adding a new application server, such as a calendaring system, at your site. This server is backed by an LDAP directory and requires certain protocol extensions from the directory. Naturally, the vendor has tested the application server with a particular LDAP server in mind—perhaps the vendor even sells an LDAP product (which, of course, is guaranteed to work with the calendar server). But as fate would have it, you've already invested a lot of time and effort in building an LDAP directory, and the directory server that supports

---

* The Kerberos administrators have confirmed that they can't come up with a working configuration, either.

the calendar server is not the directory server you've spent so much effort deploying. In this case, there are three possible solutions:

- Abandon the calendar server, since it is not supported by your existing LDAP server. However, you're probably installing the server because management wants you to do so; saying no probably isn't an option.

- Replace the existing directory with one that supports the calendar service. This solution probably doesn't involve throwing out all the work you did getting your directory service running—but you will have to redo a lot of it. And what happens the next time you're told to install an application that talks to an LDAP server? Will it be compatible with the server you've installed for the sake of the calendar service? It's clear that this isn't really an option, unless you want to spend your career playing "musical servers."

- Install a new LDAP server that supports the calendar application and include it as a subtree of your existing directory framework.

The last option is really the only option that makes sense. It allows you to augment, rather than replace, the directory infrastructure you've already built. Furthermore, sooner or later you will be forced to incorporate different LDAP servers into your network. The goal of standardization is to enable clients developed by one company to access servers developed by another; and even if this is presently a goal rather than a reality, your life will be easier if you work with this goal in mind.

The addition of a new vendor-dependent, LDAP-enabled application raises an important question: how is this solution any different than the myriad of application-specific directories of the past? The difference here is that there is a single access protocol for all clients and administration tools. The LDAP protocol is the unifying factor. While you still have applications that can talk only to a particular vendor's server, the common LDAP protocol allows you to integrate that LDAP server with the other servers on the network.

The remainder of this section explores this solution by presenting a scenario in which an OpenLDAP server is connected to an Active Directory installation. The goal is to create a virtual directory in which a user can search for an entry anywhere by querying either of the directory services, without regard for which directory holds the information. Figure 9-6 shows what we're trying to achieve.

For this exercise, you can assume the following facts:

- A working OpenLDAP has been configured with the naming context of dc=plainjoe,dc=org on the host *ldap.plainjoe.org*.

- An Active Directory domain has been created for the DNS domain *ad.plainjoe.org*. Therefore, the Active Directory LDAP service will have a naming context of dc=ad,dc=plainjoe,dc=org.

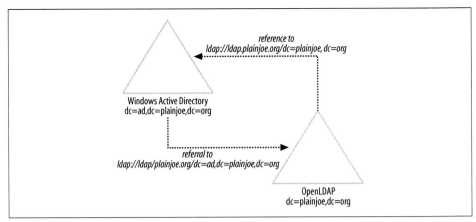

Figure 9-6. Creating a single LDAP directory using a OpenLDAP and Active Directory

You need to add two knowledge references to this system. The first will point from the Active Directory service to the OpenLDAP server; the second will refer client searches from the OpenLDAP directory to the Active Directory domain.

The ADSI Edit MMC snap-in is needed to add an LDAP referral to Active Directory. This low-level, directory-browsing utility is included in *\SUPPORT\TOOLS* on the Windows 2000 Advanced Server CD. Once the support tools have been installed (using *setup.exe*), the ADSI Edit icon should appear in the Start Menu (Start → Programs → Windows 2000 Support Tools → Tools → ADSI Edit).

The referral from the Active Directory domain to the OpenLDAP server must be created inside the `cn=Partitions,cn=Configuration,dc=ad,dc=plainjoe,dc=org` container. This directory entry is the root for all entries possessing referrals to subdomains in an Active Directory tree, as well as external referrals explicitly added by an administrator. After launching the ADSI Edit tool and navigating to the Partitions container, as illustrated in Figure 9-7, create a new `crossRef` object by right clicking within the list of existing entries and selecting the New → Object… variable from the context menu.

A Create Object wizard helps you fill in the information for the object class's mandatory attributes. The following LDIF excerpt shows what you're trying to accomplish: you need to add a node named OpenLDAP with an `nCName` attribute that has the value `dc=plainjoe,dc=org`, and a `dnsRoot` attribute that has the value `ldap.plainjoe.org`:

```
dn: cn=OpenLDAP,cn=Partitions,dc=Configuration,dc=ad,dc=plainjoe,dc=org
cn: OpenLDAP
nCName: dc=plainjoe,dc=org
dnsRoot: ldap.plainjoe.org
```

This new entry instructs the Active Directory server to return a referral of the form `ldap://ldap.plainjoe.org/dc=plainjoe,dc=org` to clients in response to an LDAP search.

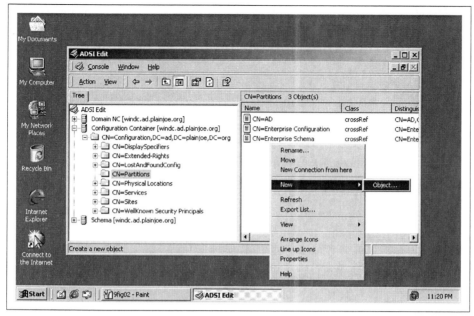

Figure 9-7. Creating a new crossRef object in the Partitions container of an Active Directory domain

Next, a corresponding knowledge reference must be added to the OpenLDAP server. This reference must point to the Active Directory domain. The following LDIF excerpt shows the reference you need to add to the OpenLDAP server:

```
dn: dc=ad,dc=plainjoe,dc=org
objectclass: referral
objectclass: dcObject
ref: ldap://ad.plainjoe.org/dc=ad,dc=plainjoe,dc=org
dc: ad
```

You can use *ldapadd* to add this entry. Assuming that the LDIF code is in the file *ad-referral.ldif*, the following command will do the trick:

```
$ ldapadd -D "cn=Manager,dc=plainjoe,dc=org" -w secret -x \
  -H ldap://ldap.plainjoe.org/ -f ad-referral.ldif
```

The ref attribute in the new entry requires that the *ad.plainjoe.org* DNS name resolve to a domain controller in the Active Directory domain. The AUXILIARY dcObject object class is included out of convention and due to a choice of RDN attributes for the entry.

The two directories are now linked in such a way that an LDAP query sent to one directory should be able to locate data stored in the other directory. To test this, start by sending an anonymous search to an Active Directory domain controller and looking for data that's stored in OpenLDAP. To do this, use OpenLDAP's *ldapsearch* command:

```
$ ldapsearch -H ldap://ad.plainjoe.org/ -x \
    -b "ou=people,dc=plainjoe,dc=org" -LLL "(uid=jerry)"

Referral (10)
Additional information: 0000202B: RefErr: DSID-031005EE, data 0, 1 access points
        ref 1: 'ldap.plainjoe.org'

Referral: ldap://ldap.plainjoe.org/ou=people,dc=plainjoe,dc=org
```

You get a referral from the Active Directory server, but you don't get any actual results: this search does not follow the referral. To see the actual results, you can perform the same search, but use the -C option to instruct the LDAP client libraries to follow the referral and print out the final results:

```
$ ldapsearch -h ad.plainjoe.org -x -C \
    -b "ou=people,dc=plainjoe,dc=org" -LLL "(uid=jerry)"

dn: cn=Gerald Carter,ou=people,dc=plainjoe,dc=org
objectClass: posixAccount
objectClass: account
objectClass: sambaAccount
cn: Gerald Carter
uidNumber: 780
uid: jerry
gidNumber: 100
homeDirectory: /home/queso/jerry
loginShell: /bin/bash
rid: 2560
acctFlags: [UX        ]
pwdLastSet: 1018451245
```

What about making a search that goes in the other direction? Can you send a search to OpenLDAP looking for data stored in Active Directory? The answer is yes, but with the same caveat that was mentioned when using pam_ldap to authenticate services against an Active Directory domain. By default, Active Directory does not support searches using an anonymous bind, except for its rootDSE. Therefore, an attempt to locate a user named *kristi* in the Active Directory domain without using some valid credentials in the bind would return only a referral to the Active Directory server itself. Login names in Active Directory are stored under the sAMAccountName attribute.

```
$ ldapsearch -x -H ldap://ldap.plainjoe.org/ \
    -b "dc=ad,dc=plainjoe,dc=org" -LLL -C "(sAMAccountName=kristi)"

# refldap://ad.plainjoe.org/CN=Configuration,DC=ad,DC=plainjoe,DC=org
```

This referral was returned by the Active Directory server itself because you did not provide valid credentials for searching deeper in the directory tree. If you would like to convince yourself that the OpenLDAP server is returning the correct referral, simply rerun the search without the -C argument:

```
$ ldapsearch -H ldap://ldap.plainjoe.org/ -x \
  -b "dc=ad,dc=plainjoe,dc=org" -LLL "(sAMAccountName=kristi)"

Referral (10)
Matched DN: dc=ad,dc=plainjoe,dc=org
Referral: ldap://ad.plainjoe.org/dc=ad,dc=plainjoe,dc=org??sub
```

To search Active Directory fully, you must employ some type of trust mechanism (e. g., Kerberos cross-realm trusts) or single-signon solution between the two LDAP servers, or allow anonymous searches of portions of the Active Directory DIT. Since anonymous searches of Active Directory were covered in "Cross-Platform Authentication Services," I won't revisit that topic here.

Metadirectories

The term *metadirectory* describes just about any solution that joins distinct, isolated data sources into a single logical volume. There are several popular metadirectory products on the market:

- MaXware MetaCenter (*http://www.maxware.com/*)
- Siemens DirXmetahub (*http://www.siemens.ie/fixedoperators/CarrierNetworks/Meta/dirxmetahub.htm*)
- Sun Microsystems SunONE MetaDirectory (*http://wwws.sun.com/software/products/meta_directory/home_meta_dir.html*)
- Novell's eDirectory and DirXML combination (*http://www.novell.com/products/edirectory/*)
- Microsoft Metadirectory Services (*http://www.microsoft.com/windows2000/technologies/directory/MMS*)

For the sake of this section, we'll assume that a metadirectory is any directory service that presents an alternate view of a data source. OpenLDAP's proxy backend provides a simple means of translating one directory server's schema into a different view, suitable for particular client applications. There is no replication or synchronization of data because the proxy provides only an alternate view of the target directory; the OpenLDAP server providing the proxy doesn't actually store the data.

Imagine an email client that expects a directory service to provide an email address using the mail attribute type. Now consider that every user in an Active Directory domain is automatically assigned a Kerberos principal name of the form *username@domain*. If the email domain is configured so that each user's email address and Kerberos principal name (userPrincipalName) are synchronized (perhaps using an LDAP proxy service), then it makes no sense to duplicate this information just to provide a directory-based address book for a picky email application.

This scenario glosses over some details, such as where the mail domain stores email addresses.

Before you can successfully create a proxy server, the Active Directory domain must meet the following requirements:

- The Active Directory domain must be configured for the DNS domain *ad.plain-joe.org*.
- The DNS name *ad.plainjoe.org* must resolve to the IP address of an Active Directory domain controller for that domain.
- An account named *ldap-proxy* must be created in the Active Directory domain for use by the proxy server when binding to a Windows domain controller.

The OpenLDAP proxy feature isn't enabled by default; it must be enabled at compile time by specifying the *--enable-ldap* and *--enable-rewrite* options to the configure script for *slapd*:

```
$ configure --enable-ldap --enable-rewrite
```

After compiling and installing the new *slapd* executable, create the new LDAP database in *slapd.conf*. Remember that a partition in *slapd.conf* begins with the database directive and continues until the next database section or the end of the file. The new proxy section begins with the declaration:

```
## Proxy backend to access Active Directory.
database        ldap
```

This declaration tells *slapd* to acquire its data from another LDAP server, allowing it to act as a proxy for that server. If OpenLDAP complains that ldap is not a valid database type, verify that *--enable-ldap* and *--enable-rewrite* were actually used when compiling the server. Even though OpenLDAP will not store any actual data for this partition, *slapd* must still be given the naming context of the database (ou=windows,dc=plainjoe,dc=org) using the standard suffix paramete:.

```
suffix          ou=windows,dc=plainjoe,dc=org
```

This is an arbitrary suffix; it does not correspond to the DN of users' container in Active Directory. The uri and suffixmassage parameters tell *slapd* about the target directory (the directory being proxied) and the request rewrite rules. Your server must replace the suffix ou=windows,dc=plainjoe,dc=org with cn=users,dc=ad,dc=plainjoe,dc=org before passing any request to the target server. If no rewriting should be performed, the suffixmassage directive can be omitted.

```
uri             ldap://ad.plainjoe.org/
suffixmassage   ou=windows,dc=plainjoe,dc=org
                cn=users,dc=ad,dc=plainjoe,dc=org
```

The binddn and bindpw parameters provide a means of specifying the credentials to use when contacting the remote LDAP directory. Here you use a simple bind. If your proxy server and remote server existed on opposite sites on an insecure, or hostile, network, it would be prudent to modify the uri parameter to use LDAPS:

```
## Active Directory also allows the userPrincipalName value to be used in LDAP binds,
## so this could be ldap-proxy@ad.plainjoe.org.
binddn    cn=ldap-proxy,cn=users,dc=ad,dc=plainjoe,dc=org
bindpw    proxy-secret
```

OpenLDAP's proxy code only provides a way to map attributes and object classes defined by its local schema to those stored in the target directory. The syntax for defining a mapping is:

```
map   attribute|objectclass [local_name|*] foreign_name|*
```

A map must define whether it applies to an *attribute* or an *objectclass*. The name of the local attribute or object class is optional, but remote names are required. The asterisk (*) character can be used to match any name. Your proxy server should map Active Directory's sAMAccountName, name, and userPrincipalName attributes to the locally defined uid, cn, and mail attributes. You also need to map the local account object class to the target user object class. Here are the map statements that perform the mapping:

```
## Map these.
map        attribute       uid      sAMAccountName
map        attribute       cn       name
map        attribute       mail     userPrincipalName
map        objectclass     account user
```

The proxy server can filter out any remaining attributes by mapping any remaining remote attributes to nothing:

```
## Remove the rest.
map        attribute       *
```

To see the results of this mapping, compare the entry returned by querying Active Directory directly to the result obtained by going through the OpenLDAP proxy. Here's what happens when you query Active Directory; the items that will be provided by the proxy server are shown in bold:

```
$ ldapsearch -H ldap://ad.plainjoe.org -x \
  -D ldap-proxy@ad.plainjoe.org -w proxy-secret -x \
  -b "cn=users,dc=ad,dc=plainjoe,dc=org" -LLL \
  "(sAMAccountName=kristi)"

dn: CN=Kristi Carter,CN=Users,DC=ad,DC=plainjoe,DC=org
accountExpires: 9223372036854775807
badPasswordTime: 0
badPwdCount: 0
codePage: 0
cn: Kristi Carter
countryCode: 0
```

```
displayName: Kristi Carter
givenName: Joe
instanceType: 4
lastLogoff: 0
lastLogon: 0
logonCount: 0
distinguishedName: CN=Kristi Carter,CN=Users,DC=ad,DC=plainjoe,DC=org
objectCategory: CN=Person,CN=Schema,CN=Configuration,DC=ad,DC=plainjoe,DC=org
objectClass: top
objectClass: person
objectClass: organizationalPerson
objectClass: user
objectGUID:: NDHKI8oYFkqN8da3Gl9a5Q= =
objectSid:: AQUAAAAAAAUVAAAAEcNfczJiHypDFwoyUwQAAA= =
primaryGroupID: 513
pwdLastSet: 126784120014273696
name: Kristi Carter
sAMAccountName: kristi
sAMAccountType: 805306368
sn: Carter
userAccountControl: 66048
userPrincipalName: kristi@ad.plainjoe.org
uSNChanged: 2963
uSNCreated: 2957
whenChanged: 20021006210839.0Z
whenCreated: 20021006210637.0Z
```

Now, issue a similar query to the proxy server—except that you'll look up a uid rather than an Active Directory sAMAccountName, and the root of your search will be the DN that you've assigned to the proxy. This time, the search can be done anonymously. Here's the result:

```
$ ldapsearch -H ldap://ldap.plainjoe.org -x  \
  -b "ou=windows,dc=plainjoe,dc=org" -LLL "(uid=kristi)"

dn: CN=Kristi Carter,ou=windows,dc=plainjoe,dc=org
objectClass: top
objectClass: person
objectClass: organizationalPerson
objectClass: account
cn: Kristi Carter
uid: kristi
mail: kristi@ad.plainjoe.org
```

When you compare the two results, you will see that:

```
objectClass: user
name: Kristi Carter
sAMAccountName: kristi
userPrincipalName: kristi@ad.plainjoe.org
```

has been mapped to:

```
objectClass: account
cn: Kristi Carter
```

```
uid: kristi
mail: kristi@ad.plainjoe.org
```

The proxy server returns something slightly different if you remove the directive that filters all the attributes that aren't explicitly mapped (map attribute *):

```
$ ldapsearch -H ldap://ldap.plainjoe.org -x \
  -b "ou=windows,dc=plainjoe,dc=org" -LLL "(uid=kristi)"

dn: CN=Kristi Carter,ou=windows,dc=plainjoe,dc=org
cn: Kristi Carter
displayName: Kristi Carter
mail: kristi@ad.plainjoe.org
givenName: Kristi
distinguishedName: CN=Kristi Carter,ou=windows,dc=plainjoe,dc=org
objectClass: top
objectClass: person
objectClass: organizationalPerson
objectClass: account
cn: Kristi Carter
uid: kristi
sn: Carter
```

While this query returns more information than the previous one, it is obvious that *slapd* is still filtering some of the attributes from the target entry. This filtering occurs because the attributes returned by the query are still controlled by the local schema defined in *slapd.conf*. If the OpenLDAP installation does not understand a given attribute or object class (for example, userAccountControl), and it has not been mapped to a known local schema item, the unknown value is filtered out.

The LDAP proxy backend supports updating the target directory, should you require it. It also supports local ACLs in the LDAP database section; these ACLs can be used to control access to an LDAP proxy that presents a view of the company's internal directory services to external clients. The *slapd-ldap(5)* manpage has more details on both of these configuration possibilities.

Push/Pull Agents for Directory Synchronization

Push/pull agents are common tools for synchronizing information between directories. In this case, a single agent manually pulls information from one directory service and massages the data to make it acceptable for upload to another directory server. Several directory vendors provide synchronization agents of this type in the form of connectors and drivers. A connector transfers data from one directory to another (see Figure 9-8) using a common format, often XML-based, while a driver translates the connector's data format to something understood by the local directory.

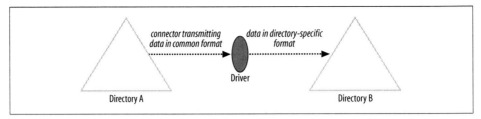

Figure 9-8. Using a connector/driver solution for synchronizing data among different directory services

A partial list of commercial connector/driver offerings includes:

- SunOne's XMLDAP (*http://wwws.sun.com/software/products/directory_srvr/*)
- Novell's DirXML (*http://www.novell.com/products/edirectory/dirxml/*)

The advantage that most commercial connector/driver solutions enjoy over in-house solutions is an inherent knowledge of when data changes in the directory. This means that the directory can trigger the connector upon any relevant change; in most cases, an external agent can detect a change only by polling the directory.

Despite this disadvantage, home-grown tools that act as middlemen between directory services can be very useful. The next chapter focuses on how to script directory operations using Perl and the Net::LDAP module.

The Directory Services Markup Language

The Extensible Markup Language (XML) has been hyped as the next big thing for several years now. Whether or not it has achieved its promise is a question I won't get into. LDAP has not been immune to the XML fever. The Directory Services Markup Language (DSML) is an XML schema for representing LDAP information using document fragments. DSML v1.0 could really only be described as an attempt to replace LDIF. With Version 2.0, however, released in May of 2002, DSML has grown up and gained some new and interesting functionality.*

DSMLv2 is designed to provide methods for representing LDAP queries, updates, and the responses to these operations in XML. This means that it would be possible for small, embedded devices to access LDAP services without relying on an LDAP client library; they only need the ability to parse XML. Because XML-based standards such as SOAP will only become more prevalent over time, the Oasis Directory Service TC has included a description of how to embed DSML requests and responses into SOAP messages.

---

* The latest information about DSML can be found at the OASIS Directory Services Technical Committee's web page (*http://www.oasis-open.org/committees/dsml/*).

It's too early to provide concrete examples of how to use this technology. Version 1.0 is only mildly interesting, and Version 2.0 of DSML is still in the early adopter phase. DSMLv2 will probably be accepted by the LDAP marketplace. Sun Microsystems will include native support for the specification in the next release of its SunOne Directory Server (Version 5.2). Microsoft is also developing a DSML development kit; this product is currently available as a beta release. Novell has also been very active in the development of DSML. All three companies have members serving on the DSML technical committee.

## CHAPTER 10

Net::LDAP and Perl

No book on system administration is complete without some coverage of scripting. For many administrators, the scripting language of choice is Perl. Perl is very good at dealing with text files (such as LDIF files), and many third-party modules make it easy to accomplish complex tasks.*

This chapter doesn't cover the basics of Perl programming. I assume that you are already comfortable with the language and its fundamental concepts, such as regular expressions, but none of the examples will require the help of a Perl guru for interpretation. Note that the scripts in this chapter are generally lax about conventions used in production Perl code, such as the use strict pragma and variable scoping (e.g., my or local).

The Net::LDAP Module

Two widely distributed Perl modules make it easy to write scripts that interact with an LDAP directory. One of these is the PerLDAP module, written by Leif Hedstrom from Netscape Communications (*http://www.mozilla.org/directory/perldap.html*). However, the last version was released in October of 2000.

A more active project, and the module that I discuss in this chapter, is Graham Barr's perl-ldap module (often referred to as Net::LDAP). The examples in this chapter are based on Version 0.26 of this module. The module's home is located at *http://perl-ldap.sourceforge.net/*, but it's simpler to get it through the Comprehensive Perl Archive Network (CPAN) at *http://search.cpan.org*. Before you install Net::LDAP, make sure that the following modules are present:

---

* For more information on Perl, visit the O'Reilly Perl web site at *http://www.perl.com/* or the Perl Monger's web site at *http://www.perl.org/*. If you're new to Perl, I recommend *Learning Perl*, by Randall Schwartz and Tom Phoenix (O'Reilly) and *Programming Perl*, by Larry Wall, Tom Christiansen, and Randall Schwartz (O'Reilly).

URI
> If you want to parse *ldap://* URIs

Digest::MD5
> For Base64 encoding

IO::Socket::SSL
> For LDAPS and StartTLS support

XML::Parser
> To read and write DSML files

Authen::SASL
> For SASL authentication support

All of these modules (and any of their requisite modules) can be downloaded from CPAN mirrors. As a convenience, several of these modules have been packaged into a single module named Bundle::Net::LDAP, which can also be download from CPAN.

 One of the easiest ways to ensure that all dependencies for a Perl module are met is to use the interactive shell provided by Andreas Koenig's CPAN module. After downloading and installing this module from *http://search.cpan.org/search?dist=CPAN*, you can learn about its features by executing the command *perldoc CPAN*.

Programming with the Net::LDAP module is not tricky. You can discover a lot about it by typing the command *perldoc Net::LDAP* at a shell prompt; additional documentation can be found under Net::LDAP::Examples and Net::LDAP::FAQ.

Connecting, Binding, and Searching

To get started with the Net::LDAP module, we will write a basic LDAP query script named *search.pl*. This script illustrates the methods used to connect to a directory server and retrieve information. It begins by importing the Net::LDAP symbols via the use pragma:

```
#!/usr/bin/perl
use Net::LDAP;
```

After the module has been included, you can create a new instance of a Net::LDAP object. To create a new Net::LDAP instance, you need the hostname of the LDAP server to which the script should connect. The constructor allows several optional arguments, of which the most common and useful are:

port
> The TCP port on which the directory server is listening. If this parameter is not defined, it defaults to the well-known LDAP port (389).

version

The LDAP version to be used when connecting to the server. The default is Version 2 in the 0.26 release. However, this is likely to change in the future. Always explicitly set the version parameter if your Perl program replies with LDAPv3 features (such as SASL or referrals).

timeout

The time in seconds that the module should wait when contacting the directory server. The default value of 120 seconds is sufficient for most situations, but for more complex searches or when communicating with a very large directory, it may be necessary to increase this value.

The next line of code establishes a connection to the host *ldap.plainjoe.org* on port 389 using Version 3 of the protocol. The returned value is a handle to a Net::LDAP object that can be used to retrieve and modify data in the directory.

```
$ldap = Net::LDAP->new ("ldap.plainjoe.org", port =>389,
                        version => 3 );
```

The script can bind to the directory after it obtains a handle to the LDAP server. By default, Net::LDAP uses an implicit anonymous bind, but it supports all the standard binds defined by the LDAPv3 RFCs (anonymous, simple, and SASL). For now, we only examine how to use a simple bind.

However, before binding to the server, call start_tls( ) to encrypt the connection; you don't want to send the user DN and password across the network in clear text. In its simplest form, the start_tls( ) method requires no parameters and appears as:

```
$ldap->start_tls( );
```

It is a good idea to check for errors after attempting to establish a secure communication channel; if start_tls( ) fails, and the script continues blindly, it might inadvertently transmit sensitive account information in the clear. To do so, save the result object returned by start_tls( ), and then use the code( ) method to find out whether start_tls( ) succeeded:

```
$result = $ldap->start_tls( );
die $result->error( ) if $result->code( );
```

If the script tries to establish transport layer security with a server that does not support this extended operation, the error check displays an error message and exits:

```
Operations error at ./search.pl line XXX.
```

The actual error from Net::LDAP::Constant is LDAP_OPERATIONS_ERROR.

Now you can safely send the sensitive data to the server. A simple authenticated bind requires only a DN and a password. If neither are provided, the call attempts to establish an explicit anonymous binding (as opposed to the implicit bind used when bind( ) is not called at all). The following line seeks to bind your client to the direc-

Checking for Errors

Most of the Net::LDAP methods return an object with two methods for obtaining the function's return status. The code( ) method retrieves the integer return value from the method call that created the object, and the error( ) method returns a descriptive character string associated with the numeric code. The constants for the various LDAP errors are contained in the Net::LDAP::Constant module. Specific error codes can be included in your code by adding a line similar to the following one:

```
use Net::LDAP::Constant qw(LDAP_SUCCESS);
```

The following code tests for an error condition after some arbitrary LDAP call:

```
if ($result->code( ) != LDAP_SUCCESS) {
        die $result->error( );
    }
```

Because most methods indicate success with a return code of zero, this error check can be shortened to:

```
die $result->error( ) if $result->code( );
```

The Net::LDAP::Util module contains a few extra functions for obtaining more error information. The ldap_error_text function returns the descriptive POD text for the error code passed in as a parameter, and ldap_error_name returns the constant name for an integer (for example, if it is passed the integer 0, it returns the string LDAP_SUCCESS).

---

tory as the entry cn=Gerald Carter,ou=people,dc=plainjoe,dc=org using the password hello. Once again, you use error( ) and code( ) to check the return status:

```
$result = $ldap->bind("cn=Gerald Carter,ou=people,dc=plainjoe,dc=org",
  password => "hello");
die $result->error( ) if $result->code( );
```

If there is no error, the script is free to search the directory. The search( ) method accepts the standard parameters that are expected from an LDAP query tool. At this point, we're interested only in the base, scope, and filter parameters. To make the script more flexible, use the first argument passed in from the command line (i.e., search.pl "Gerald Carter") to build a filter string that searches for the user's common name (cn):

```
$msg = $ldap->search(
        base => "ou=people,dc=plainjoe,dc=org",
        scope => "sub",
        filter => "(cn=$ARGV[0])" );
```

The return value of the search is an instance of the Net::LDAP::Search object. You can manipulate this object to retrieve any entries that matched the search. This object has a count( ) method that returns the number of entries, and an all_entries( )

method that returns the results as an array of Net::LDAP::Entry objects, each of which represents information associated with a single directory node. You can view the results of this query by dumping each entry from the array:

```
if ( $msg->count( ) > 0 ) {
    print $msg->count( ), " entries returned.\n";

    foreach $entry ( $msg->all_entries( ) ) {
        $entry->dump( );
    }
}
```

The output for a single entry looks like this:

```
dn:cn=Gerald Carter,ou=people,dc=plainjoe,dc=org

   objectClass: inetOrgPerson
            cn: Gerald Carter
            sn: Carter
     givenName: Gerald
             o: Hewlett-Packard
        mobile: 256.555.5309
          mail: jerry@plainjoe.org
 postalAddress: 103 Somewhere Street
             l: Some Town
            st: AL
    postalCode: 55555-5555
```

The dump( ) routine is not meant to generate valid LDIF output, as can be seen from the extra whitespace added to center the attribute/value pairs; another module, aptly named Net::LDAP::LDIF, handles that feature. We'll discuss working with LDIF files later in this chapter. For now, just printing the attribute/value pairs in any form is good enough.

What if you're interested only in a person's email address? Some entries contain many attributes, and asking a user to look through all this output in search of an email address could qualify as cruel and unusual punishment. How can you modify the script so that it displays only the attributes you want? The search( ) function has an optional parameter that allows the caller to define an array of attribute names. The search returns only the values of attributes that match names in the list. Here's how to modify the script so that it retrieves only the mail and cn attributes:

```
$msg = $ldap->search(
        base => "ou=people,dc=plainjoe,dc=org",
        scope => "sub",
        filter => "(cn=$ARGV[0])",
        attrs => [ "cn", "mail" ] );
```

And here's what you get when you dump the entry returned by the modified query:

```
dn:cn=Gerald Carter,ou=people,dc=plainjoe,dc=org

        cn: Gerald Carter
```

```
mail: jerry@plainjoe.org
```

The last line of the script invokes the unbind( ) method to disconnect from the directory:

```
$ldap->unbind( );
```

This routine effectively destroys the connection. The most portable means to rebind to an LDAP server using a new set of credentials is to call bind( ) again with the new DN and password (but only when using LDAPv3). Once the unbind( ) subroutine has been invoked, the connection should be thrown away and a new one created if needed.

The following listing shows the *search.pl* script in its entirety:

```perl
#!/usr/bin/perl
##
## Usage: ./search.pl name
##
## Author: Gerald Carter <jerry@plainjoe.org>
##
use Net::LDAP;

## Connect and bind to the server.
$ldap = Net::LDAP->new ("ldap.plainjoe.org", port =>389,
                        version => 3 )
or die $!;

$result = $ldap->start_tls( );
die $result->error( ) if $result->code( );

$result = $ldap->bind(
        "cn=Gerald Carter,ou=people,dc=plainjoe,dc=org",
        password => "hello");
die $result->error( ) if $result->code( );

## Query for the cn and mail attributes.
$msg = $ldap->search(
        base => "ou=people,dc=plainjoe,dc=org",
        scope => "sub",
        filter => "(cn=$ARGV[0])",
        attrs => [ "cn", "mail" ] );

## Print resulting entries to standard output.
if ( $msg->count( ) > 0 ) {
    print $msg->count( ), " entries returned.\n";

    foreach $entry ( $msg->all_entries( ) ) {
        $entry->dump( );
    }
}

## Unbind and exit.
$ldap->unbind( );
```

Working with Net::LDAP::LDIF

The *search.pl* script provided a simple introduction to retrieving data from an LDAP directory. However, the query results represented the state of the directory at a single point in time. The script has no good way to save the search results, and the way in which it prints the information is useful for humans, but not useful to any other LDAP tools. You need the ability to save the results in a format that can be parsed by other LDAP tools: in other words, you need to be able to read and write LDIF files directly from Perl code.

The Net::LDAP::LDIF module provides the ability to work with LDIF files. To introduce Net::LDAP::LDIF, we'll revisit *search.pl* and replace the call to dump( ) with code to produce valid LDIF output. Your first modification to the script is to add a second use pragma that imports the LDIF module:

```
use Net::LDAP::LDIF;
```

Next, the script must create a new instance of a Net::LDAP::LDIF object. Output from this object can be linked to an existing file handle such as STDOUT, as shown here:

```
$ldif = Net::LDAP::LDIF->new (scalar <STDOUT>, "w")
    or die $!;
```

It is possible to pass a filename to the new( ) method, as well as inform the module how this file will be used ("r" for read, "w" for write + truncate, and "a" for write + append). This line of code creates an LDIF output stream named *result.ldif* in the current directory:

```
$ldif = Net::LDAP::LDIF->new ("./result.ldif", "w")
    or die $!;
```

It is best to use this code after you've run the search and confirmed that it produced some results. So, you open the file after the script has tested that $msg->count( ) > 0:

```
if ( $msg->count( ) > 0 ) {
    print $msg->count( ), " entries returned.\n";

    $ldif = Net::LDAP::LDIF->new (scalar<STDOUT>, "w")
        or die $!;
```

Finally, replace the entire foreach loop that calls dump( ) on each entry with a single call to the write_entry( ) method of Net::LDAP::LDIF:

```
$ldif->write_entry($msg->all_entries( ));
```

write_entry( ) accepts either a single Net::LDAP::Entry or a one-dimensional array of these objects. The new loop is:

```
if ( $msg->count( ) > 0 ) {
    print $msg->count( ), " entries returned.\n";

    $ldif = Net::LDAP::LDIF->new (scalar<STDOUT>, "w")
        or die $!;
```

```
    $ldif->write_entry($msg->all_entries());
}
```

Now the output of the script looks like this:

```
dn: cn=Gerald Carter,ou=contacts,dc=plainjoe,dc=org
cn: Gerald Carter
mail: jerry@samba.org
```

This doesn't look like a big change, but it's an important one. Because the data is now in LDIF format, other tools such as *ldapmodify* can parse your script's output.

Once the script has created the LDIF output file, you can explicitly close the file by executing the done( ) method.

```
$ldif->done();
```

This method is implicitly called whenever a Net::LDAP::LDIF object goes out of scope.

Updating the Directory

Searching for objects in the directory is only the beginning. The real power of scripting is that it allows you to modify the directory; you can add entries, delete entries, and modify existing entries.

Adding New Entries

The first script, *import.pl*, reads the contents of an LDIF file (specified as a command-line argument) and adds each entry in the file to the directory. Here's a starting point; it resembles the last version of your *search.pl* script:

```
#!/usr/bin/perl
##
## Usage: ./import.pl filename
##
## Author: Gerald Carter <jerry@plainjoe.org>
##
use Net::LDAP;
use Net::LDAP::LDIF;

## Connect and bind to the server.
$ldap = Net::LDAP->new ("ldap.plainjoe.org", port =>389,
                            version => 3 )
or die $!;

## Secure data and credentials.
$result = $ldap->start_tls();
die $result->error() if $result->code();

## Bind to the server. The account must have sufficient privileges because you will
## be adding new entries.
$result = $ldap->bind(
```

```
        "cn=Directory Admin,ou=people,dc=plainjoe,dc=org",
        password => "secret");
die $result->error() if $result->code();

## Open the LDIF file or fail. Check for existence first.
die "$ARGV[0] not found!\n" unless ( -f $ARGV[0] );
$ldif = Net::LDAP::LDIF->new ($ARGV[0], "r")
    or die $!;
```

Once the script has a handle to the input file, you can begin processing the entries. Net::LDAP::LDIF has an eof() method for detecting the end of input. The main loop continues until this check returns true.

```
while ( ! $ldif->eof ) {
    ## Get next entry and process input here.
}
```

Retrieving the next LDIF entry in the file is extremely easy because the Net::LDAP:: LDIF module does all the work, including testing the file to ensure that its syntax is correct. If the next entry in the file is valid, the read_entry() method returns it as a Net::LDAP::Entry object.

```
$entry = $ldif->read_entry();
```

If the call to read_entry() fails, you can retrieve the offending line by invoking the error_lines() routine:

```
if ( $ldif->error() ) {
    print "Error msg: ", $ldif->error(), "\n";
    print "Error lines:\n", $ldif->error_lines(), "\n";
    next;
}
```

If no errors occur, the script adds the entry it has read from the file to the directory by invoking the Net::LDAP add() method:

```
$result = $ldap->add( $entry );
warn $result->error() if $result->code();
```

The final version of the loop looks like:

```
## Loop until the end-of-file.
while ( ! $ldif->eof() ) {
    $entry = $ldif->read_entry();

    ## Skip the entry if there is an error.
    if ( $ldif->error() ) {
        print "Error msg: ", $ldif->error(), "\n";
        print "Error lines:\n", $ldif->error_lines(), "\n";
        next;
    }

    ## Log to STDERR and continue in case of failure.
    $result = $ldap->add( $entry );
    warn $result->error() if $result->code();
```

```
    }
```

Note that you test for an error after adding the entry to the directory. You can't assume that the entry was added successfully on the basis of a successful return from read_entry( ). read_entry( ) guarantees that the entry was syntactically correct, and gives you a valid Net::LDAP::Entry object, but other kinds of errors can occur when you add the object to a directory. The most common cause of failure at this stage in the process is a schema violation.

Now that you've finished the main loop, unbind from the directory server and exit:

```
$ldap->unbind( );
exit(0);
```

Deleting Entries

The next script complements *import.pl*. It gives you the ability to delete an entire subtree from the directory by specifying its base entry. The delete( ) method of Net:: LDAP requires a DN specifying which entry to delete. The *rmtree.pl* script accepts a DN from the command line (e.g., rmtree.pl "ou=test,dc=plainjoe,dc=org") and deletes the corresponding tree.

How should you implement this script? You could simply perform a subtree search and delete entries one at a time. However, if the script exits prematurely, it could leave nodes, or entire subtrees, orphaned. A disconnected directory is very difficult to correct. A more interesting and only slightly more complex approach is to delete entries from the bottom of the tree and work your way up. This strategy eliminates the possibility of leaving orphaned entries because the tree is always contiguous: you delete only leaf entries, which have no nodes underneath them.

To implement bottom-up deletion, perform a depth-first search using recursion and allow Perl to handle the stack for you. The DeleteLdapTree( ) subroutine introduced in this script deletes an entry only after all of its children have been removed. It does a one-level search at the root of the tree to be deleted, and then calls itself on each of the entries returned by that search.

```
#!/usr/bin/perl
##
## Usage: ./rmtree.pl DN
##
## Author: Gerald Carter <jerry@plainjoe.org>
##
use Net::LDAP;

#######################################################
## Perform a depth-first search on the $dn, deleting entries from the bottom up.
## Parameters: $handle (handle to Net::LDAP object)
##             $dn       (DN of entry to remove)
sub DeleteLdapTree {
    my ( $handle, $dn ) = @_;
```

```
my ( $result );

$msg = $handle->search( base => $dn,
                        scope => one,
                        filter => "(objectclass=*)" );
if ( $msg->code() ) {
    $msg->error();
    return;
}

foreach $entry in ( $msg->all_entries ) {
    DeleteLdapTree( $handle, $entry->dn() );
}

$result = $handle->delete( $dn );
warn $result->error() if $result->code();

print "Removed $dn\n";

return;
}
```

The driver for this script begins by connecting to a directory server and binding to the server as a specific user with appropriate privileges. By now, this code should be familiar:

```
## Connect and bind to the server.
$ldap = Net::LDAP->new ("ldap.plainjoe.org", port =>389,
                        version => 3 )
or die $!;

## Secure data and credentials.
$result = $ldap->start_tls();
die $result->error() if $result->code();

## Bind to the server. The account must have sufficient privileges because you will
## be deleting new entries.
$result = $ldap->bind(
        "cn=Directory Admin,ou=people,dc=plainjoe,dc=org",
        password => "secret");
die $result->error() if $result->code();
```

To begin the deletion process, the script verifies that the DN specified on the command line points to a valid directory entry:

```
$msg = $ldap->search( base => $ARGV[0],
                      scope => base,
                      filter => "(objectclass=*)" );
die $msg->error() if $msg->code();
```

Once assured that the entry does in fact exist, the script makes a single call to the recursive DeleteLdapTree() routine, which does all the work:

```
DeleteLdapTree( $ldap, $ARGV[0] );
```

After the subtree is deleted, the script unbinds from the server and exits:

```
$ldap->unbind( );
exit(0);
```

Modifying Entries

Now that you can add and delete entries, let's look at modifying data that already exists in the LDAP tree. There are two routines for making changes to entries in the directory. The update( ) method of Net::LDAP pushes an Entry object to the directory; to use this method, get a local copy of the Net::LDAP::Entry object you want to modify, make your changes, and then push the change to the server. The modify( ) method allows you to specify a list of changes, and performs those changes directly on the server, eliminating the need to start by obtaining a copy of the entry. Each mechanism has its own advantages and disadvantages. Pushing local changes to the directory is more intuitive, but not as efficient. However, before discussing the pros and cons of these approaches, you must become acquainted with the routines for manipulating a Net::LDAP::Entry client object.

Net::LDAP::Entry

The most common way to instantiate a Net::LDAP::Entry object is to call the search( ) method of Net::LDAP. If you need a blank entry, you can create one by invoking the Net::LDAP::Entry constructor (i.e., new). You can print the contents of an Entry by calling its dump( ) method, but you can also create a custom printing method by using various methods from the Net::LDAP::Entry and Net::LDAP::LDIF modules.

We'll start this new exercise by writing a custom printing function. The new function, named DumpEntry( ), accepts a Net::LDAP::Entry object as its only parameter. It then prints the entry's DN followed by each value of each attribute that it contains. Here's a complete listing of DumpEntry( ):

```
sub DumpEntry {
    my ( $entry ) = @_;
    my ( $attrib, $val );

    print $entry->dn( ), "\n";

    foreach $attrib in ( $entry->attributes( ) ) {
        foreach $val in ( $entry->get_value( $attrib ) ) {
            print $attrib, ": ", $val, "\n";
        }
    }
}
```

This code introduces three new methods:

dn( )

When called with no arguments, the dn( ) method returns the distinguished name of the entry as a character string. If you pass it a parameter, that parameter is used to set the entry's DN.

attributes( )

This method returns an array containing the entry's attributes.

get_value( )

In its most basic form, the get_value( ) routine accepts an attribute name and returns an array of values for that attribute.

 To find out more about the Entry methods, type the following command at a shell prompt:

```
$ perldoc Net::LDAP::Entry
```

DumpEntry( ) acts just like the dump( ) method, in that it prints only the attributes and values that are stored in the local copy of the Net::LDAP::Entry object. Additional attributes may be stored in the directory.

Three methods manipulate an entry's attributes and values: add( ), delete( ), and replace( ). The add( ) method inserts a new attribute or value into an entry object. The following line of code adds a new email address for the entry represented by the scalar $e. If the attribute does not currently exist in the entry, it is added. If it does exist, the new value is added to any previous values.

```
$e->add ( "mail" => "jerry@plainjoe.org" );
```

The add( ) method does not perform any schema checking because it is working only with a local copy of the entry. If the mail attribute is not supported by the object classes assigned to the entry, you won't find out until you push the entry back to the directory server. Likewise, add( ) also allows you to assign multiple values to an attribute that allows only a single value (for example, the uidNumber attribute included in a posixAccount).

Multiple values can be assigned to a single attribute by using an array:

```
$e->add( "mail" => [ "jerry@plainjoe.org",
                     "jerry@samba.org"] );
```

The add( ) method also supports adding multiple attributes with a single call:

```
$e->add( "mail" => "jerry@plainjoe.org",
         "cn"   => "Gerald Carter" );
```

To erase an attribute from a local entry, call delete( ). This method accepts the attribute names that should be removed, either as a scalar value or as an array.

```
$e->delete ( [ "mail", "cn" ] );
```

It is possible to delete individual values from a multivalued attribute by passing an array of items to be removed. Here, I remove only *jerry@samba.org* from the entry's email addresses:

```
$e->delete( mail => [ "jerry@samba.org" ] );
```

Finally, you can delete an attribute (and all its associated values) and re-add it by calling replace( ). This method accepts attribute/value pairs in a similar fashion as add( ). The following line of code replaces all values assigned to the mail attribute with the new address *jerry@plainjoe.org*. If the attribute does not exist, it is inserted into the entry, just as if you had called add( ).

```
$e->replace( "mail" => "jerry@plainjoe.org" );
```

When working with a Net::LDAP::Entry object, remember that the client instance is only a copy, and that any changes you make affect only the local copy of the entry. The next section explains how to propagate these changes to the directory.

Pushing an updated entry back to the server

No changes made to a local copy of a Net::LDAP::Entry object are reflected in the directory until its update( ) method is called. To show how to update a directory, we will develop a simple script that allows a user to change her password. The script makes two assumptions:

- Every user has an entry in the directory; a user's Unix login name matches the value of the uid attribute (e.g., a posixAccount object).

- Every user can update their userPassword attribute values.

You need two additional modules for this program. Term::ReadKey allows you to read the user types without displaying them on the screen. Digest::MD5 provides a routine to generate a Base64-encoded md5 digest hash of a string. Here's how the script starts:

```
#!/usr/bin/perl

use Net::LDAP;
use Term::ReadKey;
use Digest::MD5 qw(md5_base64);
```

You obtain the user's login name by looking up the UID of the running process (i.e., $<):

```
$username = getpwuid($>);
print "Changing password for user ", $username, "\n";
```

The script then performs some familiar LDAP connection setup:

```
$ldap = Net::LDAP->new( "ldap.plainjoe.org",
                        version => 3)
     or die $!;
$result = $ldap->start_tls( );
die $result->error( ) if $result->code( );
```

Next, the program implicitly binds to the directory anonymously and attempts to locate the entry for the current user. The query is a subtree search using the filter (uid=$username). If the search finds multiple matches, it returns only the first entry. If no entry is found, the script complains loudly and exits.

```
$msg = $ldap->search(
                base => "ou=people,dc=plainjoe,dc=org",
                scope => "sub",
                filter => "(uid=$username)" );
die $msg->error( ) if $msg->code( );
die "No such user in directory [$username]!\n"
        if !$msg->count;
```

When you know that the user exists in the LDAP directory, prompt the user to type the old and new password strings. Ask for the new string twice, and then ensure that the user typed the same thing both times:

```
## Read old and new password strings. Use ReadMode to prevent the passwords from
## being echoed to the screen.
ReadMode( 'noecho' );
print "Enter Old Password: ";
$old_passwd = chomp( ReadLine(0) );
print "\nEnter New Password: ";
$new_passwd = chomp( ReadLine(0) );
print "\nEnter New Password again: ";
$new_passwd2 = chomp( ReadLine(0) );
print "\n";
ReadMode( 'restore' );

## Check that new password was typed correctly.
if ( "$new_passwd" ne "$new_passwd2" ) {
        print "New passwords do not match!\n";
        exit (1);
}
```

 More tidbits and code samples using the Term::ReadKey and other Perl modules can be found in *Perl Cookbook* by Tom Christiansen and Nathan Torkington (O'Reilly).

To convert the Net::LDAP::Search results to a single Net::LDAP::Entry object, the script calls the former's entry( ) method. This subroutine accepts an integer index to the array of entries produced by the previous search. In this case, we are concerned only with the first entry—in fact, we are assuming that the search returns only one entry:

```
$entry = $msg->entry(0);
```

The array of entries is not sorted in any particular order, so if you're dealing with multiple entries, this method call could conceivably return a different entry every time it is run. The best way to avoid this ambiguity is to choose an attribute that is unique within the directory subtree rooted at the search base.

You now have both the DN of the user's entry and the old password value. At this point, you can authenticate the user by binding to the directory server. If the bind fails, the script informs the user that the old password was incorrect, and exits:

```
$result = $ldap->bind( $entry->dn(),
                           password => $old_passwd );
die "Old Password is invalid!\n" if $result->code();
```

All that remains is to update the user's password in the directory. This code is pretty trivial. The script uses the md5_base64( ) function from the Digest::MD5 module to generate the new password hash:

```
## Generate Base64 md5 hash of the new passwd.
$md5_pw = "{MD5}" . md5_base64($new_passwd) . "==";
```

The "==" is appended to the password hash to pad the digest string so that its length is a multiple of four bytes. This is necessary for interoperability with other Base64 md5 digest strings and is described in the Digest::MD5 documentation. Next, over-write the old password value by calling replace( ):

```
$entry->replace( userPassword => $md5_pw );
```

To propagate the change to the directory, call the update( ) method. This method accepts a handle to the Net::LDAP object representing the directory server on which the update will be performed.

```
$result = $entry->update( $ldap );
die $result->error() if $result->code();
```

Now inform the user that her password has been updated, and exit:

```
print "Password updated successfully\n";
exit (0);
```

When executed, the output of *passwd.pl* looks similar to the standard Unix *passwd* utility:

```
$ ./passwd.pl
Changing password for user jerry
Enter Old Password: secret
Enter New Password: new-secret
Enter New Password again: new-secret
Password updated successfully
```

Modifying directory entries

Although LDAPv3 does not specify support for transactions across multiple entries, the RFCs indicate that changes to a single entry must be made atomically. When and why would you care about atomic updates? Assume that, on your network, all user accounts are created in a central LDAP directory using the posixAccount object class. Since it's a large network, you have several administrators, each of which may need to perform user management tasks at any time. You need to guarantee that their user management tool always obtains the next available numeric UID and GID without having to be concerned that two scripts running concurrently obtain the same ID number.

At this point, using the directory to store the currently available UID and GID values is the proverbial "no-brainer." What you need is a subroutine to retrieve the next free ID number and then store the newly incremented value. This operation must be atomic—that is, there must be no way for some other script to sneak in after you've read a value and read the same (unincremented) value. To support this, you need to introduce two new object classes, one for the uidPool and one for the gidPool. The schema for these two objects is illustrated in Figure 10-1.

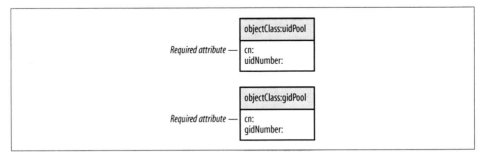

Figure 10-1. uidPool and gidPool object classes

Here's the implementation of the get_next_uid( ) function. It requires a handle to a Net::LDAP object as its only parameter. get_next_gid( ) is almost identical; I'll leave it to you to make the necessary modifications.

```
############################################################
## Get the next available UID from the idPool. Spin until you get one.
##
sub get_next_uid {
    my ( $ldap ) = @_;
    my ( $uid, $msg, $entry );
    my ( @Add, @Delete, @Changes );
```

The logic of the function is:

- Retrieve the next available uidNumber value from the uidPool entry.
- Issue an LDAP modify request that attempts to delete the original uidNumber value, and store the old value incremented by 1 as the new uidNumber.
- If the update fails, repeat the entire process until the modification succeeds.

The search and update steps are wrapped in a do...while loop to ensure that you have a valid UID upon exit. You perform a one-level search because the uidPool object is assumed to be stored directly under the search base (e.g., dc=plainjoe,dc=org). The actual location of the pool in the directory is an arbitrary choice, of course. If the search fails, either by returning an error or because of an empty list, get_next_uid( ) fails and returns an invalid UID value (-1):

```
do {
    $msg = $ldap->search(
                base => "dc=plainjoe,dc=org",
                scope => "one",
                filter => "(objectclass=uidPool)" );
    if ($msg->code ) {
        warn $msg->error;
        return -1;
    }

    if ( ! $msg->count ) {
        warn "Unable to locate uidPool entry!";
        return -1;
    }
}
```

To obtain the next available ID number, the function grabs the uidNumber attribute from the first entry returned by the search( ) call. The uidNumber attribute defined by the RFC 2307 schema is single-valued, so get_value( ) always returns a scalar value in this context:

```
$entry = $msg->entry(0);
$uid = $entry->get_value( 'uidNumber' );
```

The Net::LDAP → modify( ) method requires the DN of the entry to be changed as the first parameter:

```
modify( DN, options );
```

The *options* specify which type of update to perform: add, delete, replace, or changes. The first three options accept a reference to a hash table of attributes and values. For example, this call deletes the mail attribute value jerry@plainjoe.org:

```
$ldap->modify( $entry->dn(),
        delete => [ 'mail' => 'jerry@plainjoe.org' ] );
```

A single modify( ) call can make multiple changes of different types. Here, you delete an email address and add a phone number:

```
$ldap->modify( $entry->dn(),
        delete => { 'mail' => 'jerry@plainjoe.org' },
        add    => { 'telephoneNumber' => '555-1234' } );
```

Using separate add and delete parameters, there are no guarantees about which update will be applied first, only that all the updates will be combined into a single LDAP modify message. The ordering of changes is important to get_next_uid( ) because the delete must precede the add. For this reason, get_next_uid( ) uses the changes parameter instead because it allows the programmer to specify how the modifications will be applied.

The changes option specifies a nested array of updates. At the top dimension of the array is a pair of items: the first is the modification type (add, delete, or replace), and the second is a reference to an array composed of attribute/value pairs. The add and delete options in the previous example can be represented using the changes option like so:

```
$ldap->modify( $entry->dn( ), changes =>
        [ 'delete, [ 'mail', 'jerry@plainjoe.org' ],
          'add', ['telephoneNumber', '555-1234' ] ] );
```

It is often easier to understand these updates if they are placed in an actual array, rather than using an anonymous reference. The following code from get_next_uid( ) uses three arrays to store the changes. The first stores the delete request, the second stores the add request, and the third stores references to the previous two after indicating the type of change:

```
push ( @Delete, 'uidNumber', $uid );
push ( @Add, 'uidNumber', $uid+1 );
push ( @Changes, 'delete', \@Delete );
push ( @Changes, 'add', \@Add );

$result = $ldap->modify( $entry->dn( ),
                'changes' => [ @Changes ] );
```

If the modify( ) call fails, the script assumes that the delete operation failed because the uidNumber value did not match. Therefore, the $uid variable is set to -1 so that the loop will repeat:

```
if ( $result->code ) { $uid = -1 }

} while ( $uid == -1 );
```

Finally, the routine returns the valid numeric UID to the caller:

```
    return $uid;
}
```

To wrap things up, here is the get_next_uid( ) function in its entirety:

```
##########################################################
## Get the next available UID from the idPool. Spin until you get one.
##
sub get_next_uid {
    my ( $ldap ) = @_;
    my ( $uid, $msg, $entry );
    my ( @Add, @Delete, @Changes );

    do {
        ## Get the uidPool entry and perform error checking.
        $msg = $ldap->search(
                base => "dc=plainjoe,dc=org",
                scope => "one",
                filter => "(objectclass=uidPool)" );
        if ($msg->code ) {
            warn $msg->error;
            return -1;
        }
```

```
        if ( ! $msg->count ) {
            warn "Unable to locate uidPool entry!";
            return -1;
        }

        ## Get the next UID.
        $entry = $msg->entry(0);
        $uid = $entry->get_value( 'uidNumber' );

        ## Put the changes together to update the next UID in the directory.
        push ( @Delete, 'uidNumber', $uid );
        push ( @Add, 'uidNumber', $uid+1 );
        push ( @Changes, 'delete', \@Delete );
        push ( @Changes, 'add', \@Add );

        ## Update the directory.
        $result = $ldap->modify( $entry->dn(),
                          'changes' => [ @Changes ] );
        if ( $result->code ) { $uid = -1 }

    ## Do you need another round?
    } while ( $uid == -1 );

    ## All done
    return $uid;
}
```

This function would be invoked in a fashion similar to:

```
if ( ($nextuid=get_next_uid( $ldap )) == -1) {
    print "Unable to generate new uid!\n";
    exit 1;
}
```

Advanced Net::LDAP Scripting

At this point, we've covered all the basics: binding to a server, reading, writing, and modifying entries. The remainder of the chapter covers more advanced programming techniques. We'll start by discussing how to handle referrals and references returned from a search operation.

References and Referrals

It's important for both software developers and administrators to understand the difference between a reference and a referral. These terms are often confused, probably because the term "referral" is overused or misused. As defined in RFC 2251, an LDAP server returns a reference when a search request cannot be completed without the help of another directory server. I have called this reference a "subordinate knowledge reference" earlier in this book. In contrast, a referral is issued when the server cannot service the request at all and instead points the client to another directory that may have more knowledge about the base search suffix. I have called this link a "superior knowledge reference" because it points the client to a directory server that has superior knowledge, compared to the present LDAP server. These knowledge references will be returned only if the client has connected to the server using LDAPv3; they aren't defined by LDAPv2.

A Net::LDAP search returns a Net::LDAP::Reference object if the search can't be completed, but must be continued on another server. In this case, the reference is returned along with Net::LDAP::Entry objects. If a search requires a referral, it doesn't return any Entry objects, but instead issues the LDAP_REFERRAL return code. Both references and referrals are returned in the form of an LDAP URL. To illustrate these new concepts and their use, we will now modify the original *search.pl* script to follow both types of redirection. As of Version 0.26, the Net::LDAP module does not help you follow references or referrals—you have to do this yourself.

To aid in parsing an LDAP URL, use the URI::ldap module. If the URI module is not installed on your system, you can obtain it from *http://search.cpan.org/*. LDAP_REFERRAL is a constant from Net::LDAP::Constant that lets you check return codes from the Net::LDAP search( ) method.

```
#!/usr/bin/perl
## Usage: ./fullsearch.pl name
##
## Author: Gerald Carter <jerry@plainjoe.org>
##
use Net::LDAP qw(LDAP_REFERRAL);
use URI::ldap;
```

The script then connects to the directory server:

```
$ldap = Net::LDAP->new ("ldap.plainjoe.org",
                port => 389,
                version => 3 )
    or die $!;
```

To simplify the example, we will omit the bind( ) call (from the original version of *search.pl*) and bind to the directory anonymously. We'll also request all attributes for an entry rather than just the cn and mail values. The callback parameter is new. Its value is a reference to the subroutine that should process each entry or reference returned by the search:

```
$msg = $ldap->search(
                base => "ou=people,dc=plainjoe,dc=org",
                scope => "sub",
                filter => "(cn=$ARGV[0])",
                callback => \&ProcessSearch );

ProcessReferral( $msg->referrals( ) )
    if $msg->code( ) == LDAP_REFERRAL;
```

This code does two things: it registers ProcessSearch( ) as the callback routine for each entry or reference returned from the search and calls ProcessReferral( ) if the server replies with a referral. Both of these subroutines will be examined in turn.

All callback routines are passed two parameters: a Net::LDAP::Message object and a Net::LDAP::Entry object. ProcessSearch( ) has two responsibilities: it prints the contents of any Net::LDAP::Entry object and follows the LDAP URL in the case of a Net::LDAP::Reference object. The ProcessSearch( ) subroutine begins by assigning values to $msg and $result. If $result is not defined, as in the case of a failed search, ProcessSearch( ) can return without performing any work.

```
sub ProcessSearch {
    my ( $msg, $result ) = @_;

    ## Nothing to do
    return if ( ! defined($result) );
```

If $result exists, it must be either a Reference or an Entry. First, check whether it is a Net::LDAP::Reference. If it is, the URL is passed to the FollowURL( ) routine to continue the search. The Net::LDAP::Reference references( ) method returns a list of URLs, so you will follow them one by one:

```
if ( $result->isa("Net::LDAP::Reference") ) {
    foreach $link ( $result->refererences( ) ){
        FollowURL( $link );
    }
}
```

If $result is defined and is not a Net::LDAP::Reference, it must be a Net::LDAP:: Entry. In this case, the routine simply prints its contents to standard output using the dump( ) method:

```
else {
    $result->dump( );
    print "\n";
}
}
```

The FollowURL( ) routine merits some discussion of its own. It expects to receive a single LDAP URL as a parameter. This URL is stored in a local variable named $url:

```
sub FollowURL {
    my ( $url) = @_;
    my ( $ldap, $msg, $link );
```

Next, FollowURL( ) creates a new URI::ldap object using the character string stored in $url:

```
print "$url\n";
$link = URI::ldap->new( $url );
```

A URI::ldap object has several methods for obtaining the URL's components. We are interested in the host( ), port( ), and dn( ) methods, which tell us the LDAP server's hostname, the port to use in the new connection, and the base search suffix to use when contacting the directory server. With this new information, you can create a Net::LDAP object that is connected to the new server:

```
$ldap = Net::LDAP->new( $link->host( ),
                        port => $link->port( ),
                        version => 3 )
  or { warn $!; return; };
```

The most convenient way to continue the query to the new server is to call search( ) again, passing ProcessSearch( ) as the callback routine. Note that this new search uses the same filter as the original search, since the intent of the query has not changed.

```
    $msg = $ldap->search( base => $link->dn( ),
                          scope => "sub",
                          filter => "(cn=$ARGV[0])",
                          callback => \&ProcessSearch );
    $msg->error( ) if $msg->code( );
}
```

The first time you called search( ), you tested to see whether the search returned a referral. Don't perform this test within FollowLink( ) because the LDAP reference should send you to a server that can process the query. If the new server sends you a referral, choose not to follow it. Be aware that there are no implicit or explicit checks in this code for loops caused by chains of referrals or references.

Now let's go back and look at the implementation of ProcessReferral( ). Net:: LDAP::Message provides several methods for handling error conditions. In the case of an LDAP_REFERRAL, the referrals( ) routine can be used to obtain a list of LDAP URLs returned from the server. The implementation of ProcessReferral( ) is simple because you've already done most of the work in FollowURL( ); it's simply a wrapper function that unpacks the list of URLs, and then calls FollowURL( ) for each item:

```
    sub ProcessReferral {
        my ( @links ) = @_;

        foreach $link ( @links ) {
            FollowURL($link);
        }
    }
```

When executed, *fullsearch.pl* produces output such as:

```
$ ./fullsearch.pl "test*"
--------------------------------------------------------
dn:uid=testuser,ou=people,dc=plainjoe,dc=org

  objectClass: posixAccount
            uid: testuser
```

```
      uidNumber: 1013
      gidNumber: 1000
    homeDirectory: /home/tashtego/testuser
      loginShell: /bin/bash
              cn: testuser

ldap://tashtego.plainjoe.org/ou=test1,dc=plainjoe,dc=org
-------------------------------------------------------
dn:cn=test user,ou=test1,dc=plainjoe,dc=org

objectClass: person
          sn: user
          cn: test user
```

Scripting Authentication with SASL

In previous releases, the Authen::SASL package was bundled inside the perl-ldap distribution. Beginning in January of 2002, the Authen::SASL code became a separate module, supporting mechanisms such as ANONYMOUS, CRAM-MD5, and EXTERNAL. There is another SASL Perl module also available on CPAN, Authen::SASL::Cyrus by Mark Adamson, that uses the Cyrus SASL library. This is the one you will need if you are interested in the GSSAPI mechanism. Both modules use the same Authen::SASL framework and can be installed on a system without any conflict.

Probably the most common use of the GSSAPI SASL mechanism is to interoperate with Microsoft's implementation of Windows Active Directory. Chapter 9 discussed several interoperability issues between this server and non-Windows clients.

Updating the search script that I've developed throughout this chapter provides an excellent means of illustrating the GSSAPI package and Perl-ldap's SASL support. The only piece of code that needs to be modified is the code that binds to the directory server. Assume that you need to bind to a Windows domain with a domain controller named *windc.ad.plainjoe.org*. The Kerberos realm is named *AD.PLAINJOE.ORG*, and you'll use the principal *jerry@AD.PLAINJOE.ORG* for authentication and authorization.

First, the revised script must include the Authen::SASL package along with the familiar Net::LDAP module:

```
use Net::LDAP;
use Authen::SASL;
```

To bind to the Active Directory server using SASL, the script must create an Authen::SASL object and specify the authentication mechanism:

```
$sasl = Authen::SASL->new( 'GSSAPI',
        callback => { user => 'jerry@AD.PLAINJOE.ORG' } );
```

New Authen::SASL objects require a mechanism name (or list of mechanisms to choose from) and possibly a set of callbacks. These callbacks are used to provide information to the SASL layer during the authentication process. The GSSAPI mechanism will be handled by Adamson's module, which currently supports a limited set of predefined callback names.* The *user* callback used here is very simple; you just return the string containing the name of the account used for authentication. More information on callbacks can be found in the Authen::SASL documentation.

The code to create a new LDAP connection to the server is identical to the previous scripts that used simple binds for authentication. Remember that SASL requires the use of LDAPv3; hence the version => 3 parameter.

```
$ldap = Net::LDAP->new( 'windc.ad.plainjoe.org',
                        port => 389,
                        version => 3 )
   or die "LDAP error: $@\n";
```

At this point, you can bind to the directory server. There is no need to specify a DN to use when binding because authentication is handled by the KDC and Kerberos client libraries.

```
$msg = $ldap->bind( "", sasl => $sasl );
$msg->code && die "[",$msg->code(), "] ", $msg->error;
```

You also need to modify the search script to use the base suffix that Active Directory uses for storing user accounts. In this case, the required suffix is cn=users,dc=ad,dc=plainjoe,dc=org. If you try running the SASL-enabled search script, chances are that the result will be a less-than-helpful error message about a decoding failure:

```
$ ./saslsearch.pl 'Gerald*'
[84] decode error 28 144 at /usr/lib/perl5/site_perl/5.6.1/Convert/ASN1/_decode.pm
line 230.
```

The most common cause of this failure is the lack of a TGT from the Kerberos KDC. A quick check using the *klist* utility proves that you have not established your initial credentials:

```
$ klist -5
klist: No credentials cache file found (ticket cache FILE:/tmp/krb5cc_780)
```

If *klist* shows that a TGT has been obtained for the *principal@REALM*, another frequent cause of failure is clock skew between the Kerberos client and server. The clocks on the client and server must be synchronized to within five minutes.

Assuming that the failure occurred because you didn't establish your credentials, you need to run *kinit* to create the credentials file:

```
$ kinit
Password for jerry@AD.PLAINJOE.ORG:
```

---

* The callback names supported in Authen::SASL::Cyrus-0.06 are *user*, *auth*, and *language*.

Now when *klist* is executed, it shows that you have a TGT for the Windows domain:

```
$ klist -5
Ticket cache: FILE:/tmp/krb5cc_780
Default principal: jerry@AD.PLAINJOE.ORG

Valid starting      Expires            Service principal
06/27/02 18:27:04   06/28/02 04:27:04
                    krbtgt/AD.PLAINJOE.ORG@AD.PLAINJOE.ORG
```

This time, *saslsearch.pl* returns information about a user. I've trimmed the search output to save space.

```
$ ./saslsearch.pl 'Gerald*'
-------------------------------------------------------------
dn:CN=Gerald W. Carter,CN=Users,DC=ad,DC=plainjoe,DC=org

                  cn: Gerald W. Carter
         objectClass: top
                      person
                      organizationalPerson
                      user
       primaryGroupID: 513
          pwdLastSet: 126696214196660064
                name: Gerald W. Carter
      sAMAccountName: jerry
                  sn: Carter
  userAccountControl: 66048
   userPrincipalName: jerry@ad.plainjoe.org
```

Extensions and Controls

As mentioned in previous chapters, controls and extensions are means by which new functionality can be added to the LDAP protocol. Remember that LDAP controls behave more like adverbs, describing a specific request, such as a *sorted* search or a *sliding* view of the results. Extensions act more like verbs, creating a new LDAP operation. It is now time to examine how these two LDAPv3 features can be used in conjunction with the Net::LDAP module.

Extensions

The Net::LDAP::Extension and the Net::LDAP::Control classes provide a way to implement new extended operations. Past experience indicates that new LDAP extensions that are published in an RFC have a good chance of being included as a package or method in future versions of the Net::LDAP module. The Net::LDAP → start_tls( ) routine is a good example. Therefore, you may never need to implement an extension from scratch. However, it is worthwhile to know how it can be done.

Graham Barr posted this listing on the perl-ldap development list (*perl-ldap-dev@sourceforge.net*), discussing how to implement the Password Modify extension:[*]

```perl
package Net::LDAP::Extension::SetPassword;

require Net::LDAP::Extension;
@ISA = qw(Net::LDAP::Extension);

use Convert::ASN1;
my $passwdModReq = Convert::ASN1->new;
$passwdModReq->prepare(q<SEQUENCE {
                    user        [1] STRING OPTIONAL,
                    oldpasswd   [2] STRING OPTIONAL,
                    newpasswd   [3] STRING OPTIONAL
                    }>);

my $passwdModRes = Convert::ASN1->new;
$passwdModRes->prepare(q<SEQUENCE {
                    genPasswd   [0] STRING OPTIONAL
                    }>);

sub Net::LDAP::set_password {
    my $ldap = shift;
    my %opt = @_;

    my $res = $ldap->extension(
        name => '1.3.6.1.4.1.4203.1.11.1',
        value => $passwdModReq->encode(\%opt) );

    bless $res; # Naughty :-)
}

sub gen_password {
    my $self = shift;

    my $out = $passwdModRes->decode($self->response);
    $out->{genPasswd};
}

1;
```

The Net::LDAP → extension( ) method requires two parameters: the OID of the extended request (e.g., 1.3.6.1.4.1.4203.1.11.1) and the octet string encoding of any parameters defined by the operation. In this case, the value parameter contains the user identifier, the old string, and the new password string.

The $passwordModReq and $passwordModRes variables are instances of the Convert::ASN1 class and contain the encoding rules for the extension request and response packets. The encoding rule specified in this example was taken directly from the

[*] For more information on the Password Modify extension and how it works, refer to RFC 3062.

Password Modify specification in RFC 3062. The Convert::ASN1 module generates encodings compatible with LBER, even though it uses ASN.1. For more information on Convert::ASN, refer to the module's installed documentation.

The good news is that it's easy to invoke the extension by executing:

```
$msg = $ldap->set_password( user => "username",
                            oldpassword => "old",
                            newpassword => "new" );
```

Controls

Many controls also end up being implemented as Net::LDAP classes. The following controls are included in perl-ldap 0.26:

Net::LDAP::Control::Paged
> Implementation of the Paged Results control used to partition the results of an LDAP search into manageable chunks. This control is described in RFC 2696.

Net::LDAP::Control::ProxyAuth
> Implementation of the Proxy Authentication mechanism described by the Internet-Draft *draft-weltman-ldapv3-proxy-XX.txt*. This control, supported by Netscape's Directory Server v4.1 and later, allows a client to bind as one entity and perform operations as another.

Net::LDAP::Control::Sort, Net::LDAP::Control::SortResult
> Implementation of the Server Side Sorting control for search results described in RFC 2891.

Net::LDAP::Control::VLV, Net::LDAP::Control::VLVResponse
> Implementation of the Virtual List View control described in *draft-ietf-ldapext-ldapv3-vlv-XX.txt*. This control can be used to view a sliding window of search results. This feature is often used by address book applications.

Using the built-in controls is really just a matter of reading the documentation and following the right syntax. To show how to use these Control classes, we will extend the *saslsearch.pl* script used to search a Windows AD server.

In order to work around the size limits for searches and return large numbers of entries in response to queries, AD servers (and several other LDAP servers) support the Paged Results control, which is implemented by the Net::LDAP::Control::Paged class. The idea behind this control is to pass a pointer, or cookie, between the client and server to keep track of which results have been returned and which are left to process. To help make the implementation a little easier to swallow, we'll break the search operation into a separate function. The subroutine, called DoSearch( ), expects two input parameters: a handle to a valid Net::LDAP object already connected to the server, and a DN that will be used as the base suffix for the search:

```
sub DoSearch {
    my ( $ldap, $dn ) = @_;
    my ( $page, $ctrl, $cookie, $i );
```

The Paged Results control requires a single parameter: the maximum number of entries that can be present in a single page. In this example, you'll set the number of entries set to 4, which is more convenient for demonstration; a production script would want more entries per page:

```
$page = Net::LDAP::Control::Paged->new( size => 4 );
```

To verify that the search is being done in pages, maintain a counter and print its value at the end of each iteration (i.e., every time you read a page of results). The loop will run until all entries have been returned from the server, or there is an error.

```
$i = 1;
while (1) {
```

After the Net::LDAP::Control::Paged object has been initialized, it must be included in the call to the Net::LDAP → search( ) method. The control parameter accepts an array of control objects to be applied to the request.

```
$msg = $ldap->search( base => $dn,
                      scope => "sub",
                      filter => "(cn=$ARGV[0])",
                      callback => \&ProcessSearch,
                      control => [ $page ] );
```

The use of an LDAP control in the search does not affect the search return codes, so it is still necessary to process any referrals or protocol errors:

```
## Check for a referral.
if ($msg->code( ) == LDAP_REFERRAL) {
    ProcessReferral($msg->referrals( ));
}
## Any other errors?
elsif ($msg->code( )) {
    $msg->error( );
    last;
}
```

Finally, you need to obtain the cookie returned from the server as part of the previous search response. This value must be included in the next search request so the server will know at what point the client wants to continue in the entry list.

```
## Handle the next set of paged entries.
( $ctrl ) = $msg->control( LDAP_CONTROL_PAGED )
    or last;
$cookie = $ctrl->cookie( )
    or last;
$page->cookie( $cookie );
```

At the end of the loop, print the page number:

```
        print "Paged Set [$i]\n";
        $i++;
    }
}
```

Here's what the output looks like:

```
$ ./pagedsearch.pl '*' | egrep '(dn|Paged)'
dn:CN=Users,DC=ad,DC=plainjoe,DC=org
dn:CN=Gerald W. Carter,CN=Users,DC=ad,DC=plainjoe,DC=org
dn:CN=TelnetClients,CN=Users,DC=ad,DC=plainjoe,DC=org
dn:CN=Administrator,CN=Users,DC=ad,DC=plainjoe,DC=org
Paged Set [1]
dn:CN=Guest,CN=Users,DC=ad,DC=plainjoe,DC=org
dn:CN=TsInternetUser,CN=Users,DC=ad,DC=plainjoe,DC=org
dn:CN=krbtgt,CN=Users,DC=ad,DC=plainjoe,DC=org
dn:CN=Domain Computers,CN=Users,DC=ad,DC=plainjoe,DC=org
Paged Set [2]
dn:CN=Domain Controllers,CN=Users,DC=ad,DC=plainjoe,DC=org
dn:CN=Schema Admins,CN=Users,DC=ad,DC=plainjoe,DC=org
dn:CN=Enterprise Admins,CN=Users,DC=ad,DC=plainjoe,DC=org
dn:CN=Cert Publishers,CN=Users,DC=ad,DC=plainjoe,DC=org
Paged Set [3]
dn:CN=Domain Admins,CN=Users,DC=ad,DC=plainjoe,DC=org
dn:CN=Domain Users,CN=Users,DC=ad,DC=plainjoe,DC=org
dn:CN=Domain Guests,CN=Users,DC=ad,DC=plainjoe,DC=org
dn:CN=Group Policy Creator Owners,CN=Users,DC=ad,DC=plainjoe,DC=org
Paged Set [4]
dn:CN=RAS and IAS Servers,CN=Users,DC=ad,DC=plainjoe,DC=org
dn:CN=DnsAdmins,CN=Users,DC=ad,DC=plainjoe,DC=org
dn:CN=DnsUpdateProxy,CN=Users,DC=ad,DC=plainjoe,DC=org
```

At some point in the future, it might be necessary to implement a new control. The constructor for a generic Net::LDAP::Control object can take three parameters:

type

A character string representing the control's OID.

critical

A Boolean value that indicates whether the operation should fail if the server does not support the control. If this parameter is not specified, it is assumed to be FALSE, and the server is free to process the request in spite of the unimplemented control.

value

Optional information required by the control. The format of this parameter value is unique to each control and is defined by the control's designer. It is possible that no extra information is needed by the control.

The most common use of a raw Net::LDAP::Control object is to delete a referral object within the directory. By default, the directory server denies an attempt to delete or modify a referral object and sends the client the URL of the LDAP reference. The actual control needed to update or remove a referral entry is vendor-dependent.

OpenLDAP servers support the Manage DSA IT control described in RFC 3088. This control informs the server that the client intends to manipulate the referrals as though they were normal entries. There is no requirement that it be a critical or non-critical action. That behavior is left to the client using the control.

Creating a Net::LDAP::Control object representing ManageDSAIT simply involves specifying the OID. We'll specify that the server support the control; no optional information is required:

```
$manage_dsa = Net::LDAP::Control->(
                type => "2.16.840.1.113730.3.4.2",
                critical => 1 );
```

Net::LDAP::Constant defines a number of names that you can use as shorthand for long and unmemorable OIDs; be sure to check this module before writing code such as the lines above. These lines can be rewritten as:

```
$manage_dsa = Net::LDAP::Control->(
                type => LDAP_CONTROL_MANAGEDSAIT,
                critical => 1 );
```

This control can now be included in a modify operation:

```
$msg = $ldap->modify(
    "ou=department,dc=plainjoe,dc=org",
    replace =>
    { ref => "ldap://ldap2.plainjoe.org/ou=dept,dc=plainjoe,dc=org" },
    control => $manage_dsa );
```

It's difficult to discuss LDAP controls in detail because they are often tied to a specific server. A good place to look for new controls and possible uses is the server vendor's documentation. It is also a good idea to monitor the IETF's LDAP working groups to keep abreast of any controls that are on the track to standardization.

## PART III

Appendixes

PAM and NSS

Pluggable Authentication Modules

The concept of Pluggable Authentication Modules (PAM) was first designed by Sun Microsystems' SunSoft development group and is defined in the Open Software Foundations RFC 86.0. PAM provides a framework that allows vendors and administrators to customize the services used to authenticate users on a local computer system. For example, logging onto the console of a system may require stronger authentication than logging into a host across the network via *ssh*. Configuring systems to use different PAM modules (e.g., smart cards or passwords) for different services (e.g., *login* or *ssh*) allows administrators to implement as much or as little security as the systems require.

In practice, administrators are exposed to this framework through shared libraries that implement various security, accounting, or account management policies. On Linux and Solaris systems, you can list the installed PAM modules by examining the contents of */lib/security*. The most commonly used module for normal lookups in the system list of accounts (including */etc/shadow*) is the pam_unix.so library. Linux's PAM implementation includes a drop-in replacement module named pam_pwdb.so, which relies on the generic interface to the Password Database library (*http://linux. kernel.org/morgan/libpwdb/*).

PAM is a framework for *authentication* and *authorization*. Authentication is the process of proving you are who you say you are, while authorization is the process of determining what you are allowed do, given that you have established your identity. Applications can query the PAM interface to ask questions about a user or to inform a PAM module of a particular event. For example, "Does this password match with this login name?", "Is this user allowed to log onto this host at 10 p.m. on a Saturday?", "The user named *smitty* logged onto the local system on Thu Dec 19 21:04:27 CST 2002," or "Change this user's password to secret." In each case, the application uses a specific module to process each type of questions or event that can occur during the logon process.

Configuring PAM

PAM configuration files follow one of two formats. In modern Linux distributions, each application or service that possesses an individual configuration file is located in the directory */etc/pam.d/*. Each file is usually named after the type of service it controls. For example, Qualcomm's Qpopper server, a POP3 daemon, uses the PAM file */etc/pam.d/pop3*, and the *login* service is configured by the file */etc/pam.d/login*. Here's a valid configuration for a PAM-enabled *login* service:

```
## /etc/pam.d/login
## Log in using entries from /etc/[password|shadow].
auth        required    /lib/security/pam_unix.so
## Allow root logons only from a tty listed in /etc/securetty.
auth        required    /lib/security/pam_securetty.so
## Don't allow logins (except root) if /etc/nologin exists.
auth        required    /lib/security/pam_nologin.so

## Ensure that account and password are active and have not expired.
account     required    /lib/security/pam_unix.so

## Log username via syslog.
session     required    /lib/security/pam_unix.so

## Enforce good passwords.
password    required    /lib/security/pam_cracklib.so
## Change the password in /etc/[password|shadow].
password    required    /lib/security/pam_unix.so
```

The older type of PAM configuration file, still supported on Solaris, places information for all services in one file, */etc/pam.conf*. In the absence of the */etc/pam.d/* directory, the Linux-PAM implementation will fall back to using *pam.conf*. This file is similar to the newer PAM configuration file, except that the first entry on each line is the name of the service being configured. In newer configuration files (such as the *login* file listed above), the name of the service is taken from the filename. Given these rules, you could rewrite the *login* configuration file into an old-style *pam.conf* file like this:

```
## /etc/pam.conf
## Previous entries and comments (for other services) deleted

login   auth       required   /lib/security/pam_unix.so
login   auth       required   /lib/security/pam_securetty.so
login   auth       required   /lib/security/pam_nologin.so

login   account    required   /lib/security/pam_unix.so

login   session    required   /lib/security/pam_unix.so

login   password   required   /lib/security/pam_cracklib.so
login   password   required   /lib/security/pam_unix.so
```

The general syntax of a PAM configuration file in */etc/pam.d/* is:

```
module-type    control-flag    module-path    arguments
```

A PAM module may implement any of the four defined *module-type*s:

auth

These modules perform authentication, including the familiar password look-ups from */etc/passwd* and */etc/shadow*.

account

These modules perform certain account management functions that aren't related to authentication. For example, an account module might restrict users other than root or members of the *wheel* group from changing their user IDs (i.e., using */bin/su*). These modules often deal with authorization, but they can perform tasks that aren't related; for example, an account module might warn a user that his password is about to expire, and should be changed.

session

These modules provide session management functions before or after a user can access a particular service. For example, a session module might check for new mail or mount the user's home directory.

password

These modules update authentication tokens for the user. There is normally one password module for each auth module defined for a service when the authentication process requires some type of credentials from the user.

Each module type can accept one of four *control-flag*s that determine how the module interacts with other modules. These flags are:

required

Indicates that this module must succeed for the authentication (or authorization) to succeed. Control is not returned to the requesting application until all of the modules have been called.

sufficient

Indicates that success of this module is sufficient for authentication to succeed, assuming that no previously listed required modules have failed. In this case, no other modules in the service configuration file are executed, and control returns to the calling application. If a sufficient module fails, the authentication process continues; failure of a sufficient module doesn't deny access in and of itself.

optional

Indicates that the module's success or failure does not have any effect on the success or failure status returned to the client application. There is one exception to this rule: if no other modules return any definite success or failure status codes, the success or failure of an optional module determines whether authentication succeeds.

requisite

Indicates that the module must succeed for authentication to occur. In the event of failure, control is immediately passed back to the calling application. This is different from the required control flag, which causes all modules to be invoked before returning. This flag is not included in the original OSF-RFC 86.0.

The *module-path* component of a PAM configuration is the absolute path to the shared library that implements the authentication or authorization functions.

The last option listed in a PAM configuration line supplies any additional arguments that should be passed to the module upon invocation. The module must parse and process these arguments. The nature of these arguments varies from module to module; however, a few standard arguments are normally supported by all PAM modules:

debug

Enables generation of debugging information either to standard output or via the *syslogd* daemon.

no_warn

Disables authentication failure logging.

use_first_pass

Instructs the module to use the password entered for the previous module and to return failure if the password does not succeed.

try_first_pass

Instructs the module to attempt to use the password entered for the previous module. If authentication fails, the user should be prompted to enter the password for this module.

PAM administrators frequently specify stacked configurations of modules, forcing a user to be approved by multiple services. With your new understanding of module types and control flags, the previously listed */etc/pam.d/login* file should make more sense. Here are the auth lines from it:

```
auth       required    /lib/security/pam_unix.so
auth       required    /lib/security/pam_securetty.so
auth       required    /lib/security/pam_nologin.so
```

Any authentication attempt must be approved by all three in order for authentication to succeed. The first PAM module performs standard user and password authentication according to entries in */etc/passwd*. The second module, pam_securetty.so, causes a root login to fail unless it is on a terminal listed in */etc/securetty*. The final PAM module, pam_nologin.so, results in all logins except root failing if the file */etc/nologin* exists.

These modules are processed in order. You should examine for yourself what will occur in the following scenario. Assuming that the file */etc/nologin* exists, what users will be able to log onto the system? The answer is that only the *root* account will be able to log on but only from a secure console. How would this be different if the control flag in the first line was changed from required to sufficient? (The *root* would be able to log in from anywhere, and the */etc/nologin* file would have no affect.)

Name Service Switch (NSS)

The Name Service Switch (NSS) framework was designed to let administrators specify which files or directory services to query to obtain information. For example, it's frequently used to specify whether a system should perform hostname lookups in */etc/hosts*, NIS, or DNS. Here's an entry from a typical NSS configuration file, named */etc/nsswitch.conf*. It instructs the local machine to check its own */etc/hosts* file first and to consult DNS only if the entry is not located. NIS is not consulted at all.

```
hosts:      files dns
```

NSS can provide similar services for many different administrative databases. The following databases are generally defined in */etc/nsswitch.conf*:

passwd
shadow
group
hosts
ethers
networks
protocols
rpc
services
netgroup
aliases
automount

You can configure a different lookup method for each database. An NSS module does not need to support all of the databases listed above. Some lookup modules support only user accounts. The libnss_dns.so library is designed to resolve only hostnames and network addresses.

A typical NSS configuration for an LDAP-enabled host would appear as:

```
# /etc/nsswitch.conf
# Legal entries are:
#
# nisplus or nis+: Use NIS+ (NIS Version 3)
# nis or yp: Use NIS (NIS Version 2)
# dns: Use DNS (Domain Name Service)
# files: Use the local files
# db: Use the local database (.db) files
# compat: Use NIS on compat mode
# hesiod: Use Hesiod for user lookups
# ldap: Use PADL's nss_ldap
```

```
## How to handle users and groups
passwd:     files ldap
shadow:     files ldap
group:      files ldap

## DNS should be authoritative; use files only when DNS is not available.
hosts:      dns [NOTFOUND=return] files

bootparams: ldap files

ethers:     ldap files
netmasks:   ldap files
networks:   ldap files
protocols:  ldap files
rpc:        ldap files
services:   ldap files

netgroup:   files ldap
automount:  files ldap
aliases:    files
```

More information can be found on the *nsswitch.conf(5)* manpage.

OpenLDAP Command-Line Tools

Debugging Options

Most OpenLDAP tools provide an option for setting the log level during execution. Table B-1 lists the information recorded with each level. Log levels are additive, so a log level of 24 means to print packets sent and received as well as logging all connection management functions.

Table B-1. OpenLDAP logging levels

Level	Information recorded
-1	All logging information
0	No logging information
1	Trace function calls
2	Packet-handling debugging information
4	Heavy trace debugging
8	Connection management
16	Packets sent and received
32	Search filter processing
64	Configuration file processing
128	Access control list processing
256	Statistics for connection, operations, and results
512	Statistics for results returned to clients
1024	Communication with shell backends
2048	Entry-parsing debugging information

Slap Tools

The collection of slap tools included with OpenLDAP are provided to import and export data directly from the DB files used for supporting an OpenLDAP server.

slapadd(8c)

This tool reads LDIF entries from a file or standard input and writes the new records to a *slapd* database (see Table B-2).

Table B-2. Summary of slapadd command-line arguments

Option	Description
-c	Continues processing input in the event of errors.
-b suffix -n integer	Specify which database in the configuration file to use by the directory's suffix (-b) or by its location (-n) in the *slapd.conf* file (the first database listed is numbered 0). These options are mutually exclusive.
-d integer	Specifies which debugging information to log. See the `loglevel` parameter in *slapd.conf* for a listing of log levels.
-f filename	Specifies which configuration file to read.
-l filename	Specifies the LDIF file to use for input. In the absence of this option, *slapadd* reads data from standard input.
-v	Enables verbose mode.

slapcat(8c)

This tool reads records from a *slapd* database and writes them to a file or standard output (see Table B-3).

Table B-3. Summary of slapcat command-line arguments

Option	Description
-c	Continues processing input in the event of errors.
-b suffix -n integer	Specify which database in the configuration file to use by the directory's suffix (-b) or by its location (-n) in the *slapd.conf* file (the first database listed is numbered 0). These options are mutually exclusive.
-d integer	Specifies which debugging information to log. See the `loglevel` parameter in *slapd.conf* for a listing of log levels.
-f filename	Specifies which configuration file to read.
-l filename	Specifies the name of the file to which the LDIF entries should be written. In the absence of this option, *slapcat* writes data to standard output.
-v	Enables verbose mode.

slapindex(8c)

This tool regenerates the indexes in a *slapd* database (see Table B-4).

Table B-4. Summary of slapindex command-line arguments

Option	Description
-c	Continues processing input in the event of errors.
-b suffix -n integer	Specify which database in the configuration file to use by the directory's suffix (-b) or by its location (-n) in the *slapd.conf* file (the first database listed is numbered 0). These options are mutually exclusive.

Table B-4. Summary of slapindex command-line arguments (continued)

Option	Description
-d integer	Specifies which debugging information to log. See the `loglevel` parameter in *slapd.conf* for a listing of log levels.
-f filename	Specifies which configuration file to read.
-v	Enables verbose mode.

slappasswd(8c)

This tool generates a password hash suitable for use as an *Lq* in *slapd.conf* (see Table B-5).

Table B-5. Summary of slappasswd command-line arguments

Option	Description
-c crypt-salt-format	Defines the format of the salt used when invoking the `crypt( )` function to generate a password suitable for use with {CRYPT}. The string must be in the `snprintf( )` format and must contain a single %s conversion.
-h hash	Defines the hash algorithm to use. Possible values are {CRYPT}, {MD5}, {SMD5}, {SSHA}, and {SHA}. The default is {SSHA}.
-s secret	Specifies the password to hash.
-u	Instructs *slappasswd* to generate password syntaxes for the userPassword attribute (the default) and is included for forward compatibility. No other syntaxes are currently supported.
-v	Enables verbose mode.

LDAP Tools

OpenLDAP's set of LDAP client tools can be used to communicate with any LDAPv3 server (see Table B-6).

Table B-6. Command-line options common to ldapsearch, ldapcompare, ldapadd, ldapdelete, ldapmodify, and ldapmodrdn

Option	Description
-d integer	Specifies what debugging information to log. See the `loglevel` *slapd.conf* parameter for a listing of log levels.
-D binddn	Specifies the DN to use for binding to the LDAP server.
-e [!]ctrl[=ctrlparam]	Defines an LDAP control to be used on the current operation. See also the -M option for the manageDSAit control.
-f filename	Specifies the file containing the LDIF entries to be used in the operations.
-H URI	Defines the LDAP URI to be used in the connection request.
-I	Enables the SASL "interactive" mode. By default, the client prompts for information only when necessary.
-k	Enables Kerberos 4 authentication.

Table B-6. Command-line options common to ldapsearch, ldapcompare, ldapadd, ldapdelete, ldapmodify, and ldapmodrdn (continued)

Option	Description
-K	Enables only the first step of the Kerberos 4 bind for authentication.
-M -MM	Enable the Manager DSA IT control. This option is necessary when modifying an entry that is a referral or an alias. *-MM* requires that the Manager DSA IT control be supported by the server.
-n	Does not perform the search; just displays what would be done.
-O security_properties	Defines the SASL security properties for authentication. See previous information on the `sasl-secprops` parameter in *slapd.conf*.
-P [2|3]	Defines which protocol version to use in the connection (Version 2 or 3). The default is LDAP v3.
-Q	Suppresses SASL-related messages such as how the authentication mechanism is used, username, and realm.
-R sasl_realm	Defines the realm to be used by the SASL authentication mechanism.
-U username	Defines the username to be used by the SASL authentication mechanism.
-v	Enables verbose mode.
-w password	Specifies the password to be used for authentication.
-W	Instructs the client to prompt for the password.
-x	Enables simple authentication. The default is to use SASL authentication.
-X id	Defines the SASL authorization identity. The identity has the form dn:*dn* or u:*user*. The default is to use the same authorization identity that the user authenticated.
-y passwdfile	Instructs the *ldap* tool to read the password for a simple bind from the given filename.
-Y sasl_mechanism	Tells the client which SASL mechanism should be used. The bind request will fail if the server does not support the chosen mechanism.
-Z -ZZ	Issue a StartTLS request. Use of *-ZZ* makes the support of this request mandatory for a successful connection.

ldapadd(1), ldapmodify(1)

These tools send updates to directory servers (see Table B-7).

Table B-7. ldapadd/ldapmodify options

Option	Description
-a	Adds entries. This option is the default for *ldapadd*.
-r	Replaces (or modifies) entries and values. This is the default for *ldapmodify*.
-F	Forces all change records to be used from the input.

ldapcompare(1)

This tool asks a directory server to compare two values:

```
ldapcompare [options] DN <attr:value|attr::b64value>.
```

There are no additional command-line flags for this tool.

ldapdelete(1)

This tool deletes entries from an LDAP directory (see Table B-8).

Table B-8. ldapdelete [option] DN

Option	Description
-r	Deletes the subtree whose root is designated by DN. The delete is not performed atomically.

ldapmodrdn(1)

This tool changes the RDN of an entry in an LDAP directory (see Table B-9).

Table B-9. ldapmodrdn [options] [dn rdn]

Option	Description
-c	Instructs *ldapmodrdn* to continue if errors occur. By default, it terminates if there is an error.
-r	Removes the old RDN value. The default behavior is to add another value of the RDN and leave the old value intact. The default behavior makes it easier to modify a directory without leaving orphaned entries.
-s new_superior_node	Defines the new superior, or parent, entry under which the renamed entry should be located.

ldappasswd(1)

This tool changes the password stored in a directory entry (see Table B-10).

Table B-10. ldappasswd [options] [user]

Option	Description
-a secret	The old password value
-A	Prompt for the old password
-s new_secret	The new password value
-S	Prompt for the new password

ldapsearch(1)

This tool issues LDAP search queries to directory servers (see Table B-11).

Table B-11. ldapsearch [options] [filter [attributes...]]

Option	Description
-a [never|always|search|find]	Specifies how to handle aliases when they are located during a search. Possible values include never (default), always, search, or find.
-A	For any entries found, returns the attribute names, but not their values.
-b basedn	Defines the base DN for the directory search.
-F prefix	Defines the URL prefix for filenames. The default is to use the value stored in $LDAP_FILE_URI_PREFIX.
-l limit	Defines a time limit (in seconds) for the server in the search.
-L -LL -LLL	Print the resulting output in LDIF v1 format. -LL causes the result to be printed in LDIF format without comments. -LLL prints the resulting output in LDIF format without comments and without version information.
-s [sub|base|one]	Defines the scope of the search to be base, one, or sub (the default).
-S attribute	Causes the *ldapsearch* client to sort the results by the value of *attribute*.
-t -tt	Write binary values to files in a temporary directory defined by the -T option. -tt specifies that all values should be written to files in a temporary directory defined by the -T option.
-T directory	Defines the directory used to store the resulting output files. The default is the directory specified by $LDAP_TMPDIR.
-u	Includes user-friendly entry names in the output.
-z limit	Specifies the maximum number of entries to return.

Common Attributes and Objects

This appendix is provided as a quick reference for schema items used throughout this book. It is by no means a complete set of attributes and object classes that you may encounter in the wild. The schema items not listed here should not be assumed to be less important or less commonly used. These are just the primary ones I have focused on in the examples.

Schema Files

Table C-1 tells you where you can find schema files.

Table C-1. Where to find schema files

Software	Schema files included
Bind 9 (schema file located at *http://www.venaas.no/ldap/bind-sdb/*)	*dnszone.schema*
LDAP System Administration (*http://www.oreilly.com/catalog/ldapsa/*)	*idpool.schema* *printer.schema*
OpenLDAP (*http://www.openldap.org/*)	*core.schema* *corba.schema* *cosine.schema* *inetorgperson.schema* *java.schema* *misc.schema* *nis.schema* *openldap.schema*
Samba (*http://www.samba.org/*)	*samba.schema*
Sendmail (*http://www.sendmail.org/*)	*sendmail.schema*
FreeRadius (*http://www.freeradius.org*)	*RADIUS-LDAPv3.schema*

Attributes

Table C-2 outlines some common attributes presented in this book.

Table C-2. Common attributes presented in this book

Name	Single value	Description
cn		Common name of entity
dc		Single domain component of an FQDN
displayName	✓	Preferred name to use when displaying entry
gidNumber	✓	Numeric Unix group ID
givenName		First name by which an entity is known
mail		Email address represented as an RFC 822 mailbox
ou		`organizationalUnit` to which this entry belongs
sn		Last name by which an entity is known
telephoneNumber		Telephone number (supports international dialing format)
uid		Login name for a user account
uidNumber	✓	Numeric Unix user ID
userPassword		Password asssociated with an entry

Object Classes

This section describes some object classes presented in this book.

account

(cosine.schema)

Type	STRUCTURAL
Parent	top
Attributes	*Mandatory:* uid *Optional:* description, seeAlso, localityName, organizationName, organizationalUnitName, host

dcObject

(core.schema)

Type	AUXILIARY
Parent	top
Attributes	*Mandatory:* dc *Optional:* None

dNSZone

(dnszone.schema)

Type	STRUCTURAL
Parent	top

Attributes	*Mandatory:* zoneName, relativeDomainName
	Optional: DNSTTL, DNSClass, ARecord, MDRecord, MXRecord, NSRecord, SOARecord, CNAMERecord, PTRRecord, HINFORecord, MINFORecord, TXTRecord, SIGRecord, KEYRecord, AAAARecord, LOCRecord, NXTRecord, SRVRecord, NAPTRRecord, KXRecord, CERTRecord, A6Record, DNAMERecord

gidPool
(idpool.schema)

Type	AUXILIARY
Parent	top
Attributes	*Mandatory:* gidNumber, cn
	Optional: None

inetLocalMailReciptient
(misc.schema)

Type	AUXILIARY
Parent	top
Attributes	*Mandatory:* None
	Optional: mailLocalAddress, mailHost, mailRoutingAddress

inetOrgPerson
(inetorgperson.schema)

Type	STRUCTURAL
Parent	organizationalPerson
Attributes	*Mandatory:* None
	Optional: audio, businessCategory, carLicense, departmentNumber, displayName, employeeNumber, employeeType, givenName, homePhone, homePostalAddress, initials, jpegPhoto, labeledURI, mail, manager, mobile, o, pager, photo, roomNumber, secretary, uid, userCertificate, x500uniqueIdentifier, preferredLanguage, userSMIMECertificate, userPKCS12

nisMap
(nis.schema)

Type	STRUCTURAL
Parent	top
Attributes	*Mandatory:* nisMapName
	Optional: description

nisNetgroup
(nis.schema)

Type	STRUCTURAL
Parent	top
Attributes	*Mandatory:* cn
	Optional: nisNetgroupTriple, memberNisNetgroup, description

nisObject

Type	STRUCTURAL
Parent	top
Attributes	*Mandatory:* cn, nisMapEntry, nisMapName
	Optional: description

nprintHostPrinter

Type	AUXILIARY
Parent	top
Attributes	*Mandatory:* None
	Optional: printer-name, nprintPrinterName, nprintLocation

nprintNetworkPrinterInfo

Type	AUXILIARY
Parent	top
Attributes	*Mandatory:* None
	Optional: nprintDNSName, nprintHardwareQueueName, nprintQueue Port

nprintPortPrinterInfo

Type	AUXILIARY
Parent	top
Attributes	*Mandatory:* None
	Optional: nprintDeviceName, nprintDeviceFlags, nprintFilter

organizationalPerson

Type	STRUCTURAL
Parent	person
Attributes	*Mandatory:* None
	Optional: title, x121Address, registeredAddress, destinationIndicator, preferredDeliveryMethod, telexNumber, teletexTerminalIdentifier, telephoneNumber, internationaliSDNNumber, facsimileTelephoneNumber, street, postOfficeBox, postalCode, postalAddress, physicalDeliveryOfficeName, ou, st, l

organizationalUnit

Type	STRUCTURAL
Parent	top
Attributes	*Mandatory:* ou
	Optional: userPassword, searchGuide, seeAlso, businessCategory, x121Address, registeredAddress, destinationIndicator,

preferredDeliveryMethod, telexNumber, teletexTerminalIdentifier, telephoneNumber, internationaliSDNNumber, facsimileTelephoneNumber, street, postOfficeBox, postalCode, postalAddress, physicalDeliveryOfficeName, st, l, description

person
(core.schema)

Type	STRUCTURAL
Parent	top
Attributes	*Mandatory:* sn, cn
	Optional: userPassword, telephoneNumber, seeAlso, description

posixAccount
(nis.schema)

Type	AUXILIARY
Parent	top
Attributes	*Mandatory:* cn, uid, uidNumber, gidNumber, homeDirectory
	Optional: userPassword, loginShell, gecos, description

posixGroup
(nis.schema)

Type	STRUCTURAL
Parent	top
Attributes	*Mandatory:* cn, gidNumber
	Optional: userPassword, memberUid, description

printerAbstract
(printer.schema)

Type	ABSTRACT
Parent	top
Attributes	*Mandatory:* None
	Optional: printer-name, printer-natural-language-configured, printer-location, printer-info, printer-more-info, printer-make-and-model, printer-multiple-document-jobs-supported, printer-charset-configured, printer-charset-supported, printer-generated-natural-language-supported, printer-document-format-supported, printer-color-supported, printer-compression-supported, printer-pages-per-minute, printer-pages-per-minute-color, printer-finishings-supported, printer-number-up-supported, printer-sides-supported, printer-media-supported, printer-media-local-supported, printer-resolution-supported, printer-print-quality-supported, printer-job-priority-supported, printer-copies-supported, printer-job-k-octets-supported, printer-current-operator, printer-service-person, printer-delivery-orientation-supported, printer-stacking-order-supported, printer-output-features-supported

printerIPP
(printer.schema)

Type	AUXILIARY
Parent	top
Attributes	*Mandatory:* None *Optional:* printer-ipp-versions-supported, printer-multiple-document-jobs-supported

printerLPR
(printer.schema)

Type	AUXILIARY
Parent	top
Attributes	*Mandatory:* printer-name *Optional:* printer-aliases

printerService
(printer.schema)

Type	STRUCTURAL
Parent	printerAbstract
Attributes	*Mandatory:* None *Optional:* printer-uri, printer-xri-supported

printerServiceAuxClass
(printer.schema)

Type	AUXILIARY
Parent	printerAbstract
Attributes	*Mandatory:* None *Optional:* printer-uri, printer-xri-supported

radiusprofile
(RADIUS-LDAPv3.schema)

Type	STRUCTURAL
Parent	top
Attributes	*Mandatory:* cn *Optional:* radiusArapFeatures, radiusArapSecurity, radiusArapZoneAccess, radiusAuthType, radiusCallbackId, radiusCallbackNumber, radiusCalledStationId, radiusCallingStationId, radiusClass, radiusClientIPAddress, radiusFilterId, radiusFramedAppleTalkLink, radiusFramedAppleTalkNetwork, radiusFramedAppleTalkZone, radiusFramedCompression, radiusFramedIPAddress, radiusFramedCompression, radius-FramedIPAddress, radiusFramedIPNetmask, radiusFramedIPXNetwork, radiusFramedMTU, radiusFramedProtocol, radiusCheckItem, radiusReplyItem, radiusFramedRoute, radiusFramedRouting, radiusIdleTimeout, radiusGroupName, radiusHint, radiusHuntgroupName,

radiusLoginIPHost, radiusLoginLATGroup, radiusLoginLATNode,
radiusLoginLATPort, radiusLoginLATService, radiusLoginService,
radiusLoginTCPPort, radiusLoginTime, radiusPasswordRetry,
radiusPortLimit, radiusPrompt, radiusProxyToRealm, radiusRealm,
radiusReplicateToRealm, radiusServiceType, radiusSessionTimeout,
radiusStripUserName, radiusTerminationAction,
radiusTunnelAssignmentId, radiusTunnelClientEndpoint,
radiusIdleTimeout, radiusProfileDn, radiusSimultaneousUse,
radiusTunnelMediumType, radiusTunnelPassword, radiusTunnelPreference,
radiusTunnelPrivateGroupId, radiusTunnelServerEndpoint,
radiusTunnelType, radiusUserCategory, radiusVSA, radiusExpiration,
dialupAccess

referral

Type	STRUCTURAL
Parent	top
Attributes	*Mandatory:* ref
	Optional: None

sambaAccount

(samba.schema)

Type	AUXILIARY
Parent	top
Attributes	*Mandatory:* uid, rid
	Optional: cn, lmPassword, ntPassword, pwdLastSet, logonTime, logoffTime, kickoffTime, pwdCanChange, pwdMustChange, acctFlags, displayName, smbHome, homeDrive, scriptPath, profilePath, description, userWorkstations, primaryGroupID, domain

sendmailMTA

(sendmail.schema)

Type	STRUCTURAL
Parent	top
Attributes	*Mandatory:* None
	Optional: sendmailMTACluster, sendmailMTAHost, Description

sendmailMTAAlias

(sendmail.schema)

Type	STRUCTURAL
Parent	sendmailMTA
Attributes	*Mandatory:* None
	Optional: sendmailMTAAliasGrouping, sendmailMTACluster, sendmailMTAHost, Description

sendmailMTAAliasObject

Type	STRUCTURAL
Parent	sendmailMTAAlias
Attributes	*Mandatory:* sendmailMTAKey, sendmailMTAAliasValue *Optional:* sendmailMTAAliasGrouping, sendmailMTACluster, sendmailMTAHost, Description

sendmailMTAClass

Type	STRUCTURAL
Parent	sendmailMTA
Attributes	*Mandatory:* sendmailMTAClassName, sendmailMTAClassValue *Optional:* sendmailMTACluster, sendmailMTAHost, Description

sendmailMTAMap

Type	STRUCTURAL
Parent	sendmailMTA
Attributes	*Mandatory:* sendmailMTAMapName *Optional:* sendmailMTACluster, sendmailMTAHost, Description

sendmailMTAMapObject

Type	STRUCTURAL
Parent	sendmailMTAMap
Attributes	*Mandatory:* sendmailMTAMapName, sendmailMTAKey, sendmailMTAMapValue *Optional:* sendmailMTACluster, sendmailMTAHost, Description

shadowAccount

Type	AUXILIARY
Parent	top
Attributes	*Mandatory:* uid *Optional:* userPassword, shadowLastChange, shadowMin, shadowMax, shadowWarning, shadowInactive, shadowExpire, shadowFlag, description

uidPool

Type	AUXILIARY
Parent	top
Attributes	*Mandatory:* uidNumber, cn *Optional:* None

LDAP RFCs, Internet-Drafts, and Mailing Lists

Requests for Comments

RFC documents are available online at *http://www.rfc-editor.org/*. The list here includes LDAPv3-related RFCs in numerical order.

RFC 1274
"The COSINE and Internet X.500 Schema". P. Barker and S. Kille. November 1991. Status: Proposed Standard.

RFC 2079
"Definition of an X.500 Attribute Type and an Object Class to Hold Uniform Resource Identifiers (URIs)". M. Smith. January 1997. Status: Proposed Standard.

RFC 2247
"Using Domains in LDAP/X.500 Distinguished Names". S. Kille et al. January 1998. Status: Proposed Standard.

RFC 2251
"Lightweight Directory Access Protocol (v3)". M. Wahl, T. Howes, and S. Kille. December 1997. Status: Proposed Standard.

RFC 2252
"Lightweight Directory Access Protocol (v3): Attribute Syntax Definitions". M. Wahl et al. December 1997. Status: Proposed Standard.

RFC 2253
"Lightweight Directory Access Protocol (v3): UTF-8 String Representation of Distinguished Names". M. Wahl, S. Kille, and T. Howes. December 1997. Status: Proposed Standard.

RFC 2254
"The String Representation of LDAP Search Filters". T. Howes. December 1997. Status: Proposed Standard.

RFC 2255

"The LDAP URL Format". T. Howes and M. Smith. December 1997. Status: Proposed Standard.

RFC 2256

"A Summary of the X.500(96) User Schema for use with LDAPv3". M. Wahl. December 1997. Status: Proposed Standard.

RFC 2293

"Representing Tables and Subtrees in the X.500 Directory". S. Kille. March 1998. Status: Proposed Standard.

RFC 2294

"Representing the O/R Address Hierarchy in the X.500 Directory Information Tree". S. Kille. March 1998. Status: Proposed Standard.

RFC 2307

"An Approach for Using LDAP as a Network Information Service". L. Howard. March 1998. Status: Experimental.

RFC 2377

"Naming Plan for Internet Directory-Enabled Applications". A. Grimstad et al. September 1998. Status: Informational.

RFC 2589

"Lightweight Directory Access Protocol (v3): Extensions for Dynamic Directory Services". Y. Yaacovi, M. Wahl, and T. Genovese. May 1999. Status: Proposed Standard.

RFC 2596

"Use of Language Codes in LDAP". M. Wahl and T. Howes. May 1999. Status: Proposed Standard.

RFC 2649

"An LDAP Control and Schema for Holding Operation Signatures". B. Greenblatt and P. Richard. August 1999. Status: Experimental.

RFC 2696

"LDAP Control Extension for Simple Paged Results Manipulation". C. Weider et al. September 1999. Status: Informational.

RFC 2713

"Schema for Representing Java™ Objects in an LDAP Directory". V. Ryan, S. Seligman, and R. Lee. October 1999. Status: Informational.

RFC 2714

"Schema for Representing CORBA Object References in an LDAP Directory". V. Ryan, R. Lee, and S. Seligman. October 1999. Status: Informational.

RFC 2798

"Definition of the inetOrgPerson LDAP Object Class". M. Smith. April 2000. Status: Informational.

RFC 2829

"Authentication Methods for LDAP". M. Wahl et al. May 2000. Status: Proposed Standard.

RFC 2830

"Lightweight Directory Access Protocol (v3): Extension for Transport Layer Security". J. Hodges, R. Morgan, and M. Wahl. May 2000. Status: Proposed Standard.

RFC 2849

"The LDAP Data Interchange Format (LDIF)—Technical Specification". G. Good. June 2000. Status: Proposed Standard.

RFC 2891

"LDAP Control Extension for Server Side Sorting of Search Results". T. Howes, M. Wahl, and A. Anantha. August 2000. Status: Proposed Standard.

RFC 3045

"Storing Vendor Information in the LDAP root DSE". M. Meredith. January 2001. Status: Informational.

RFC 3062

"LDAP Password Modify Extended Operation". K. Zeilenga. February 2001. Status: Proposed Standard.

RFC 3088

"OpenLDAP Root Service: An experimental LDAP referral service". K. Zeilenga. April 2001. Status: Experimental.

RFC 3112

"LDAP Authentication Password Schema". K. Zeilenga. May 2001. Status: Experimental.

RFC 3296

"Named Subordinate References in Lightweight Directory Access Protocol (LDAP) Directories". K. Zeilenga. July 2002. Status: Proposed Standard.

RFC 3377

"Lightweight Directory Access Protocol (v3): Technical Specification". J. Hodges and R. Morgan. September 2002. Status: Proposed Standard.

RFC 3383

"Internet Assigned Numbers Authority (IANA) Considerations for the Lightweight Directory Access Protocol (LDAP)". K. Zeilenga. September 2002. Status: Best Common Practices.

Internet-Drafts (I-Ds) are temporary by nature, although this often does not stop vendors from implementing parts or all of the functionality that a draft outlines. The I-Ds listed here are included for their relevance to topics covered in one or more chapters in this book. The absence of an I-D from this list should not be interpreted to mean it may or may not be relevant in future LDAP deployments.

Nonexpired I-Ds can be found at *http://rfc-editor.org/*. Expired drafts can be found online at various archive sites, such as *http://www.watersprings.org/*. Search engines such as Google.com are normally able to locate several such archives.

draft-lachman-laser-ldap-mail-routing-xx.txt
> "LDAP Schema for Intranet Mail Routing". H. Lachman and G. Shapiro. Expires: July 2001.

draft-ietf-ldapext-ldap-c-api-xx.txt
> "The C LDAP Application Program Interface". M. Smith (ed.) et al. Expires: May 2001.

draft-weltman-ldapv3-proxy-xx.txt
> "LDAP Proxied Authorization Control". R. Weltman. Expires: November 2002.

draft-fleming-ldap-printer-schema-xx.txt
> "Lightweight Directory Access Protocol (LDAP): Schema for Printer Services". Pat Fleming and I. McDonald. Expires: December 2002.

draft-howard-rfc2307bis-xx.txt
> "An Approach for Using LDAP as a Network Information Service". L. Howard and M. Ansari. Expires: April 2003.

draft-ietf-ldapext-ldapv3-vlv-xx.txt
> "LDAP Extensions for Scrolling View Browsing of Search Results". D. Boreham, J. Sermersheim, and A. Kashi. Expires: November 2002.

draft-ietf-ldapext-acl-model-xx.txt
> "Access Control Model for LDAPv3". E. Stokes et al. Expires: January 2001.

Mailing Lists

OpenLDAP.org hosts several public mailing lists, all of which are described at *http://www.openldap.org/lists/*. The two most frequented lists are *openldap-software* (discussions about software created as part of the OpenLDAP project) and *openldap-devel* (technical discussions relating to OpenLDAP development). You can subscribe to a list by sending an email to *openldap-<list>-request@OpenLDAP.org,* in which *<list>* is either *software* or *devel*, with the word "subscribe" in the body of the message.

The University of Michigan hosts a general LDAP mailing list. You can subscribe to its list by sending email to *ldap-request@umich.edu* with the word "subscribe" as the subject or by accessing the web interface found at *http://listserver.itd.umich.edu/*.

slapd.conf ACLs

This appendix is provided as a quick reference to the access control rule syntax used in *slapd.conf*. The general syntax of an access control rule is:

```
access to what {by who how-much [control]}+
```

Three syntax items are referred to frequently in the tables found in this appendix:

dnstyle
> Can be one of [regex | base | one | subtree | children]

style
> Can be one of [regex | base]

regex
> Will be expanded as described by the *regex(7)* manpage

What?

Table E-1 presents a summary of access rule targets.

Table E-1. Summary of access rule targets

What?	Description
*	Everything
dn[.*dnstyle*]=*regex*	The entries specified by the *style* beginning at the suffix *regex*
filter=*ldapfilter*	The entries returned by applying the RFC 2254 LDAP filter to the directory
attrs=*attribute_list*	The list of attributes specified

Who?

Table E-2 presents a summary of access rule entities.

Table E-2. Summary of access rule entities

Who?	Description
*	Everyone (including anonymous connections)
anonymous	Non-authenticated connections
users	Authenticated connections
self	The user represented by the DN of the target entry
dn[*dnstyle*]=*regex*	The user represented by the specified DN.
dnattr=*attribute_name*	The user represented by the DN stored in the specified attribute in the target entry
group[/*obj*[/*attr*]][.*style*]=*pattern*	The members of the group represented by *pattern*
peername[.*style*]=*pattern* sockname[.*style*]=*pattern* domain[.*style*[,*modifier*]]=*pattern* sockurl[.*style*]=*pattern*	Host-/filesystem-based access mechanisms
ssf=*n* transport_ssf=*n* tls_ssf=*n* sasl_ssf=*n*	Defined minimum security levels for access to be granted

How Much?

OpenLDAP supports two modes of defining access. The general form of the access specifier clause is:

```
[self]{level|priv}
```

The special modifier self implies special access to self-owned attributes such as the member attribute in a group.

While the access level model implements incremental access (higher access includes lower access levels), the privilege model requires that an administrator explicitly define access for each permission using the =, +, and - operators to reset, add, and remove permissions, respectively (see Table E-3).

Table E-3. Summary of access and privilege levels from most (top) to least (bottom)

Access level	Privilege	Permission granted
write	w	Access to update attribute values (e.g., change this telephoneNumber to 555-2345).
read	r	Access to read search results (e.g., Show me all the entries with a telephoneNumber of 555*).
search	s	Access to apply search filters (e.g., Are there any entries with a telephoneNumber of 555*?).

Table E-3. Summary of access and privilege levels from most (top) to least (bottom) (continued)

Access level	Privilege	Permission granted
compare	c	Access to compare attributes (e.g., Is your telephoneNumber 555-1234?).
auth	x	Access to bind (authenticate). This requires that the client send a username in the form of a DN and some type of credentials to prove his or her identity.
none		No access.

Control flow from one access rule to the next can be managed by the keywords stop, continue, and break (see Table E-4).

Table E-4. Control flow keywords in access rules

Keyword	Meaning
break	Allows other access clauses to be processed
continue	Allows additional "who" clauses within the current access rule to be processed
stop	Stops access check upon a match (default)

Examples

Grant authenticated users the capability to read the cn attribute with the following:

```
access to attrs=cn
    by users read
```

Grant a single, specified user the capability to write to all posixAccount entries below the ou=people container with the following. This does not include permission to add new entries directly below ou=people.

```
access to dn.children="ou=people,dc=plainjoe,dc=org"
    filter=(objectclass=posixAccount)
    by dn="uid=admin,ou=people,dc=plainjoe,dc=org" write
```

Grant everyone the capability to attempt to authenticate against an entry's password with the following. The owner of the entry should also be given read and write access.

```
access to attrs=userPassword
    by * +x continue
    by self +rw
```

Restrict access to the administration organizational unit to members of the admin groupOfNames object with the following:

```
access to dn.subtree="ou=administration,dc=plainjoe,dc=org"
    by group/groupOfNames/member=
        "cn=admin,ou=group,dc=plainjoe,dc=org" write
    by * none
```

Index

Symbols

: (colon), in LDIF files, 12
, (comma), 13
" (double quote), 13
< or > (angle brackets), 13
+ (plus character), 13
\ (see backslash)
(see pound character)
; (semicolon), 13
\~ (tilde), associating with a home
    directory, 163

A

abstract object classes, 20
access control entries (ACEs), 120
access control lists (see ACLs)
access_attr parameter (rlm_ldap
    module), 175
access_attr_used_for_allow parameter (rlm_
    ldap module), 175
access_db feature (Sendmail), 140
account object class, 262
    schema for, 116
ACEs (access control entries), 120
ACLs (access control lists), 55–58
    SASL user IDs and, 98
    slapd.conf (see slapd.conf file, ACLs)
    summary of access levels, 56
Active Directory, 31
    anonymous searches and, 196
    authenticating Unix requests, 194
    changing the user's password, 195

gateways and, 193
Kerberos and, 203
OpenLDAP server scenario, 205–209
posixAccount object class and, 195
proxy servers and, 210
relaxing access control lists, 196
schema, extending, 198
StartTLS and, 197
uid attribute and, 195
user accounts, 195
Active Directory Schema MMC snap-in, 200
AD4Unix configuration application, 201
AD4Unix plugin, 199
Adamson, Mark, 239
add( ) method (Net::LDAP), 224, 228
add keyword, 75
administrative boundaries as reason for
    distributed directories, 27
ADSI Edit MMC (Microsoft Management
    Console) snap-in, 206
alias (symbolic link), 29
aliases database, 253
aliases (see Sendmail, aliases)
ALIAS_FILE definition (Sendmail), 143
AliasFile option (sendmail.cf file), 141
allow option (slapd.conf file), 48–49
all_sysadmin netgroup, 118
alternate schema syntaxes and matching
    rules, 95
angle brackets (< or >), 13
anonymous authentication, 25
ANONYMOUS mechanism, 239

We'd like to hear your suggestions for improving our indexes. Send email to *index@oreilly.com*.

C

cache option (Postfix), 152
cache_expiry option (Postfix), 152
cache_size option (Postfix), 152
cachesize parameter (slapd.conf file), 54
calls, start_tls( ), 218
CA.pl Perl script, 45
Carnegie Mellon University, 33
case-sensitivity and DNs, 14
certificates, generating, 45
challenge/response authentication
    methods, 166
change log, dependencies between slapd
    daemon, slurpd replication helper,
    and, 80
changetype keyword, 75
    in LDIF file, 74
CIFS (Common Internet File System), 165
classes
    account (see account object class)
    creating new, 95
    dcObject (see dcObject object class)
    dNSZone, 262
    gidPool, 263
    inetLocalMailReciptient, 263
    inetOrgPerson (see inetOrgPerson object
        class)
    nisMap (see nisMap object class)
    nisNetgroup (see nisNetgroup object
        class)
    nisObject (see nisObject object class)
    nprintHostPrinter, 264
    nprintNetworkPrinterInfo, 264
    nprintPortPrinterInfo, 264
    organizationalPerson (see
        organizationalPerson object class)
    organizationalUnit (see
        organizationalUnit object class)
    person (see person object class)
    posixAccount (see posixAccount object
        class)
    posixGroup, 265
    printerAbstract, 265
    printerIPP, 266
    printerLPR, 266
    printerService, 266
    printerServiceAuxClass, 266
    radiusprofile, 266
    referral (see referral object class)
    sambaAccount, 267

    sendmailMTA, 267
    sendmailMTAAlias, 267
    sendmailMTAAliasObject, 268
    sendmailMTAClass, 268
    sendmailMTAMap, 268
    sendmailMTAMapObject, 268
    shadowAccount, 268
    uidPool, 268
cn attribute, 13, 262
    using as the RDN for each entry, 62
    using organizational unit to avoid
        collisions, 62
code( ) method (Net::LDAP), 219
collisions of common names (cn),
    avoiding, 62
colon (:) in LDIF files, 12
comma (,), 13
command-line tools (OpenLDAP), 255–260
Common Internet File System (CIFS), 165
common name atttribute (see cn attribute)
compare_check_items parameter (rlm_ldap
    module), 175
Comprehensive Perl Archive Network
    (CPAN), 216
config organizational unit, removing a printer
    entry from, 185
configure file (Exim), 155
configure script
    informing which libraries are
        installed, 108
    locating LDAP libraries, 164
    OpenLDAP, 36
confLDAP_DEFAULT_SPEC variable
    (Sendmail), 140, 143
connectors and drivers for
    synchronization, 213
contact information, 59
    identifying the data that should be placed
        in an employee's entry, 60
    (see also data, adding initial directory
        entries; directories, building a
        company directory for storing
        employee contact information)
controls
    defined, 241
    (see also Net::LDAP::Control)
Corba objects, storing in LDAP directory, 40
CORBA Schema for Representing CORBA
    Object References in an LDAP
    Directory (see RFC 2714)

inheritance, 96
integration
    defined, 192
    versus interoperability, 192
internationalization support in LDAPv3, 32
Internet Directory-Enabled Applications,
        naming plan for (see RFC 2377)
Internet-Drafts (I-Ds), 271
    nonexpired, 272
interoperability, 191–215
    common solutions, 192
    versus integration, 192

J

Java
    objects, storing in LDAP directory, 40
    Schema for Representing Java Objects in
        an LDAP Directory (see RFC 2713)
Java LDAP Browser/Editor, 78
java.schema file, 40
    where to find, 261
JNDI reference, storing in LDAP
        directory, 40

K

Kerberos
    MIT distribution, 35
    plug-ins, 35
    v4, 26
    v5 authentication
        GSSAPI, 97
        protecting passwords, 119
    various distributions, 203
Kerberos, Heimdal, 35
kill -9 command, 65

L

lastmod option (slapd.conf file), 52
lber*.h library, 38
LCUP (LDAP Client Update Protocol), 79
LDAP (Lightweight Directory Access
        Protocol)
    attributes (see attributes)
    attributes and RADIUS attributes,
        mapping between, 179
    authentication (see authentication,
        specific to LDAP)
    backend used to store the persistent data,
        distinction between, 7
    best practices (see RFC 3383), 271

client utilities, adding initial directory
        entries, 66
client, server, and data storage facility,
        relationship between, 7
comparing namespaces, 103
connectionless version, 6
controls, 26
defined, 5–8
directory tree, 12
    example, 10
intended function of, 8
mailing lists, 272
models, 9
    functional, 10
    information, 9
    naming, 9
namespaces (see namespaces)
outlining need for, 4
SDK, 108
search filter syntax, 91
server, backend storage for a web
        server, 8
standardization, 29
ldap admin dn parameter (smb.conf
        file), 167
LDAP Authentication Password Schema (see
        RFC 3112)
LDAP Client Update Protocol (LCUP), 79
LDAP Control Extension for Server Side
        Sorting of Search Results (see RFC
        2891)
LDAP Data Interchange Format (see LDIF)
LDAP Duplication/Replication/Update
        Protocols (LDUP) working
        group, 29
ldap filter parameter (smb.conf file), 167
LDAP Interchange Format (see LDIF)
ldap keyword (Postfix), 150
ldap keyword (sendmail.cf file), 138
LDAP (Lightweight Directory Access
        Protocol)
    models, security, 10
    URIs, defining, 29
LDAP over SSL (LDAPS - tcp/636), 26
LDAP over TCP/IP versus X.500 over OSI, 6
LDAP Password Modify Extended Operation
        (see RFC 3062)
ldap port parameter (smb.conf file), 167
LDAP Schema Viewer, 23
ldap server parameter (smb.conf file), 167
ldap ssl parameter (smb.conf file), 167
ldap suffix parameter (smb.conf file), 167

About the Author

Gerald Carter has been a member of the SAMBA Development Team since 1998. His involvement with systems and network administration of Unix systems began in 1995. He currently works on embedded printing appliances at HP. He has published articles with various web-based magazines and teaches instructional courses as a consultant for several companies and conferences. Gerald has also written books for SAMS Publishing.

Gerald (Jerry to his friends) first became interested in computers in 1983 when he was introduced to a Commodore 64 and a copy of *Zork I: The Great Underground Empire*, which he now carries on his Palm III (Zork I, not the C64). In 1997, he received his master's degree in Computer Science from Auburn University, where he continues to pursue his Ph.D., also in Computer Science.

Gerald's hobbies include running, hiking, and playing music. He lives near Lake Martin in Dadeville, Alabama, with his wife, Kristi, and Smitty, their cat. If you would like to contact him, Gerald's email address is *jerry@plainjoe.org*, and his web site is *http://www.plainjoe.org/*.

Colophon

Our look is the result of reader comments, our own experimentation, and feedback from distribution channels. Distinctive covers complement our distinctive approach to technical topics, breathing personality and life into potentially dry subjects.

The animal on the cover of *LDAP System Administration* is a mink (*Mustela vison*). Mink are found throughout the United States and Canada except in Arizona, the Arctic, and some offshore islands. A mink's fur is mostly brown with some white spots around the throat, chin, and chest. Its coat is thick, soft, and waterproof (thanks to guard hairs covered with an oily protective substance). Its body is stream-lined and skinny with short legs and an elongated face. As part of its water-loving nature, a mink's toes are partially webbed. Body length varies but is usually around two feet. The tail comprises almost half of a mink's total length.

Females become fertile during the winter and give birth in April or May. A typical litter ranges between one and eight offspring. *M. vison* is a solitary species; males are particularly intolerant of each other. They mark their territories with a pungent, musky secretion from their oversized anal glands. They are especially active at night and are skilled swimmers and climbers. Mink dig burrows in banks of lakes and rivers, or they may occupy abandoned dens of other mammals, such as muskrats. Their tastes in food changes from season to season, but they tend to dine on small mammals such as mice, rabbits, and shrews, along with fish and duck.

The main threat to the mink's existence continues to be the fur industry. Most U.S. states and all of Canada have limited trapping seasons with strict quotas on catch size. These provisions help keep mink population densities constant. Mink have few natural enemies other than humans. Occasionally, they will be hunted by coyotes, bobcats, and other meat-eaters.

Matt Hutchinson was the production editor and copyeditor for *LDAP System Administration*. Genevieve d'Entremont proofread the book. Genevieve d'Entremont, Emily Quill and Mary Anne Weeks Mayo provided quality control. Jamie Peppard provided production assistance. Julie Hawks wrote the index.

Emma Colby designed the cover of this book, based on a series design by Edie Freedman. The cover image is a 19th-century engraving from the Dover Pictorial Archive. Emma Colby produced the cover layout with QuarkXPress 4.1 using Adobe's ITC Garamond font.

Bret Kerr designed the interior layout, based on a series design by David Futato. This book was converted by Joe Wizda to FrameMaker 5.5.6 with a format conversion tool created by Erik Ray, Jason McIntosh, Neil Walls, and Mike Sierra that uses Perl and XML technologies. The text font is Linotype Birka; the heading font is Adobe Myriad Condensed; and the code font is LucasFont's TheSans Mono Condensed. The illustrations that appear in this book were produced by Robert Romano and Jessamyn Read using Macromedia FreeHand 9 and Adobe Photoshop 6. The tip and warning icons were drawn by Christopher Bing. This colophon was written by Matt Hutchinson.

Get even more for your money.

Join the O'Reilly Community, and register the O'Reilly books you own. It's free, and you'll get:

- $4.99 ebook upgrade offer
- 40% upgrade offer on O'Reilly print books
- Membership discounts on books and events
- Free lifetime updates to ebooks and videos
- Multiple ebook formats, DRM FREE
- Participation in the O'Reilly community
- Newsletters
- Account management
- 100% Satisfaction Guarantee

Signing up is easy:

1. **Go to: oreilly.com/go/register**
2. **Create an O'Reilly login.**
3. **Provide your address.**
4. **Register your books.**

Note: English-language books only

To order books online:
oreilly.com/store

For questions about products or an order:
orders@oreilly.com

To sign up to get topic-specific email announcements and/or news about upcoming books, conferences, special offers, and new technologies:
elists@oreilly.com

For technical questions about book content:
booktech@oreilly.com

To submit new book proposals to our editors:
proposals@oreilly.com

O'Reilly books are available in multiple DRM-free ebook formats. For more information:
oreilly.com/ebooks

Spreading the knowledge of innovators   oreilly.com

Have it your way.

CPSIA information can be obtained at www.ICGtesting.com
Printed in the USA
BVOW061419191212

308694BV00006B/172/P